WIN
OR ELSE

SOVIET FOOTBALL IN MOSCOW AND BEYOND, 1921–1985

LARRY E. HOLMES

EDITED BY SAMANTHA LOMB

INDIANA UNIVERSITY PRESS

This book is a publication of

Indiana University Press
Office of Scholarly Publishing
Herman B Wells Library 350
1320 East 10th Street
Bloomington, Indiana 47405 USA

iupress.org

© 2024 by Marsha Hobbs

All rights reserved
No part of this book may be reproduced or utilized in any form or by any means, electronic or mechanical, including photocopying and recording, or by any information storage and retrieval system, without permission in writing from the publisher. The paper used in this publication meets the minimum requirements of the American National Standard for Information Sciences—Permanence of Paper for Printed Library Materials, ANSI Z39.48–1992.

Manufactured in the United States of America

First printing 2024

Cataloging information is available from the Library of Congress.

978-0-253-06962-7 (hdbk.)
978-0-253-06963-4 (pbk.)
978-0-253-06964-1 (web PDF)

Larry Holmes (1942–2022) and his rescue dog, Kali.

Larry E. Holmes was a professor emeritus at the University of South Alabama, a leading expert on Stalinism and Soviet education, and a pioneer in regional studies. Larry was born in Chicago and raised in Kansas. Larry's love of sports began early, and by the time he was a student at McPherson College, he had become an outstanding pitcher with dreams of going pro. He decided instead to apply to Eastern New Mexico University to study to become a lawyer. While at Eastern New Mexico University, Larry was offered funding to study history, and he jumped at the offer. He returned to the University of Kansas for his PhD and studied under Russian medievalist Oswald P. Backus and Soviet historian Herbert J. Ellison. After graduation, he accepted a job at the University of South Alabama in 1968.

Larry was on faculty at the University of South Alabama for thirty-eight years. His time there was marked by great success and great troubles. Over the course of his career, Larry became an award-winning teacher and scholar, president of the faculty senate, president of the Southern Slavic Association, and a kind mentor to his students. He used his love of sports to connect with his students, frequently taking them to local baseball games and leading a running group at the university. But he had contentious relations with the university administration because of his political activities, which included protesting against the Junior Miss pageant, supporting migrant workers and the civil rights movement, and writing a sports column (under the alias "Baseballs") for the underground student newspaper, *The Rearguard*. In 1972, the university—with the tacit support of the FBI, who had sent an informant to spy on Larry's classes—tried to deny him tenure for his political activity. The Alabama Education Association along with support from Larry's colleagues, students, and a sympathetic judge saved his job.

While working at the University of South Alabama, Larry wrote several books on the history of education in the Soviet Union and post–Soviet Russia, including *The Kremlin and the Schoolhouse: Reforming Education in Soviet Russia, 1917–1931* (1991) and *Stalin's School: Moscow's Model School No. 25, 1931–1937* (1999), a microhistorical study of the school attended by children of party elites in Moscow. In the late 1990s, Larry came to Kirov for the first time and fell in love with the city and its people. For the next twenty-plus years, he would divide his time between Kirov and Alabama.

Larry's arrival in Kirov kicked off a second stage of his academic career as he produced several groundbreaking works based on the rich local archives after he retired in 2006. These works emphasized the tension between local power structures and central authorities and how important regional context is to studying history. *Grand Theater: Regional Governance in Stalin's Russia, 1931–1941* (2009) looks at Kirov's regional educational bureaucracy during the 1930s, including during the repression years. *War, Evacuation, and the Exercise of Power: The Center, Periphery, and Kirov's Pedagogical Institute 1941–1952* (2012) and the acclaimed *Stalin's World War II Evacuations: Triumph and Troubles in Kirov* (2017) both focus on tensions created by the massive influx of evacuees and evacuated enterprises during World War II. Larry returned to his dissertation topic with *Revising the Revolution: The Unmaking of Russia's Official History of 1917* (2021), which focuses on how regional historians of Viatka (the pre-1934 name for Kirov) had to revise their writings on the October 1917 revolution to comply with the center's demands. For his last book, the one you are currently reading, Larry dug deep into both the rich historical sources in Kirov and his love of sports to produce a history of his beloved Kirov football team, Dinamo.

When in Kirov, Larry planned his schedule around sporting events, whether it was a hockey match in nearby Kirovo-Cheptetsk, a bandy match (hockey played with a ball), or a football match featuring Dinamo. An avid supporter of local teams, he always wore his blue-and-white Dinamo scarf to the archives, where he was a frequent visitor as a researcher and friend who enjoyed lively discussions with the archivists over lunch. Larry was also an avid dog rescuer. At his home in Alabama, he had a menagerie of rescue dogs, and he was a frequent shelter volunteer. His keen wit, great sense of humor, enthusiasm for life, and kindness will be greatly missed.

Samantha Lomb
Assistant Professor
Vyatka State University

CONTENTS

Foreword xi
Acknowledgments xiii
Note on Transliteration xv

Introduction 1

PART I. THE SHAPE OF SOVIET FOOTBALL, 1917–1985
1. Not a Sporting Affair 23
2. Winning Is Everything 39
3. The System and Its Fault Lines 72

PART II. FOOTBALL IN RUSSIA'S DEPTHS, 1979–1985
4. Kirov's Dinamo 97
5. Success! 112
6. Foul Play 129
7. The First League 144
8. Dead Last 161
9. Fallen from Grace 175

Conclusion 180
Epilogue 193

Select Bibliography 197
Index 203

FOREWORD

In this book, I almost invariably refer to the sport that dominates its pages as football rather than soccer.

I begin with a discussion of the main features of Soviet football as they developed from 1917 to the early 1980s. I then turn my attention to a minor-league professional football team, Kirov's Dinamo, and its history over a span of six years from 1979 to 1985. It was a period when the club played at its worst and best. I seek to explain the reasons for its sudden success, then abrupt failure.

Dinamo represented the region and the city of Kirov, located about 550 miles northeast of Moscow. Both the province and the municipality were known as Viatka before the assassination in December 1934 of Sergei Mironovich Kirov, a prominent member of the Bolshevik Party who headed its apparatus in Leningrad. Beginning in the 1930s, factories in the military-industrial complex dominated the city and region.

ACKNOWLEDGMENTS

Kirov's sports journalists, Viktor Andreevich Chudinovskikh and Boris Aronovich Kolomensky, graciously shared information and their insights about the history of sports in the Kirov region. The archivists at the State Archive for the Kirov Region (GAKO) and the State Archive for the Social and Political History of the Kirov Region (GASPI KO) located materials and photographs. I am especially indebted to the latter's Elena Nikolaevna Chudinovskikh, Vladimir Sergeevich Zharavin, and Liubov' Gennad'evna Poptsvoa. Kirov's Herzen State Public Library brought innumerable books and newspapers immediately on request. They also found photographs of importance to this work. I am especially indebted to Svetlana Shutova for research in Moscow's archives at a time when first COVID-19 restrictions and then the war in Ukraine prevented me from doing so.

Research for this book could not have been completed without the help of Deborah Cobb and the staff of the interlibrary loan department at the University of South Alabama's library.

Viktor Chudinovskikh and Lev Nikolaevich Isupov, the latter a player for Dinamo, kindly provided numerous photographs. I am indebted to Vladimir Kuragin for his assistance in procuring other illustrations. Keith Holmes expertly enhanced the quality of many of them.

Special thanks to my friends in Kirov, Tat'iana Kuragina, Irina Ovechkina, Konstantin Tokarev, Andrei Pervushev, and Svetlana Shutova, who suffered quietly while I babbled on about Dinamo and its past.

I could not have completed this book without the website https://footballfacts.ru. I thank its managers and sponsors for providing a vast amount of information about the zones, leagues, players, coaches, administrators, and stadiums of football teams in the USSR's major and minor leagues. Unfortunately, the site now provides far fewer details, especially about a single team's performance in any given year.

All errors of fact and judgment are, of course, exclusively mine.

Larry E. Holmes
Professor Emeritus of History
University of South Alabama

NOTE ON TRANSLITERATION

I use the Library of Congress transliteration system with several exceptions. Surnames that end in "skii" such as Kolomenskii or Dunaevskii have been changed to "sky," thus Kolomensky or Dunaevsky. In the reference notes, I use the following abbreviations when citing Russian archival material: f. for collection (*fond*), op. for inventory (*opis'*), d. for file or folder (*delo*), l. (*list*) for page and ll. (*listy*) for pages, and ob. (*oborot*) for the reverse side of a page. I use a capital letter for Soviet football's Higher League as well as First League but not for the second league. Capital letters are used for the Sports Committee of the USSR and of the Russian Republic but not for regional committees.

WIN
OR ELSE

INTRODUCTION

"Soccer is never just soccer."[1] Football is a game, a lived experience, for fans, players, coaches, and administrators. It is what Robert Edelman, historian of Soviet and Russian sport, has called "serious fun."[2] For the fans, especially, it is a chance to let off steam, to forget about political scandals, economic woes, and the humdrum banality of everyday life. Any scholarly approach to the sport, whatever its intent and focus, must acknowledge, then appreciate this, football's transcendent appeal or what some observers would call the game's "soul." And so it is, I trust, with this book. I hope that it conducts a scholarly examination of football's political underbelly with a requisite understanding that the game is an emotional phenomenon for fans, players, sports correspondents, and administrators. I write this book both as a historian and as a fan. In it, the two are inextricably joined.

Game On

Not long ago, most intellectuals, academics prominent among them, dismissed sports—and professional sport, in particular—as an inappropriate subject of study. The subject was without a "history," "culture," or "sociology." That has certainly changed. Over the past few decades, professional football, among other forms of sport, has become fair game for historians, sociologists, anthropologists, political scientists, psychologists, feminists, and investigative journalists. They have written extensively about its intertwining with a whole host of topics: politics, business, the drug trade (narco-football), sexuality, ideology, religion, diplomacy, gender, fashion (sportswear), self-identity, national identity, and ethnic prejudice.[3] However, as literary theorist Hans Ulrich

Gumbrecht has remarked, "Even scholars who love sports often wind up feeling obliged to interpret it as a symptom of highly undesirable tendencies."[4] They have, therefore, often written it off as "a despicably Other" and have felt compelled to discount the pleasure it brings its viewers.[5] As Gumbrecht well knows, these analysts have forgotten that sports have become corrupted precisely because they are such an immensely popular form of entertainment. Fortunately, an increasing number of scholars have made an appreciation of football as a game part of their epistemological arsenal when examining the sport's sleaze.

A fascination with football as performed on the playing field explains the origins of this, the present study, and the motivation for its completion as I discovered time and again football's disappointing side. The sport's beauty and shabbiness pushed me to and fro, with considerable stress as the result. I decided to continue nevertheless, this book being a testament to my choice to do so. Devotees of the sport who experienced the same unease but plowed on have greatly helped me along the way to combine critical analysis with an admiration for "the beautiful game."[6]

It was precisely the game's emotional appeal that attracted novelist Nick Hornby to it. He described it well in his 1992 book *Fever Pitch*, which was about the author's passion for Arsenal in England's Premier League.[7] As a social critic, Hornby acknowledged that his obsession gave him "a quick way to fill a previously empty trolley in the Masculinity Supermarket." Arsenal was a kind of opiate, a religion. Hornby became a "born again member of the Church of Latterday Championship Believers." But as a fan, Hornby wistfully admitted that surrender to passion for his team made him not an analyst but "a moron." Whether watching in the stadium or at home, he lost his critical faculties. "I rarely think. . . . There is no analysis or self-awareness, or mental rigour going on at all." Hornby wrote, "It worries me, the prospect of dying in mid-season."[8]

In 2006, novelist Jean-Philippe Toussaint expressed similar sentiments in his book *Football*. He had hoped initially to analyze the sport and simultaneously to express his enjoyment of it. The result, Toussaint warned his readers at the outset, might be a book "that no one will like—not intellectuals, who aren't interested in football, or football-lovers, who will find it too intellectual." As a critic, Toussaint admitted that football encouraged its fans to vent their chauvinism, "a non-duped, second-level nationalism." He admitted that he was not immune to disreputable thoughts and behavior. "During a match, I am in a state of simple-minded comfort, the more flavoursome for being accompanied by a temporarily acceptable intellectual regression . . . I give free rein to the impulses of violence and aggression that normally have no place in my personality." Toussaint acknowledged the depravities associated with football:

"racism, homophobia, hooliganism, and exorbitant salaries of players." But as a passionate fan of the game, Toussaint hastened to add, he did not want to dwell on such horrors. "I will not devote more than a parenthesis to them (oof, tired already—end of parenthesis)."[9]

In 2014, Toussaint decided to avoid football altogether and focus completely on writing a novel. Moored in Corsica, far from football's World Cup in Brazil, he was determined to avoid any television or radio transmission of the great event "to devote myself exclusively to literature." Toussaint managed to do so for a week. But one morning, he went on the internet to glance—no more than that—at the previous day's scores. It was then that he discovered the phenomenon of live streaming. He could not help himself. It was "as if a sly and devastating virus had managed to slip into my workplace ... [to] take control of my work tool and infect my computer."[10] He watched all of the remaining games.

Eduardo Galeano, left-wing journalist, novelist, and "the unofficial poet laureate of the game," described his similarly complex relationship with football. He did so in a charming collection of vignettes of people and events, *Soccer in the Sun and Shadow*.[11] Football in the shadow represented the dark and malodorous side of the game: xenophobia, racism, commercialization, monetization, corporatization, corruption, and a "pagan mass." But critics who focused on the "dark side" failed, Galeano interjected, to see what transpired in the sun. They missed "the simple truth ... that soccer is a game, and those who really play it feel happy and make us happy too." Galeano recalled his behavior on the first day of the 2010 World Cup: "I hung a sign on the door of my house that said: 'Closed for soccer.' When I took it down a month later, I had played sixty-four matches, beer in hand, without budging from my favorite chair."[12]

In his 2015 book *What We Think about When We Think about Soccer*, professor of philosophy Simon Critchley likewise expressed contrasting feelings about the sport. The scholar in Critchley attested to the "intrinsic connection" of football with violence, colonialism, racism, and sexism that "props up a crumbling sense of masculinity." Football was a "powerful opiate, a form of mass psychology that can license the most egregious forms of tribalism ... and the ugliest nationalism." "My only religious experience" Critchley confessed, "is to Liverpool Football Club," a team in England's Premier League. "Liking football as much as I do—as many of us do," he admitted, "is really dumb, and part of the enormous appeal of the game is our completely willing submission to something that is pretty stupid." But for all that, it remained for Critchley a game dominated by "the beauty of the players, the splendour of play itself, and the fans with their songs, weird outfits, and flag-coloured facepaint." "The stupid" could be "the beautiful." Critchley decided to write his book to affirm the "poetics of football experience."[13]

An appreciation of football as a sport could lead to less uplifting observations such as those by Bill Buford in his book *Among the Thugs*.[14] From 1982 to 1990, Buford engaged in an extreme form of participatory journalism by immersing himself among English fans who engaged in multiple acts of violence against people and property. After searching for a grand political or economic explanation for their behavior, Buford arrived at something far less "academic." He concluded that his subjects acted on little more than the desire to experience, in turn, first the excitement, then the pleasure, and finally the addictive high of collective aggression. A specialist in anthropology, Gary Armstrong, largely agreed with Buford in his study of hooliganism perpetrated by supporters of England's Sheffield United during the 1980s and 1990s: "Academic theory," he concluded, "*cannot* provide one single and simple explanation."[15] Unlike Buford, however, he insisted that "hooligan culture" in this somewhat later period severely limited the extent of violence, often reducing it to little more than performance art. Young men "enjoy the *performance* aspects of a threat." When some form of physical altercation happened to occur, it was "consistently devoid of hatred or vicious sadism."[16]

Many analysts have forgotten that sport has made a large imprint on society and has become corrupted precisely because it is such a popular form of entertainment. Football as a reflection of larger society is a key point in this work. As such, analysts who have combined a critical approach to the game with an appreciation of its aesthetic appeal inspired me to start this project.

A Personal Journey

This book originated long ago with my emotional investment in a professional football team, Dinamo, in Russia's provincial city of Kirov, located 550 miles northeast of Moscow. In 1993, following a tip from a colleague from Kirov about the wealth of material in the city's archives, I went there to find out for myself. I discovered, as he had promised, a vast treasure trove of documentation. Those riches resulted from a local tradition, one predating the 1917 revolution, of collecting and preserving more materials than people elsewhere thought possible or appropriate. During World War II, Germans never threatened the region, and unlike in Moscow and other areas at or near the front, documents in Kirov were neither burned nor inevitably lost during their removal to safer areas.

In the fall of 2000, I began eleven consecutive months of research in Kirov's archives. Since then, until the outbreak of the COVID-19 pandemic, I have spent four to six months of every calendar year working in the city. Kirov became something of a second home where my professional and personal lives merged. I adopted its people and institutions as well as its sports teams as my own. In particular, I became an avid fan of the city's minor-league football team, Dinamo.

At first, Dinamo rewarded me and my fellow faithful with a decent, if not spectacular, showing. At season's end, the team usually occupied a place in the middle of its zone's standings. But then, regrettably, its performance went from mediocre to bad to worse. Beginning in 2008, Dinamo finished near the bottom of the league. It ingloriously occupied dead last at the end of the 2015–2016 and 2016–2017 seasons. The club ceased to exist in mid-2017, a mercy killing of sorts. (Dinamo was actually resurrected by the regional government in 2023 and is expected to field a team again in the 2023–2024 season. Sadly, Larry will not get to see his beloved team rise from the ashes.) Until then, I had doggedly remained committed to "my" team. Any return to the United States in midseason prompted a panic attack whatever Dinamo's position in the standings. I would miss the game, and, to be honest, I thought that my presence helped Dinamo, even at its worst, make a decent showing.

I was not the only long-suffering devotee. But my sporting brethren mitigated their despair at every turn with tall tales, so I thought at the time, of Dinamo's greatness in what seemed like the distant past. But they could not tell me precisely the who, what, when, or how of it. So I decided to find out for myself.

It was not difficult. It first took only an examination of the team's official history and additional information readily available on the internet. The glory years followed an earlier, equally miserable period in Dinamo's history, the 1970s. From 1976 to 1979, the team consistently occupied the bottom of its zone, one of several in the USSR's second league. In 1979, the club managed only a twenty-first finish among twenty-four entrants in one of six zones in a league of 142 teams.

Then, in 1980, Dinamo, heretofore one of the worst teams in the entire Soviet Union, suddenly vaulted into third place in its zone. The next year, it took first place, overwhelming the next-best finisher by an astounding six wins and eight points. In the ensuing playoffs, it won promotion into the prestigious First League of only twenty-two teams. Kirov, a relatively small city with a population of 362,000 in 1980, now competed with clubs from such major Soviet municipalities as Moscow, Iaroslavl', Riga, Rostov-on-Don, L'vov, Volgograd, and Kiev.[17]

Then bad things began to happen. In 1982, Dinamo finished in fifteenth place. Even that unenviable position failed to tell the whole story. The team avoided relegation to the second league from whence it had just come by winning three of its final four games. Despite the miracle finish, Dinamo won a mere fifteen of forty-two games.

No season-ending miracle occurred the following year. Dinamo finished dead last, winning five of forty-two games. It returned to the second league. The following year, the team managed no more than a twelfth-place finish among the seventeen teams in its zone in a league with 149 entrants.

Such basic information about Dinamo's past performance was easy to come by. As a fan, I wanted to know more. How, from 1979 through 1984, could Dinamo alternately lose, then win, then lose so spectacularly? I knew what to do: interview former players, coaches, and sports correspondents; examine documents in Kirov's archives; read reports in the city's major newspapers; and study the transcripts of transmissions from Kirov's radio and television stations. In doing so, I discovered more than I expected. The historian in me overwhelmed the fan. Dinamo's play ceased to be entertaining and fun; it had now become part of a story of sordid politics and cutthroat economics designed for a club to win at any cost or else. I also realized that Dinamo's tale could best be understood only after a larger study of the history of Soviet football, an effort that uncovered many of the same depressing problems on a national scale.

I should have known. Sports journalist Igor' Rabiner had already warned anyone who cared to listen about the pain that could accompany a critical appraisal of the sport and especially of one's own team. In 2011, he wrote eloquently of the psychological toll he had endured describing the travails of his beloved Moscow's Spartak in the first decade of the twenty-first century. Coming from a long line of devoted Spartak supporters, Rabiner mused that he might have "pronounced the word 'Spartak' for the first time after I said 'Mummy' and 'Daddy.'"[18] Now his team had fallen on hard times. To write about it "was unpleasant and painful . . . I couldn't get rid of a feeling of discomfort."[19]

Structure

This book consists of two parts. The three chapters of part 1, "The Shape of Soviet Football," set forth the chief characteristics of the professional game, its governance, and its public reception until Mikhail Gorbachev's ascent to power in 1985. As early as the 1920s, football culture in the USSR defied official ideological and political imperatives. An authoritarian party-state that claimed governance over a socialist society could not prevent the sport's rapid progression toward something more akin to capitalism than to socialism. A fiercely competitive system emerged in which clubs, coaches, and players responded to the unforgiving demands of supply and demand. Six chapters in part 2, "Football in Russia's Depths," examine the history of Kirov's Dinamo football team from 1979 to 1985. They demonstrate how Kirov's minor-league squad and the provincial game more generally exemplified the chief attributes of Soviet football.

Chapter 1, "Not a Sporting Affair," analyzes how initial doubts about competitive sport gave way to a form of football that allowed, then encouraged a robust professionalism. Beginning in the 1920s, clubs enticed players with fictional jobs, bonuses, and other benefits. Chapter 2, "Winning Is Everything," emphasizes a fixation on victory in international competition. At first, in a sharp contradiction with the competitive spirit, that demand meant games with far inferior, often amateur squads or frequent avoidance altogether of play in the international arena. In the 1930s and thereafter, defeat or victory following matches with foreign clubs prompted hyperbolic braggadocio or self-deprecating disappointment. Chapter 3, "The System and Its Fault Lines," covers the center's failure to prevent an unchecked growth in the number of teams and to limit the costs involved in their operation. Of particular importance, it failed to curb demands by coaches and players for multiple and exorbitant forms of compensation, many of which were "off the books." In this environment, some teams thrived in the quest for victory while others, a majority, eked out a mere survival.

Chapter 4 examines the origins of Kirov's Dinamo and the sources of the club's funding. The dismal season of 1979 confronted regional authorities and the club's administrators with a fateful choice. They could continue to disappoint their fans with annual disasters, or they could somehow find the means to spend far more resources on the team to field a championship team. They chose the latter.

With enhanced financial support, much of it off the books, Dinamo recruited better coaches and players. Chapter 5, "Success!," follows Dinamo's remarkably successful play in 1980 and 1981. Much to the delight of fans, reporters, and local party and state officials, the team's performance in 1981 earned it promotion to the prestigious First League. Stiffer competition there, however, required ever-greater financial support from legitimate as well as illicit sources. And that need came precisely at a time when party and state administrators in Moscow renewed spasmodic efforts to limit payment of improper benefits to players and coaches, the subject of chapter 6, "Foul Play." Fortunately for

Dinamo, the center directed its ire primarily at clubs with losing records. For the moment, through evasion and dissimulation, Kirov's Dinamo wriggled free of any punishment for illegal behavior thanks to its winning ways.

Kirov's citizens looked forward to their team's play the following year with great enthusiasm. As chapter 7, "The First League," demonstrates, the club's performance initially justified fans' fondest hopes. Dinamo played reasonably well even as doubts arose about the long-term effect of its coach's tactics. The season then unraveled; the team seemed doomed to relegation. A miracle finish saved the day. Dinamo would live to see yet another year in the First League.

Improved play required even greater financial backing. It was not forthcoming in 1983 as chapter 8, "Dead Last," attests. A poor choice of new and costly recruits added to the team's woes. Dinamo finished at the bottom of the league and suffered relegation. The loss provoked the disgust of its fans and sports correspondents. It also prompted the condemnation of the team, now a loser, by regional governing bodies and serious charges of fiscal mismanagement by the sport's governing organs in Moscow.

Chapter 9 covers Dinamo's fall from grace. Stripped of most of its financing and the support of fans, the team stumbled badly in its zone in the second league. Never again would Dinamo achieve anything resembling the glorious years of 1980 and 1981.

Sources

The discussion in part 1 of football in the Soviet Union relies extensively on reports in newspapers and journals. It cites repeatedly the scholarship of such historians as Robert Edelman, James Riordan, and Barbara Keys. I am especially indebted to archivist and historian Mikhail Iur'evich Prozumenshchikov. I am not the only specialist to appreciate the importance of his efforts. Ekaterina Emeliantseva recently wrote that "among Russian language publications, Prozumenshchikov's work remains the most extensive study of Soviet sport's direct dependence on political bodies and of the personal interference of political leaders in sporting matters from Stalin to Gorbachev."[20] Of particular importance, in 2004, Prozumenshchikov published *Big-Time Sports and Big-Time Politics*, with a chapter devoted to Soviet football. Its athletes, he argued, were dependent on "tough and sometimes cruel" political factors. Sport and its practitioners had become "the hostages of big politics."[21] In 2017, Prozumenshchikov as the deputy director of the Russian State Archive of Contemporary History (RGANI) and its director Natal'ia Georgievna Tomlina compiled and edited *The Game of Millions under Party Control: Soviet Football in Documents of the Communist*

Party's Central Committee. A volume devoted solely to Soviet football, it consists of over 250 of the archive's recently declassified documents that repeatedly reveal the political and financial machinations so prevalent in the history of that sport.[22]

Part 2 relies extensively on reports in the mass media (newspapers, radio, television) and archival documents. Two local newspapers dominated Kirov's newsstands. *Kirovskaia pravda*, a publication of the regional party committee, appeared six days a week. *Komsomol'skoe plemia*, sponsored by the party's youth arm for adolescents, the Young Communist League, thrice weekly. During the football season, *Kirovskaia pravda* printed multiple articles on Dinamo's performance by its chief sports correspondent Viktor Andreevich Chudinovskikh. *Komsomol'skoe plemia* published similar items by its reporter, Boris Aronovich Kolomensky. They understood that their job involved much more than the mere transmission of scores and the club's place in the standings. When the team played well, they shared their anxiety that it might not continue to do so. And when Dinamo performed poorly, both correspondents published biting and sarcastic criticism of players, coaches, and occasionally administrators. In so doing, they created what could be called "a little habitat" of freedom of expression, a topic to which I will return at length in this book's conclusion.[23]

The national weekly, *Futbol-Khokkei*, a sixteen-page Sunday supplement to the daily *Sovetskii sport*, evaluated Dinamo's performance from time to time. The publication had begun as *Futbol* in 1960 but expanded its coverage to include hockey in response to the considerable interest in the sport by the Communist Party's general secretary, Leonid Brezhnev. It changed its name to *Futbol-Khokkei* in 1967.[24]

Kirov's two main archives contain an immense amount of material about Dinamo. The two recently merged to become the Central State Archive of the Kirov Region (TsGAKO). To best indicate the location of documents, I cite in the reference notes below each depository separately: the State Archive for the Social and Political History of the Kirov Region (GASPI KO) and the State Archive of the Kirov Region (GAKO). GASPI KO holds records from the region's Dinamo society, the organization that supervised the football team. It also houses transcripts of transmissions from Kirov's radio and television stations. Its collection (*fond*) No. 6777 contains thousands upon thousands of letters submitted to *Kirovskaia pravda* by its readers. But that cache of letters proved to be a major disappointment. We know that Dinamo's fans sent multiple items of praise and complaint to *Kirovskaia pravda*. Occasionally, the newspaper encouraged them to do so by announcing contests for the best submission. Unfortunately, for the period under study here, the daily did not save those remarks. Rather, it archived almost exclusively letters of complaint about public services (transportation, housing, sewerage, roads, water) and letters with poetry submitted for publication (almost all of which were rejected, sometimes rudely so). The disparity between preserving such items and trashing others (those about sport, in particular) resulted from the editorial board's understanding of its newspaper's role in municipal and regional governance. Editors considered *Kirovskaia pravda* as something akin to an ombudsman for people with complaints about the ills of public services. It accordingly sent copies of grievances about such matters to the appropriate state organs. Sometimes it proceeded to investigate on its own. It did not regard Dinamo and professional sport as part of its oversight function. Perhaps it thought games were insignificant when compared to a breakdown in public utilities. Or perhaps the editorial board believed that it should tread warily with a team that was the creature of the regional branch of the powerful Ministry of Internal Affairs. *Kirovskaia pravada* did, however, occasionally print a summary of letters, some of them harshly critical, submitted about Dinamo's play. It also sometimes mentioned one or more specific items from happy or distraught fans. And, as noted above, the sports correspondents of both *Kirovskaia pravda* and *Komsomol'skoe plemia* were bold enough to scold the team and its administrators. Their brutal postmortems that followed a disappointing season included criticism, if only implicitly, of officials at the regional Ministry of Internal Affairs.

GAKO holds the records, reports, and rulings about Dinamo by Kirov's regional soviet and its executive committee. That material includes the soviet's correspondence with the Council of Ministers of both the Russian Republic and the USSR. Of particular importance is GAKO's collection of items from the regional soviet's committee for physical culture and sport (the sports committee), including correspondence with the sports committee of both the Russian Republic and the USSR. Unfortunately, most of the records of the region's Ministry of Internal Affairs, Dinamo's chief sponsor, are not accessible. Other lacunae exist as well. Available documentation at the GAKO reveals much about the regional government's financial support of efforts to improve the physical fitness of the public at large and of organized amateur sport. It provides, however, scant detail about the funding of its professional football team, Dinamo. It also tells us very little about the revenue generated at the gate when Dinamo played at home. Moreover, available documentation provides almost nothing about the salaries and other benefits Dinamo's coaches and players received from the Dinamo society and the regional soviet, including that soviet's branch of the Ministry of Internal Affairs.

In Moscow, the State Archive of the Russian Federation (GARF) yielded a trove of documents from the USSR's Sports Committee that are essential to this book's part 2.[25] There I found records of the deliberations of the presidium of the USSR's Football Federation and other administrative organs under the USSR's Sports Committee. I also discovered the committee's correspondence with the Central Committee and regional party and state authorities. That collection also holds reports from football inspectors who attended games and informed Moscow about the quality of play; the behavior of players, referees, and fans; and the condition of the playing field and stadium. It also contains testimony about alleged misdeeds by a number of teams and the demand that Kirov's Dinamo, among other clubs, verify the absence on its part of any such misbehavior.

Unfortunately, the archival record for the years 1979–1985 of the Russian Republic's Sports Committee and of the governing organs of the Dinamo society for the Russian Republic and the USSR are not yet accessible.[26] However, I found items from these organizations, including their deliberations and correspondence, in Kirov's archives (another instance when the provinces tell us more about the center than the latter at present is willing to reveal about itself).

For the years 1979–1985, Moscow's Russian State Archive for Contemporary History (RGANI) contains materials of the Central Committee's organ for the supervision of sports, its Propaganda Department, including its correspondence with regional party committees and the USSR's Sports Committee.[27] In concert or separately, these agencies discussed measures for disciplining players, coaches, and officials (and sometimes an entire team and sponsors) for a wide range of sins, especially when the club in question played poorly.

Looking Back

The history of Kirov's Dinamo illustrates at the regional level much about the nature and place of professional sports in the USSR. In particular, Dinamo's story reveals an obsession by clubs and their sponsors with winning at any cost and a concomitant exercise of political power in the late Soviet Union to make it so. It is not my first study of the uses and abuses of power in the history of the Kirov/Viatka region. My examination of the region's educational bureaucracy, *Grand Theater: Regional Governance in Stalin's Russia, 1931–1941*, published in 2009, found that during the 1930s, teachers, school directors, inspectors, and local officials in Kirov turned to theatrical displays of their own presumed authority to defend their interests in a party-state that otherwise rendered them powerless.[28]

My work that followed—a history of Kirov's Pedagogical Institute from 1941 to 1952—uncovered a tangled web of alliances in which state and party organs exercised power in a way irrespective of their purported place in a monolithic structure of authority arranged vertically from the top, Moscow, to the bottom, Kirov.[29] The people and governing institutions of the province and city of Kirov often pursued their own agenda. A subsequent book that assessed Soviet evacuation during World War II found that Kirov's citizens and institutions resented the hardships that the central government and evacuation required of them. While not directly challenging the Soviet system, they vigorously advanced their own interests and, in the case of officials, the welfare of the institutions and regions they represented.[30] More recently, my book *Revising the Revolution: The Unmaking of Russia's Official History of 1917* focused on the contested discussion in the capital, Moscow, and in a province, Viatka (Kirov), during the 1920s and early 1930s over the standards of historical scholarship and the interpretation of the 1917 revolution.[31] The center's Commission for the Study of the October Revolution and Party History (Istpart) in Moscow and the periphery's Istpart local in Viatka sharply disagreed over how best to adjudicate the demands of politics, ideology, and the scholarly canon in writing a useful history of 1917. Much to Moscow's consternation, Viatka had its own historical narrative to tell.

Kirov's Dinamo likewise has its own distinctive story, which, as we will see, was an integral part of a national obsession to win (or else).

Looking Ahead

With minor modifications from 1936 through 1971, professional football in the USSR consisted of a hierarchy of teams arranged at the top in what was called a Group A or Class A league with eight to twenty-six teams and a Group B or Class B league of many teams subdivided into additional categories. From 1971 through 1991, Soviet football consisted of three divisions: a Higher League of 18 clubs; the First League of 22–24; and the second league of around 150 divided into multiple geographic zones. In any given year, the best teams in a league earned *promotion* to the next higher league, and the worst underwent *relegation* to a lower league.

The Dinamo society was officially created on April 18, 1923, on Felix Dzerzhinsky's initiative and under the sponsorship of the State Political Directorate (GPU), which was the predecessor of the People's Commissariat of Internal Affairs (NKVD) and later the Ministry of Internal Affairs (MVD) and the Committee for State Security (KGB). The name given to the sports society was Latin and was meant to signify power in motion, a name not coincidentally given by Belgian inventor Zenobe Gramme to the electrical generator. The Dinamo society created a series of union-wide sport and fitness clubs, of which the Kirov branch was part. The Dinamo team in Kirov was controlled by the regional Dinamo society, an organization that promoted physical fitness as well as amateur and professional sports. It was, in turn, part of a larger Dinamo organization for the Russian Republic and the USSR as a whole. The Dinamo society at every level was affiliated with the MVD.

The story that follows is very much one of clubs' efforts to win by enticing players with illegal as well as legal benefits. Then as now, the age of a professional athlete determined in part their value. In the contemporary world of professional sports, advanced conditioning and diet allow athletes to remain prized possessions well into their thirties, a few even beyond. Football players in the period covered in this volume were not so fortunate. They "aged" far more quickly. In 1989, Nikolai Petrovich Starostin, the famous architect on and off the field of Moscow's Spartak who merits considerable attention in the following chapters, put it well. A football player experiences three stages in a career. The first occurs when they are eighteen to twenty-three years when their head does not always keep pace with their legs. The second, at twenty-four to twenty-eight when their head and legs work well together. The third, from the age of twenty-nine on when their legs do not always keep pace with their head.[32]

Readers conversant with Soviet football are acquainted with many of the sport's chief attributes as outlined in this volume. They will find surprising, however, the intensity already in the 1920s of a professionalization of the Soviet game and of an open market for the services of players by promises of multiple illicit benefits. They will find remarkable the number of scandals involving individual players and entire clubs and the persistent defiance of the center by many football clubs, including the one in the provincial depths of Kirov. An elaborate bureaucracy for the administration of sports, one obsessed with its own power of diktat, could not in fact control what it sought to regulate.

Historians of sport know well that fans, administrators, coaches, and players of almost all clubs embraced the preeminent importance of victory. But more so than acknowledged in existing historical literature, the seamier aspects of Soviet football as discussed here originated with and were fueled by an overwhelming need to win and keep on winning . . . or else. Specialists will also find it revelatory that several Soviet commentators suggested a fundamental reform of Soviet football as a prerequisite for a club's competitive success at home and, above all, for the USSR's national team in the international arena. Their recommendations included an allowance for individual creativity and imagination on the playing field. They may well have hoped that their suggestions might lead to modest changes in Soviet governance and society.

NOTES

1. Simon Kuper, *Soccer against the Enemy*, 2nd ed. (New York: Nation Books, 2006), 1.

2. Robert Edelman, *Serious Fun: A History of Spectator Sports in the USSR* (New York: Oxford University Press, 1993).

3. For analyses of sport in general and football in particular, see essays in a special issue of the journal *Historical Social Research* 31, no. 1 (115) (January 2006) and in Heather L. Dichter and Andrew L. Johns, eds., *Diplomatic Games: Sport, Statecraft and International Relations since 1945* (Lexington: University Press of Kentucky, 2014); Tamir Ban-On, *The World through Soccer: The Cultural Impact of Global Sport* (New York: Rowman and Littlefield, 2014); Eric Dunning and Chris Rojek, eds., *Sport and Leisure in the Civilizing Process: Critique and Counter-Critique* (Toronto: University of Toronto Press, 1992); Eric Dunning and Kenneth Sheard, *Barbarians, Gentlemen and Players*, 2nd ed. (New York: Routledge, 2005); Bero Rigauer, *Sport and Work*, trans. Allen Guttmann (New York: Columbia University Press, 1981). See also Pierre Bourdieu, *Distinction: A Social Critique of the Judgment of Taste*, trans. Richard Nice (Cambridge, MA: Harvard University Press, 1984), for an argument that the "class body" determines an individual's preference for a particular type of food, dress, and sport. The author's emphasis on the dominant class's aversion to participation in and observance of team sports now seems most outdated (see 169–225). David Goldblatt has written a number of important volumes: David Goldblatt, *The Ball Is Round: A Global History of Soccer* (New York: Riverhead Books, 2008); Goldblatt, *The Game of Our Lives: The Meaning and Making of English Football* (New York: Penguin, 2015); and Goldblatt, *The Age of Football: Soccer and the 21st Century* (New York: W. W. Norton, 2020). For a radical treatment of the culture of sport and masculinity, see Varda Burstyn, *The Rites of Men: Manhood, Politics, and the Culture of Sport* (Toronto: University of Toronto Press, 2000), especially the sections "Football, Masculinity, and Militarization" (69–75) and "Hypermasculinity and Football Hooliganism," (194–201); Kimberly B. George, "A Feminist Football Fan: On the Psychic Life of Spectatorship," in *Football, Culture and Power*, ed. David J. Leonard, Kimberly B. George, and Wade Davis (New York: Routledge, 2017). See also Franklin Foer, *How Soccer Explains the World: An Unlikely Theory of Globalization* (New York: HarperCollins, 2004) and John Sugden and Alan Tomlinson, "Football, *Ressentiment* and Resistance in the Break-Up of the Former Soviet Union," *Culture, Sport, Society* 2, no. 2 (Summer 2000): 89–108. On football as business, see especially: Kieran Maguire, *The Price of Football: Understanding*

Football Club Finance (Newcastle: Agenda, 2020) and Daniel Geey, *Done Deal: An Insider's Guide to Football Contracts, Multi-Million Pound Transfers and Premier League Big Business* (London: Bloomsbury, 2019). On the politics of football generally, see Simon Kuper, *Soccer against the Enemy: How the World's Most Popular Sport Starts and Fuels Revolutions and Keeps Dictators in Power* (New York: Bold Type Books, 1994 [2006]). A special issue of the journal *Sociological Review* 39, no. 3 (August 1991) was devoted to a sociological and anthropological examination of fan violence. Allen Guttmann reviewed scholarship published in a number of languages in his "Sport, Politics, and the Engaged Historian," *Journal of Contemporary History* 38, no. 3 (July 2003): 363–375. A more recent review of scholarship on Russian sport is in Ekaterina Emeliantseva, "Russian Sport and the Challenges of Its Recent Historiography," *Journal of Sport History* 38, no. 3 (Fall 2011): 361–372. Zoologist Desmond Morris, best known for his wildly successful *The Naked Ape* (1967) wrote a breezy account of the behavior of players, managers, referees, and fans as expressions of tribal rites and rituals: Desmond Morris, *The Soccer Tribe* (London: Jonathan Cape, 1981).

4. Hans Ulrich Gumbrecht, *In Praise of Athletic Beauty* (Cambridge, MA: Belknap, 2006), 25. Gumbrecht's is a book written by a fan and philosopher that underscores the beauty and aesthetic appeal of the sport. In a discussion of the book, Hayden White declared, "Likening watching sports to a religious experience, as Gumbrecht does, diverts attention from the sleaziness and ugliness of the institutions of college sports." Gumbrecht replied by reemphasizing the sport's "aesthetic appeal, as powerful as the experience of a beautiful work of music or art." See the comments by White and Gumbrecht in "The Place and Value of College Sports: 2 Views," *Chronicle of Higher Education* 52, no. 42 (June 23, 2006): B10. In a follow-up book, an unrepentant Gumbrecht spoke of "the special elation of the stadium" and that "being part of a crowd sets free potentialities which are normally dormant": Hans Ulrich Gumbrecht, *Crowds: The Stadium as a Ritual of Intensity*, trans. Emily Gooding (Stanford, CA: Stanford University Press, 2021), 63, 107. At the outset of a book on art and ideology in Russia and the USSR, Tim Harte wrote, "I have tried to take sports at face value and not follow the example of scholars, artists, and others who have construed sports as veiled metaphors for labor, war, or sex." Tim Harte, *Faster, Higher, Stronger, Comrades! Sports, Art, and Ideology in Late Russian and Early Soviet Culture* (Madison: University of Wisconsin Press, 2020), xi.

5. Hans Ulrich Gumbrecht, "Allure Constrained by 'Ethics'? How Athletic Events Have Engaged Their Spectators," in *The Allure of Sports in Western Culture*, ed. John Zilcosky and Marlo Burks (Toronto: Toronto University Press, 2019), 3. Gumbrecht added that these scholars cannot take seriously the pleasure of watching sports (37). See also in that volume Annette Vowinckel, "The Ethics and Allure of the Foul in Football," in which the author argues that for spectators

"the intriguing moments or real football" occur with the violation on the field of the game's rules (237).

6. Not every devotee of sport, of course, appreciates football or soccer as a game. American political columnist Ann Coulter sarcastically dismissed soccer as foreign to the American way and hardly the beautiful game: "Everyone just runs up and down the field and, every once in a while, a ball accidentally goes in. That's when we're supposed to go wild. I'm already asleep." Ann Coulter, "America's Favorite National Pastime: Hating Soccer," June 25, 2014, https://anncoulter.com/2014/06/25/americas-favorite-national-pastime-hating-soccer/.

7. Nick Hornby, *Fever Pitch* (New York: Riverhead Books, 1992). Hornby's book inspired the commercial film by the same name, released in 1997 and then remade in 2005. The later version, however, was about an individual's addiction to the American baseball team the Boston Red Sox.

8. Hornby, *Fever Pitch*, quotations in succession on 80, 227, 10–11, 71. Gumbrecht has expressed a similar sentiment: "When I am actually watching sports, I am not pursuing any intellectually (or even ethically) edifying ends. I simply enjoy the moments of intensity that such events provide." Gumbrecht, *In Praise of Athletic Beauty*, 31–32. One critic has called Hornby's book "part of the culture of the male-confessional that took shape at the time against a background of discussion of male roles after the impact of feminism": Dave Russell, *Football and the English: A Social History of Association Football in England, 1963–1995* (Preston: Carnegie, 1997), 230.

9. Jean-Philippe Toussaint, *Soccer*, trans. Shaun Whiteside (New Brunswick, NJ: Rutgers University Press, 2019), quotations in succession vii, 13, 14, 22.

10. Toussaint, *Soccer*, 67. With pained humor, Toussaint describes his efforts to follow the semifinal match between the Netherlands and Argentina teams. Just when a penalty shootout to determine the winner began, a storm interrupted the streaming. Toussaint began to listen on the radio. Then the electricity went out. He found a transistor radio just in time to follow the final and deciding kick (71–73).

11. On Galeano, see John Foster, "Tell Me How You Play and I'll Tell You Who You Are," in *Soccer and Philosophy: Beautiful Thoughts on the Beautiful Game*, ed. Ted Richards (Chicago: Open Court, 2010), 254.

12. Eduardo Galeano, *Soccer in Sun and Shadow*, trans. Mark Fried (New York: Nation Books, 2013), quotations in succession 7, 256, 269. Galeano the leftist could not help but repeat—and in a delightfully humorous way—the refrain: "Well-informed sources in Miami were announcing the imminent fall of Fidel Castro, it was only a matter of hours."

13. Simon Critchley, *What We Think about When We Think about Soccer* (New York: Penguin Books, 2017), quotations in succession 9, 12, 161, 160, 19, 82, xvi, 106. See a lengthy review of Critchley's book in Aleksei S. Titkov, "Petushinye boi na 'Enfilde': Anatomiia rituala poznaniia," *Sotsiologiia vlasti* 30, no. 2 (2018):

231–246. Titkov acknowledges the author's multidimensional approach to the game, while he, Titkov, analyzes Critchley's work from sociological, anthropological, and philosophical perspectives. For articles on football by specialists in the field of philosophy that speak far more about philosophy than the game itself, see Richards, *Soccer and Philosophy*.

14. Bill Buford, *Among the Thugs* (New York: W. W. Norton, 1992). For the most part, Buford avoids any sociological analysis of fan violence that would attribute it to any one class and in particular to the working class. Galeano wrote that "rowdy crowds insult soccer the way drunks insult wine." Galeano, *Soccer in Sun and Shadow*, 189. Buford has continued his career as a participatory journalist in the realm of cuisine: Bill Buford, *Heat: An Amateur's Adventures as Kitchen Slave, Line Cook, Pasta Maker, and Apprentice to a Dante-Quoting Butcher in Tuscany* (New York: Alfred A. Knopf, 2006) and Buford, *Dirt: Adventures in Lyon as a Chef in Training, Father, and Sleuth Looking for the Secret of French Cooking* (New York: Alfred A. Knopf, 2020).

15. Gary Armstrong, *Football Hooligans: Knowing the Score* (New York: Berg, 1998), 295. Armstrong denounces, unfairly in my view, Buford's work as "a poor book that was more fictional than a novel" (19). For a far different account, one similar to Buford's, see reminiscences of hooligans associated with southeast London's Millwall football club in Andrew Woods, *No-One Likes Us, We Don't Care: True Stories from Millwall, Britain's Most Notorious Football Hooligans* (London: John Blake, 2011). As recalled there, these individuals used assorted weapons from razors and knives to bricks and hammers in pitched battles with their rivals during the 1970s and 1980s. A sociological examination of football hooliganism in the same period concluded that violence was the product chiefly of "youth and young men from the 'rougher' sections of the working class." They were determined to defend their territory in and beyond the stadium. See chap. 9, "The Social Roots of Aggressive Masculinity," in Eric Dunning, Patrick Murphy, and John Williams, *The Roots of Football Hooliganism: An Historical and Sociological Study* (New York: Routledge, 1988), 184–216, quote on 213. The authors argue more generally that since the mid-1960s, a minority of workers faced with economic insecurity, violence in their own lives, and discrimination—those who are "unincorporated" in society—have associated football with their own acts of violence (see especially 230–237). For an earlier view that contends that football violence is the result of efforts by "the rump"—essentially the lumpenproletariat—to assert control over professional players and a game that no longer represents it, the rump, see Ian Taylor, "'Football Mad': A Speculative Sociology of Football Hooliganism," in *Sport: Readings from a Sociological Perspective*, ed. Eric Dunning (Toronto: University of Toronto Press, 1971), 352–377.

16. Armstrong, *Football Hooligans*, 249, 295, 300. Even the "hardest" were "most discriminatory in their violence" (249). In an article coauthored with Richard Giulianotti, Armstrong reached similar conclusions: Gary Armstrong

and Richard Giulianotti, "Legislators and Interpreters: The Law and 'Football Hooligans,'" in *Entering the Field: New Perspectives on World Football* (New York: Berg, 1997), 175–191. "Partisan fanship is part of a complex and social process which is constructed and played out almost as carnival" (175). "Though the performers periodically enjoy the performance aspects of threat and disorder, this leads to violence and serious injury only on rare occasions" (181). For relatively minor forms of misbehavior by football fans in Moscow during the late 1970s and early 1980s, see John Bushnell, *Moscow Graffiti: Language and Subculture* (Boston: Unwin Hyman, 1990), 29–65.

17. On Kirov city's population, see a report by its radio station, October 29, 1980, in Gosudarstvennyi arkhiv sotsial'no-politicheskoi istorii Kirovskoi oblasti, f. R-6818, op. 5, d. 1362, l. 102. The region was home to 1,660,000 people.

18. Igor' Rabiner, "Fallen Idol," *Blizzard: The Football Quarterly*, no. 3 (December 1, 2011).

19. Igor' Rabiner, *Spartakovskie ispovedi* (Moscow: Olma, 2011), 7. His books: Igor' Rabiner, *Kak ubivali "Spartak": Sensatsionnye podrobnosti padeniia velikogo kluba* (Moscow: "Sekret firmy," 2006) and Rabiner, *Nasha futbol'naia Rossiia* (Moscow: Olma, 2008).

20. Emeliantseva, "Russian Sport and the Challenges of Its Recent Historiography," 367. Robert Edelman also singles out Prozumenshchikov's work for praise: R. Edel'man, S. A. Bondarenko, and O. V. Kil'danov, "Sport pomogaet nam otvetit' na fundamental'nye voprosy: Interv'iu s Robertom Edelmanom," *Sotsiologicheskoe obozrenie* 16, no. 2 (2017): 282.

21. M. Iu. Prozumenshchikov, *Bol'shoi sport i bol'shaia politika* (Moscow: ROSSPEN, 2004), quotes on 9 and 10. The chapter on football: "The Games around the Game of Millions," 345–395, relies largely on documents in the Russian State Archive of Modern History (RGANI, in abbreviated Russian) and covers the years from 1953 to 1985. On the history, holdings, publications, and personnel of the archive, see Mikhail Iur'evich Prozumenshchikov, "Rossiiskii gosudarstvennyi arkhiv noveishei istorii (RGANI): Kratkie itogi poslednikh let i blizhaishie perspektivy," *Biulleten' Germanskogo isotricheskogo instituta v Moskve*, no. 4 (2010): 12–22.

22. N. G. Tomilina and M. Iu. Prozumenshchikov, *Igra millionov pod partiinym kontrolem: Sovetskii futbol po dokumentam TsK KPSS* (Moscow: Mezhdunarodnyi fond "Demokratiia," 2017). See Prozumenshchikov's valuable introductory article, "Obratnaia storona sovetskogo futbola," 5–37. Also "Interv'iu s M. Iu. Prozumenshchikovym," *Sotsiologicheskoe obozrenie* 17, no. 2 (2018): 173–194.

23. My use of *habitat* is a rough adaptation of Pierre Bourdieu's "habitus." My argument is that in the realm of Soviet professional football, a consciousness, a set of attitudes prevailed among the many agents involved in the sport on and off the playing field. These agents embraced the possibility, even the necessity, of

expressing their own thoughts and feelings about the way the game was administered and played. I give more agency to these actors than Bourdieu, who argued that the actions of such individuals "are the product of a *modus operandi* of which they are not the producer and have no conscious mastery." Pierre Bourdieu, *Outline of a Theory of Practice*, trans. Richard Nice (Cambridge, MA: Harvard University Press, 1977), 79.

24. The official explanation for the renaming attributed it to the growth in the popularity of hockey: *Igra millionov*, 692–693. On Brezhnev's love for sport, see Mikhail Prozumenshchikov, "Action in the Era of Stagnation: Leonid Brezhnev and the Soviet Olympic Dream," in *The Whole World Was Watching: Sport in the Cold War*, ed. Robert Edelman and Christopher Young (Stanford, CA: Stanford University Press, 2020), 73–84.

25. State Archive of the Russian Federation (GARF), f. R-7576, op. 31, 34, and 35, especially 31. I am indebted to Svetlana Borisovna Shutova for research in this archive and in the Russian State Archive of Contemporary History (Rossiiskii gosudarstvennyi arkhiv noveishei istorii, hereafter RGANI). Twice in 2021, first in the spring, then in the fall, within days of my departure to Moscow, Russia's COVID-19 restrictions intervened to abort my plan for travel. In 2022, two days before departure, Russia's invasion of Ukraine caused the flight to be canceled.

26. For the Russian Republic's Sports Committee: GARF, f. A-564. For Dinamo society's governing council of the Russian Republic and the USSR, respectively: GARF, f. A-558 and GARF, f. R-8410.

27. RGANI, f. 5, especially opis' 77 and 88.

28. Larry E. Holmes, *Grand Theater: Regional Governance in Stalin's Russia, 1931–1941* (Lanham, MD: Lexington Books, 2009).

29. Larry E. Holmes, *War, Evacuation, and the Exercise of Power: Kirov's Pedagogical Institute, 1941–1952* (Lanham, MD: Lexington Books, 2012).

30. Larry E. Holmes, *Stalin's World War II Evacuations: Triumph and Troubles in Kirov* (Lawrence: University Press of Kansas, 2017).

31. Larry E. Holmes, *Revising the Revolution: The Unmaking of Russia's Official History of 1917* (Bloomington: Indiana University Press, 2021).

32. Nikolai Petrovich Starostin, *Futbol skvoz' gody* (Moscow: Molodaia gvardiia, 1989), 195.

PART I
THE SHAPE OF SOVIET FOOTBALL, 1917–1985

NOT A SPORTING AFFAIR

Novelist and sports historian James Riordan has observed that the infant Soviet state hoped to create a "new pattern of sports relations" based neither on competitive sports nor on individual records but rather on "physical culture."[1] For the new government, winning was not important; it was entirely beyond the socialist pale. Rather, it sought to encourage physical activity for the development of well-rounded Soviet citizens suitable for a new socialist society. Such "new Soviet persons" would make the workplace a more productive unit and would possess the will and ability to defend socialism against enemies at home and abroad. Not everyone agreed. Some officials and athletes thought such ideas inappropriately disparaged competitive sport.[2]

Physical Culture or Sport?

Soon after the 1917 revolution, the Soviet republic placed all sports societies and clubs under Moscow's Universal Military Training Administration (*Vsevobuch*, in abbreviated Russian). During its existence from 1918 to 1923, it compelled daily training for all males from eighteen to forty.[3] Other organizations, among them factories; schools; and the party's youth arms, the Young Communist League (Komsomol) and, after 1922, the Pioneers organization, encouraged physical exercise. The 1926 film *Stride, Soviet* by Soviet director Dziga Vertov presented physical fitness as essential to the nation's victory over social decadence. Near the film's end, a section titled "In a Deadly Battle with a Rotten Dying Form of Everyday Life" contrasted calisthenics, skating, and skiing on the one hand, with drinking, smoking, and modern dance on the other.[4] "The Soviet body was a battlefield," historian Tricia Starks has observed, "in the war

Viatka's Sports Club for Universal Military Training, c. 1922. *Courtesy of Herzen Public State Library.*

against sloth, disease, alcohol, tobacco, poor hygiene, improper sexual urges, religion, and political lethargy."[5] And the effort was very much a gendered affair. The whole complex of activities that fell under the heading of physical culture, Starks noted, sought in particular to prepare males "for leadership and domination."[6]

The role of competitive sport within the field of physical culture was an especially contested subject. In 1920, the Soviet republic created a Supreme Council of Physical Culture explicitly avoiding the word *sport* in its title. Radical voices condemned almost all forms of contests. The Proletarian Culture and Educational Organizations (Proletkul't), founded in 1917, was one such voice. It insisted on the replacement of so-called bourgeois culture with a proletarian one. Proletkul't dismissed competition as "bourgeois" and "foreign." Any so-called sporting activity, it said, should avoid a specialization in it by its participants, desist from keeping and setting records, and involve the public at large. Proletkul't would allow "sport" primarily in the form of pageants to celebrate revolutionary holidays and in the performance of so-called labor gymnastics to enhance productivity on the shop floor.[7]

Proletkul't did not get its way. Vladimir Lenin and other prominent Bolsheviks rejected the very notion of a distinct proletarian culture at least for the foreseeable future. They preferred instead an aggressive appropriation of those aspects of the bourgeois legacy deemed useful in advancing the interests of the Soviet state and society. Organized sports and athletic contests would qualify, but only in a new revolutionary form.

The Soviet state refused to participate in the "bourgeois" Olympics. It opted rather for extravaganzas organized by the Red Sports International (Sportintern), created in Moscow in 1921 as an auxiliary of the Communist International. In these venues, people of varied ability participated in such pursuits as gymnastics, tumbling, calisthenics, grenade throwing, and hiking.[8] In August 1928, Sportintern conducted the First All-Union Summer Spartakiad, held in Moscow to compete with the Summer Olympics in Amsterdam. More than seven thousand athletes, including several hundred foreigners, participated in twelve events (including football). To be sure, individual records in some events were kept and broken in the Spartakiad and other, similar celebrations. These games were nevertheless "alternatives to modern sport," as Barbara Keys has written, "collectivist rather than competitive, mass-based rather than elitist."[9]

The Party Speaks

In 1925, the Communist Party's Central Committee expressed its unease with competition and the setting of records. Its decree "On the Tasks of the Party in Physical Culture," issued on July 13, avoided the word *sport* completely. It advanced what it called "physical culture" as a means to promote public health and the "cultural, economic, and military training of youth." It did not, however, dismiss competition altogether. It acknowledged its importance, but only as "one of the means of involving the public in physical culture and of promoting the achievements of individuals and especially of entire collectives."[10]

Many party officials nevertheless preferred something more than a conditional embrace of competition.[11] Over the next ten years, the party shifted its position on the subject, lurching first in one direction, then in the other. Less than fourteen months after the Central Committee's decree in mid-1925, the party's Fifteenth Party Conference (October 26 to November 3, 1926) expressed doubts about a dismissive attitude toward athletic contests. A "bookish approach toward physical culture," the conference declared, had reduced it to "hygiene, exercises, and choreographed movements." The conference condemned what it called a "scornful attitude toward competitive methods." Moreover, it questioned the wisdom of a "struggle against recordmania and sportmania." Denigration of sports had discouraged workers' participation

Relay Race, Viatka, June 1929. Physical Culture or Competitive Sport? *Courtesy of Herzen Public State Library.*

in athletic activity and had driven them "to seek relief in bars and on the street."[12]

In January 1928, the Supreme Council of Physical Culture launched a weekly *Physical Culture and Sport*. Yet despite the word *sport* in the journal's name, the initial issue's editorial avoided the word while extolling the virtues of physical culture for economic development and national defense.[13] In September 1929, the party's Central Committee denounced "a deviation toward recordmania."[14] It called for the creation of an agency that did not confuse physical culture with competitive sports. The following April, the presidium of the USSR's Central Executive Committee did just that with the formation of an All-Union Council of Physical Culture, explicitly avoiding *sport* in its title.[15]

In 1930, former Commissar of Education from 1917 to 1929 Anatolii Vasil'evich Lunacharsky joined the conversation. In a short book, *My Thoughts about Sport*, he dismissed the highly competitive and spectator sports popular in the West. They were forms of entertainment that diverted the working class's focus away from the creation of a just and equitable society.[16] Lunacharsky preferred the USSR's brand of physical culture with an emphasis, as he understood it, on non-competitive exercise, personal hygiene, nutrition, healthy conditions at work, and communal rather than individual household duties.[17] Yet Lunacharsky acknowledged that competition among teams might be useful if it avoided the evils of individualism and prioritized teamwork as a prerequisite for victory. Then, surprisingly, at the end of his essay, he extolled the most individualistic of sports, boxing, as a potentially healthy endeavor in a socialist society. The sport required, he wrote, physical conditioning and perseverance. Its strict rules, when properly enforced in the ring by a referee, compelled pugilists to regard each other as comrades, not opponents.[18] Sport remained a way to build physical fitness and comradeship rather than a field where competition and rivalry were encouraged.

Sport Victorious

In 1931, on the initiative of the Komsomol, the state introduced the program Ready for Labor and Defense of the USSR. Best known by the abbreviation GTO, it encouraged physical exercise among adolescents and adults by awarding them badges for achievements in a variety of activities. It remained an important state-sponsored affair in the decades that followed. At the same time, Moscow made highly specialized and professionalized sport a top priority. In May 1934, the Central Executive Committee, which four years earlier had refused to use *sport* in the title of its newly formed All-Union Council of Physical Culture, now blessed the word with the creation of the honor Master of Sport, to be awarded to the nation's top, implicitly record-breaking, athletes.[19] Soviet commentators now repeatedly spoke of a necessary quest to surpass bourgeois records.[20] Cities and regions opened sports schools to train a new generation of specialists. In June 1936, the council added the word *sport* to its title to become the All-Union Council of Physical Culture and Sport (the Sports Committee) subordinate to the USSR's Council of Peoples Commissars.[21] That year, fifty athletes and sport administrators received orders and medals. In 1937, the state awarded the sports clubs Dinamo and Spartak the Order of Lenin.

These awards accompanied a larger cultural and political shift in the USSR. Historian Katerina Clark has emphasized the transition from the valorization of the masses in the 1920s to a glorification of hierarchy and the individual hero in the 1930s.[22] Little men and women could suddenly become "big." Through miraculous achievements on the job, Stakhanovites became larger than life. On an even grander level, Soviet explorers conquered the Arctic North and aviators set numerous world records for distance, height, and speed. In June 1937, Valerii Pavlovich Chkalov set a world record by flying for sixty-three hours nonstop from Moscow to Vancouver, Washington. In the artistic realm, the emphasis during the 1920s on the simultaneous movement of multiple bodies gave way in

Deineka, *Soccer Player* (1931).

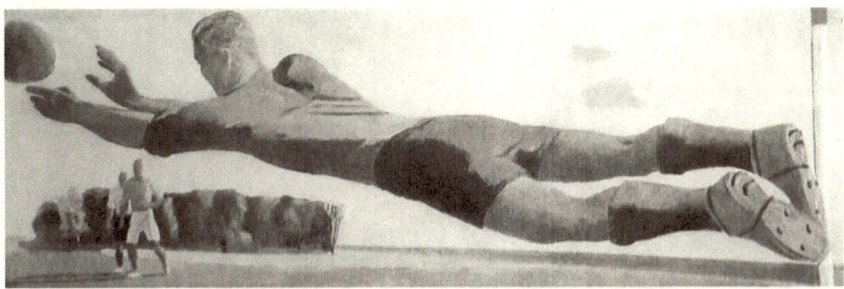

Deineka, *Goalkeeper* (1934).

the 1930s to a portrayal of individual athletes often in a state of flight.[23] Painter Aleksandr Aleksandrovich Deineka portrayed it well in his *Soccer Player* (1931) and *Goalkeeper* (1934).[24]

Professionalization

During the early 1920s, the Soviet press denounced football as one of the bourgeois sports injurious to mind and body. It hardly helped matters that many of the football matches that did occur featured excessively rough play and fights by athletes and spectators alike. Inexperienced and unqualified referees (as well as the militia) could neither prevent nor easily quash the ensuing bedlam.[25] And yet the sport grew in popularity despite the violence; an absence of comfortable seating (when seating was available at all); an insufficient number of public toilets; few food stands that, when present, offered stale products; and dusty, pockmarked playing surfaces. Cities and regions organized their own teams. By the late 1920s, football had become the most popular spectator sport in the USSR. Few events at Moscow's Spartakiad in 1928 elicited the public's interest except for football matches. Over fifty thousand spectators attended the final between squads representing Moscow and the Ukrainian SSR.[26]

The sport's popularity went hand in hand with its rapid professionalization. That had been precisely the case decades earlier in England and Scotland, as historian Tony Collins has so well demonstrated. The formation there of a football league created a fan base now certain of a set schedule of games and a quality product performed by players who were assessed on their merit rather than their social status. Professionalism, Collins concluded, "was the rocket fuel that propelled soccer into the stratosphere."[27] And so it was in the first decade of Soviet power. As a chronicler of this phenomenon, Sergei Butov

Spring Transfers "Amateur Athletes" Seek the Best Deal. The recruiter for Dinamo sits behind the desk in the upper-left-hand corner. *Fizkul'tura i sport*, no. 18 (May 5, 1928), 16.

has shown that as early as the 1920s, clubs enticed players with fictional jobs, bonuses, and other benefits to include apartments or rooms in a hotel rather than in a dormitory. Players transferred from one team to the next in search of the best deal they could find. The Soviet press made no secret of this professionalization of the sport even as it frequently condemned it.[28]

In the early and mid-1920s, Soviet professional teams ventured abroad to engage amateur teams that, on the demands of Sportintern, consisted of members of the working class. They were hardly a match for their "less socialist" guests.[29] In 1923, the Soviet entry won all three games against amateur workers' clubs in Germany by a cumulative score of 26–1. The result appropriately elicited the scorn of the host and Sportintern.[30]

Reasonably objective Soviet observers understood that the nation's teams, including its national squad formed in 1924, played weak foreign clubs and could hardly match the expertise of "bourgeois" clubs abroad. Some critics thought it should remain so, thus avoiding, they hoped, a more serious case of the disease of professionalism. At least a few domestic teams went even further in their disdain for commercialization of the sport. In 1930, a newly appointed director of a factory in Moscow summoned his enterprise's club and asked its players who, in fact, earned their salaries by actually working on the shop floor. When no one among the assembled could respond in the affirmative, the director fired them all.[31] He was not alone. But his and other amateur clubs suffered a string of defeats at the hands of their well-compensated opponents. "In the end," as Keys has noted, "proletarian *fizkultura* lost to capitalist soccer."[32]

As football's popularity grew in the Soviet Union, governing organs at the municipal, regional, and national levels increased their financial support of the game. At the center, Soviet leaders understood that the sport could be used, especially if thoroughly professionalized and thereby victorious, to advance the nation's prestige. In October 1934, despite fears of defeat abroad, the national squad played for the first time a frankly professional team, Zhidenitse, which led the Czech football league at the time, in the Czech city of Brno. Surprisingly, the visitor won by a score of 3–2.[33] More trips followed in 1935 to compete against European professional teams. On January 1, 1936, the city of Moscow's collective played the well-known Parisian club, Racing, which consisted of athletes from France's colonies, France, and several other European countries. The loss by only a score of 2–1 to this especially strong professional squad was a cause for joy. It nevertheless elicited concern about the wisdom of competing abroad.[34] Thereafter, competition beyond the confines of the USSR continued on a hit-and-miss basis as the nation's leadership, despite pressure to act otherwise from the USSR's Sports Committee, feared defeat at the hands of foreign "bourgeois" teams.[35] Games in the USSR with a team of Basques in 1937, to be discussed below, validated their belief in the relative weakness internationally of Soviet football.

To ensure improved performance at home and, when possible, abroad, players called for greater professionalization of their sport by prolonged periods of training and greater benefits for players. They got their way. In 1935, the leading sports newspaper, *Krasnyi sport*, a publication of the USSR's Committee for Physical Culture, openly discussed the sale and transfer of players in which athletes as well as clubs reaped considerable financial rewards. At the end of 1935, Komsomol's Central Committee and the Committee for Physical Culture condemned the practice. It continued nevertheless. By this time, Butov concluded, Soviet football "had become a full-fledged profession."[36]

Professionalization was further enhanced with the formation of a major football league in 1936 "modeled after similar leagues in capitalist countries."[37] Consisting of seven teams, it quickly expanded to over twenty. Minor leagues were also formed. In April 1936, the USSR's Sports Committee with the endorsement of the Central Committee's Politburo planned to invite a prominent British professional team to play several games in the Soviet Union. It hoped to bring if not Manchester City, then Chelsea or Glasgow's Rangers.[38] Sadly, the event could not be successfully organized. That failure hardly dampened popular enthusiasm for the sport. In 1938, an average of nineteen thousand fans attended games in the USSR's major league. By the end of the decade, matches of Moscow's top teams attracted up to one hundred thousand spectators. Teams' sponsors rewarded their best players ever more handsomely. While readily acknowledging the professional nature of the game, the Soviet press nevertheless meticulously avoided specifying just how much players earned.[39]

Yet controversy over sport, especially over its professionalized version and an alleged preoccupation with victory, persisted. The tension was evident in the Soviet film released in January 1937, *The Goalkeeper* (*Vratar'*). The character of the goalie, Anton Kandidov, personified both the evils and the virtues of compensated stardom. His play for pay for a squad that did not represent his home factory merited condemnation (and an inglorious defeat on the field when he allowed a goal). But his subsequent performance for the Soviet national team against black-shirted foreign professionals, in which he blocked shot after shot, earned redemption (and he got the girl). In the contest's final seconds, Kandidov made a game-saving stop of a penalty kick. Then, as the film's audience presumably suspended disbelief, Kandidov dribbled the ball from his end to the opponent's and scored the game-winning goal as time expired.[40]

Heralded songwriters Vasily Lebedev-Kumach and Isaac Dunaevsky forecast the great event in music written for the movie, the "Sportsman's March." Just before the big game with the foreign opponent, Soviet players sang the final stanza that summoned their goalkeeper to defend the USSR from all foreign enemies.

> Hey you, goalie, prepare for battle!
> You're a watchman by the gate!
> Just imagine, that behind you
> The borderline must be kept safe![41]

The star for Moscow's Spartak in the 1950s, Nikita Siminoian, recalled how as an adolescent he and his friends watched *Vratar'* on multiple occasions. They believed that Kandidov in fact had existed and had allowed a total of only one goal in his entire life.[42]

In the early years of the Soviet Union, there was intense disagreement on how to approach sport and what role it would play in the new socialist society. Organizations such as Proletkul't, which focused on remaking society, felt that competitive sport had no place in Soviet society and instead, the focus should be on group events that helped promote physical fitness. High-ranking party members such as Lunacharsky promoted this view. But others, such as Lenin, supported co-opting bourgeois culture, including competitive sport as a way of promoting mass engagement. Throughout the 1920s, top party, state, and cultural organizations waffled over including competitive sports or sports at all (as opposed to physical culture) in official programs policies and organizations. Despite party and state leaders' indecisiveness on the issue, Soviet football increased rapidly in popularity with the masses, particularly once leagues had been established and the sport started to professionalize. By the mid-1930s, the pendulum had swung in favor of including and promoting competitive sports as part of Soviet life, though as demonstrated in the abovementioned film, playing professionally for hire was still officially discouraged. Players were supposed to be motivated by their love of and loyalty to the organization they represented or their country.

NOTES

1. James Riordan, "The Sports Policy of the Soviet Union, 1917–1941," in *Sport and International Politics: Impact of Fascism and Communism on Sport*, ed. Pierre Arnaud and James Riordan (New York: Routledge, 1998), 67. The concept of "physical culture" predated in Russia its embrace by Soviet authorities. For its earlier manifestation, see Louise McReynolds, *Russia at Play: Leisure Activities at the End of the Tsarist Era* (Ithaca, NY: Cornell University Press, 2003), 87–95.

2. See the discussion of the role of competition in Soviet physical culture in the 1920s in John Read, "Physical Culture and Sport in the Early Soviet Period," *Australian Slavonic and East European Studies* 10, no. 1 (1966): 59–84. See also James Riordan, "Worker Sport within a Worker State: The Soviet Union," in *The Story of Worker Sport*, ed. Arnd Krüger and James Riordan (Champaign, IL: Human Kinetics, 1996), 43–65. So-called hygienists argued that such activities as football, boxing, and field events were harmful to physical and mental health.

3. On Vsevobuch and subsequent squabbles among agencies and officials over the administration of physical culture in the 1920s, see Susan Grant, "The Politics and Organization of Physical Culture in the USSR during the 1920s," *Slavonic and East European Review* 89, no. 3 (July 2011): 494–515. On the linkage between physical culture and the new "Soviet man," see David L. Hoffmann, "Bodies of Knowledge: Physical Culture and the New Soviet Man," in *Language and Revolution: Making Modern Political Identities*, ed. Igal Halfin (London: Frank Cass, 2002), 228–242.

4. The section is shown with about eleven minutes remaining in the sixty-nine-minute film.

5. Tricia Starks, *The Body Soviet: Propaganda, Hygiene, and the Revolutionary State* (Madison: University of Wisconsin Press, 2008), 164.

6. Starks, *Body Soviet*, 193. Kateryna Kobchenko argues that in the 1920s, Soviet authorities attempted to involve women in physical culture as an act of emancipation. By the end of the decade, she acknowledges, these attempts "remained only declarations of intent." Kateryna Kobchenko, "Emancipation within the Ruling Ideology: Soviet Women in Fizkul'tura and Sport in the 1920s and 1930s," in *Euphoria and Exhaustion: Modern Sport in Soviet Culture and Society*, ed. Nikolaus Katzer, Sandra Budy, Alexandra Köhring, and Manfred Zeller (New York: Campus, 2010), 255–256, quote on 256.

7. James Riordan, "Sport in Soviet Society: Fetish or Fair Play?," in *Home, School, and Leisure in the Soviet Union*, ed. Jenny Brine, Maureen Perrie, and Andrew Sutton (Boston: Allen & Unwin, 1980), 224. For an extended discussion of Proletkul't's early years, see Sheila Fitzpatrick, *The Commissariat of Enlightenment: Soviet Organization of Education under Lunacharsky, October 1917–1921* (New York: Cambridge University Press, 1970), 89–109. For a history of Proletkul't that gives little attention to its position on physical education and sport, see Lynn Mally, *Culture of the Future: The Proletkult Movement in Revolutionary Russia* (Berkeley: University of California Press, 1990).

8. André Gounot has written extensively on the Red Sports International: André Gounot, "Between Revolutionary Demands and Diplomatic Necessity: The Uneasy Relationship between Soviet Sport and Worker and Bourgeois Sport in Europe from 1920 to 1937," in *Sport and International Politics: Impact of Fascism and Communism on Sport*, ed. Pierre Arnaud and James Riordan (New York: Routledge, 1998), 184–209; Gounot, "Sport or Political Organization? Structures and Characteristics of the Red Sport International, 1921–1937," *Journal of Sport History* 28, no. 1 (Spring 2001): 23–39; Gounot, "Social Democratic and Communist Influences on Workers' Sport across Europe (1893–1939)," *Labour History Review* 80, no. 1 (April 2015): 1–29; Gounot, "Sport und Inszenierung des sozialistischen Aufbaus: Das Projekt der Weltspartakiade in Moskau (1934–1934)," in *Sport zwischen Ost und West: Beiträge zur Sportgeschichte Osteuropas im 19. und 20. Jahrhundert* (Osnabrück: Fibre, 2007), 75–91. Gounot emphasizes the Comintern's dominance over Sportintern's clubs and resistance from below by workers who wanted sporting activity relatively free of calls for revolutionary change and class warfare. See also David Steinberg, "The Workers' Sport Internationals, 1920–1928," *Journal of Contemporary History* 13, no. 2 (April 1978): 233–35 and A. V. Khorosheva, "Deiatel'nost' Krasnogo sportivnogo Internatsionala v 1933–1937 gg.," *Rossiiskaia istoriia*, no. 5 (September–October 2018): 105–115. Sportintern competed with the socialist Lucerne Sports International that organized Workers Olympics, the first held in Frankfurt in 1925, the second in Vienna in 1931. On the creation and the subsequent relationship between the two sports internationals, see A. I. Avrus and A. A. Vasil'ev, *Protivostoianie ili sotrudnichestvo: Mezhdunarodnye sviazi sovetskikh*

sportsmenov v 1920-e gody (Saratov: Izdatel'stvo Saratovskogo universiteta, 2002), 21–58 and E. A. Mel'nikov, *V edinom stroiu internatsionalistov: Iz istorii sovetskikh sektsii mezhdunarodnykh organizatsii rabochego klassa (1919–1939 gg.)* (Leningrad: Izdatel'stvo Leningradskogo universiteta, 1982), 54–59, 108–117, 151–156.

9. Barbara J. Keys, *Globalizing Sport: National Rivalry and International Community in the 1930s* (Cambridge, MA: Harvard University Press, 2006), 3. Such an attitude toward physical exercise as opposed to *sport* was hardly singularly *red* or *Soviet*. On a heightened emphasis in Great Britain on national fitness above and beyond *sport*, see Peter J. Beck, *Scoring for Britain: International Football and International Politics, 1900–1939* (London: Frank Cass, 1999), 220–223. In his address in New York at the National Football Foundation and Hall of Fame banquet, December 5, 1961, US president John F. Kennedy declared, "I must confess that I view the growing emphasis on professionalism and specialization in amateur sports without great enthusiasm.... There are more important goals than winning contests, and that is to improve on a broad level the health and vitality of all of our people." Kennedy then spoke of the formation of the President's Council on Youth Fitness. Kennedy's speech in *The Sporting Spirit: Athletes in Literature and Life*, ed. Robert J. Higgs and Neil D. Isaacs (New York: Harcourt Brace Jovanovich, 1997), 215–216.

10. I. D. Chudinov, ed., *Osnovnye postanovleniia, prikazy i instruktsii po voprosam fizicheskoi kul'tury i sporta, 1917–1957* (Moscow: Fizkul'tura i sport, 1959), 12.

11. Barbara Keys has commented that the debates over "the role of sport in the system of physical culture, over the proper balance between collectivism and competition, and over the relationship with 'bourgeois' sport were never definitively settled, and contradictory tendencies co-existed throughout the 1920s." See Barbara Keys, "Soviet Sport and Transnational Mass Culture in the 1930s," *Journal of Contemporary History* 38, no. 3 (July 2003): 419.

12. Chudinov, *Osnovnye postanovleniia*, 15.

13. *Fizkul'tura i sport*, no. 1 (January 4, 1928), 1. To be sure, an appeal for subscriptions was addressed to all those engaged in physical culture and in sport, 7.

14. Chudinov, *Osnovnye postanovleniia*, 17.

15. Chudinov, *Osnovnye postanovleniia*, 18–22. On July 28, 1931, the Executive Committee of the International Organization of Assistance to Warriors of Revolution (MOPR, in abbreviated Russian and commonly referred to as International RedAid) issued a set of directives on sport. Sports organizations in capitalist countries and their competitions were, it said, chauvinistic exercises for the preparation of war. The committee thought it possible, nevertheless, to recruit athletes into MOPR for the purpose of organizing and guarding its demonstrations. The directives are in *10 let MOPR: V rezoliutsiiakh i dokumentakh* (Moscow: Izdanie TsK MOPR SSSR, 1932), 99–103.

16. A. V. Lunacharsky, *Mysli o sporte* (Moscow: Ogonek, 1930), 23–25. The booklet was published in a generous press run of twenty thousand copies.

Lunacharsky wrote critically of "European sport that smells of blood" (16) and a "fetishization of sport" in the West (26).

17. Lunacharsky, *Mysli*, 23–37.

18. Lunacharsky, *Mysli*, 42–44. Several years earlier, Lunacharsky had been instrumental in lifting a ban on the sport imposed by Leningrad's Regional Council of Physical Culture: G. S. Demeter, *Ocherki po istorii otechestvennoi fizicheskoi kultur'y i olimpiiskogo dvizheniia* (Moscow: Sovetskii sport, 2005), 191. In 1937, the popular weekly *Ogonek* published the article "In the Ring." After taking note of the sport's popularity in the USSR, the author hastened to add that there, unlike the version abroad, boxing was free of blood and gambling. *Ogonek*, June 30, 1937, 21–22.

19. Chudinov, *Osnovnye postanovleniia*, 22.

20. Keys, "Soviet Sport," 420.

21. "The new nomenclature indicated a shift from pure physical culture to physical culture combined with competitive sport": James Riordan, *Sport in Soviet Society: Development of Sport and Physical Education in Russia and the USSR* (New York: Cambridge University Press, 1977), 127.

22. Katerina Clark, *The Soviet Novel: History as Ritual*, 3rd ed. (Bloomington: Indiana University Press, 2000), 118–119, 131; Clark, *Petersburg, Crucible of Cultural Revolution* (Cambridge, MA: Harvard University Press, 1995), 282. Clark writes of the portrayal in literature and film of "hyperbolically positive human beings" and the reverse, "hyperbolically negative human beings": Clark, *Moscow, the Fourth Rome: Stalinism, Cosmopolitanism, and the Evolution of Soviet Culture, 1931–1941* (Cambridge, MA: Harvard University Press, 2011), 213.

23. For a discussion of the rendition of sport in art, see Nina Sobol Levent, *Healthy Spirit in a Healthy Body: Representations of the Sports Body in Soviet Art of the 1920s and 1930s* (New York: Peter Lang, 2004) and Mike O'Mahony, *Sport in the USSR: Physical Culture-Visual Culture* (London: Reaktion Books, 2006). O'Mahony discusses especially well multiple depictions of athletes in Moscow's metro, in chap. 4, "Going Underground," 97–121. See also Sandra Budy, "Changing Images of Sport in the Early Soviet Press," in *Euphoria and Exhaustion: Modern Sport in Soviet Culture and Society*, ed. Nikolaus Katzer, Sandra Budy, Alexandra Köhring, and Manfred Zeller (New York: Campus, 2010), 71–87. See also Roman Strožek, "The Footballer as the Figure of the New Man in Italian and Russian Avant-Garde, 1910s–1930s," in *Picturing the Beautiful Game: A History of Soccer in Visual Culture and Art*, ed. Daniel Haxall (New York: Bloomsbury Visual Arts, 2019), especially the section "Footballer—the Soviet Icarus," 101–111.

24. See a discussion of both paintings as representative of the nation's conquest of the past and advance into the future in Tim Harte, *Faster, Higher, Stronger, Comrades! Sports, Art, and Ideology in Late Russian and Early Soviet Culture* (Madison: University of Wisconsin Press, 2020), 222–223.

25. Sergei Valer'evich Butov, "Razvitie sovetskogo futbola v 1921–1941 gg." (PhD diss., Sibirskii gosudarstvennyi tekhnologicheskii universitet, Krasnoiarsk, 2007), 56–58.

26. Butov, "Razvitie sovetskogo futbola," 126–127.

27. Tony Collins, *How Football Began: A Global History of How the World's Football Codes Were Born* (New York: Routledge, 2019), 60. The formation of professional leagues threw off "the straitjacket of gentlemanly amateurism" (63).

28. Butov, "Razvitie sovetskogo futbola," 59–61. During the 1920s, "it became clear," Avrus and Vasil'ev have concluded, "that pure amateurism could not exist at the summit of sporting competition": Avrus and Vasil'ev, *Protivostoianie ili sotrudnichestvo*, 99.

29. In September 1922, a Moscow team defeated a Finnish squad 7–1. Also that year, three Soviet teams played six games against a Finnish club winning five and losing one. The next year, Soviet teams won all seven matches in Finland. See A. Perel, *Football in the U.S.S.R.* (Moscow: Foreign Languages Publishing House, 1958), 26–27.

30. Butov, "Razvitie sovetskogo futbola," 95–96. This history with Germans repeated itself in 1925, 1926, and 1927: Butov, "Razvitie sovetskogo futbola," 79–80, 99 and Avrus and Vasil'ev, *Protivostoianie ili sotrudnichestvo*, 63, 66–67. In 1925, a team from Khar'kov (Kharkiv) won seven and tied one with teams in Germany by a cumulative score of 47–4 (Avrus and Vasil'ev, *Protivostoianie ili sotrudnichestvo*, 63) In 1926, the Soviet national team won all seven matches in Germany by a combined score of 64–10 (66). The following year, it won all eight contests in Germany (67).

31. See a discussion of this factory in M. P. Sushkov, *Futbol'nyi teatr* (Moscow: Molodaia gvardiia, 1981), 116–117. The team was one of 222 football squads in the city of Moscow alone: 114. A single large enterprise might sponsor five or six teams: Leonid Pavlovich Pribylovsky, *Trenery bol'shogo futbola* (Moscow: Fizkul'tura i sport, 1980), 28.

32. Keys, *Globalizing Sport*, 158.

33. Butov, "Razvitie sovetskogo futbola," 87–88, 104–105.

34. For a description of the game and its significance, see Martyn Merzhanov, *Eshche raz pro futbol* (Moscow: Fizkul'tura i sport, 1972), 19–21. Merzhanov, a sports correspondent at the time, later recalled that Soviet administrators and coaches, who were wedded to outmoded tactics, bore much of the blame for a justifiable fear of defeat abroad: especially 21. Merzhanov would become the chief editor of the weekly *Futbol* at its founding in 1960.

35. Butov, "Razvitie sovetskogo futbola," 108–109, 120–122, 132.

36. Butov, "Razvitie sovetskogo futbola," 49, 106–107, 132, quote on 129.

37. Robert Edelman, *Spartak Moscow: A History of the People's Team in the Workers' State* (Ithaca, NY: Cornell University Press, 2009), 78. Until then in the

1930s, teams representing six Soviet cities had competed in a first division and forty-five in a second division: Perel, *Football*, 10.

38. *Igra millionov*, 480–481. The Young Communist League's Central Committee backed the plan. Negotiations for the visit of a British team began at the end of 1935. A problem arose with the Soviet Union's failure to become a member of the International Federation of Association Football (FIFA), the "bourgeois" football organization. *Igra millionov*, 573n5. England, however, had not been a member of FIFA since 1928.

39. Butov, "Razvitie sovetskogo futbola," 65. Butov reported that his research in the periodical press and in archives did not reveal the amount of pay these athletes earned: Butov, "Razvitie sovetskogo futbola," 130, 133. He estimated that some players earned ten times more than the average worker: 134. In his memoir, Petr Dement'ev, who played for Leningrad's Dinamo in the 1930s, recalled that all players in the league's top division officially received the same relatively modest salary. Dement'ev proceeded, however, to acknowledge that a club lavished other benefits on its athletes, especially its best players. Dement'ev received a handsome apartment. He also acknowledged that such benefits were offered to entice players to transfer to another team. See a downloaded copy in Word format of Petr Dement'ev, *Peka o sebe, ili Futbol nachinaetsia v detstve* (Moscow: Izvestiia, 1995), 19, 32, 38, https://royallib.com/book/dementev_petr/peka_o_sebe_ili_futbol_nachinaetsya_v_detstve.html.

40. The film was first shown at a private session at the end of December. See a discussion of the film in John Haynes, "Film as Political Football: The Goalkeeper (1936)," *Studies in Russian and Soviet Cinema* 1, no. 3 (2007): 283–297 and Butov, "Razvitie sovetskogo futbola," 65–67. The screenplay's author, Lev Kassil', expanded the story into a full-blown novel serialized in the Soviet press beginning in 1937. On the novel, see Keith A. Livers, "The Soccer Match as Stalinist Ritual: Constructing the Body Social in Lev Kassil's *The Goalkeeper of the Republic*," *Russian Review* 60, no. 4 (October 2001): 592–613. For an earlier, somewhat similar rendition of a Soviet goalie's heroic exploits against a foreign team, see Iurii Oleshov's 1927 novel *Envy*, as discussed in Harte, *Faster, Higher*, 207–211.

41. Translation in James von Geldern and Richard Stites, *Mass Culture in Soviet Russia: Tales, Poems, Songs, Movies, Plays, and Folklore, 1917–1953* (Bloomington: Indiana University Press, 1995), 236.

42. Nikita Simonian, *Futbol—tol'ko li igra?* (Moscow: Agenstvo "FAIR," 1998), 19. Robert Edelman comments, "To this day, *The Goalkeeper* is fondly remembered, a reminder of a moment of optimism and possibility, since embracing football meant embracing modernity": Bob Edelman, "*The Goalkeeper*. Directed by S. Timoshenko, Screenplay by Lev Kassil. USSR. Lenfilm, 1936," *Soccer & Society* 12, no. 1 (January 2011): 42.

2

WINNING IS EVERYTHING

The continuing allure of competition, records, and victory at home and abroad quickly overwhelmed even the pretense of amateurism. Sportintern ceased to exist in April 1937.[1]

Traveling All-Stars

In 1937, an all-star team of Basque players, "professionals of the highest rank," as historian Robert Edelman has described them, toured Europe. They played some of the continent's top professional teams to raise funds for the republican cause in the Spanish Civil War.[2] On June 15, an honor guard of students from the Stalin Institute of Physical Culture and the deputy chair of the USSR's Sports Committee, Elena L'vovna Knopova, greeted the Basques upon their arrival by train in Moscow. A "sea of people" then showered them with flowers.[3] The Soviet host knew full well that the guests were a gifted lot, praising the Basques for their considerable skills and tactics. Days before the team's trip to the USSR, Soviet newspapers published encomiums about their dexterity, quickness, speed, and ball handling. A majority of the squad's members had played for the Spanish national team. Soviet commentators took special note of the visitors' contests with the aforementioned club, Racing.[4] The Basques had won two of the games and in the third, when the visitors had fielded something less than their best players, earned a tie. Nevertheless, Soviet sports administrators expected their teams to match if not overwhelm their guests. Accordingly, *Pravda*, the daily organ of the party's Central Committee, and *Trud*, the daily arm of the USSR's Council of Trade Unions, published the Basques' captain's and general manager's remarks and tributes, albeit courteously pro forma, regarding the speed and energy of their Soviet rivals.[5]

The first two contests were scheduled for Moscow's Dinamo stadium on June 24 and 27. Soviet organizers arranged for far more than a game. Before each contest, a stirring rendition of the Spanish national anthem and then "The Internationale" brought everyone to attention. Before kickoff on June 24, a plane dropped a large bouquet of flowers by parachute to the players below. At halftime, athletes competed in a 1,500-meter race. Preceding the second match, organizers staged races at various distances in the stadium. About ninety thousand spectators attended each game, considerably more than the arena's official seating capacity. Twenty-eight buffets offered an extended menu while in the stands, three hundred vendors hawked ice cream, sandwiches, oranges, and pastries. Fourteen photographers and seven film operators worked the initial contest that was broadcast live over Soviet radio.[6] There was, however, one major problem. The honored guests failed to cooperate. They stole the show.

On June 24, a Thursday, the Basques played Lokomotiv, a team in the Soviet major league. Its coach had acknowledged that the Basque team was better than his but promised that his squad would put on a good show.[7] It did not happen. The guest led 4–1 at halftime and 5–1 at game's end. Soviet writer and journalist Tat'iana Tess reported that the Basques played "with a gallant unfeigned joy."[8] On June 27, the visitors played Moscow's Dinamo, the team that had just won the Soviet Union's major league. Although the capital's squad played well, dominating the first half, the Basques prevailed 2–1. The visitors then proceeded to Leningrad for a game on June 30 against a collective of players from the city's two top professional squads also in the major league. The guests traveled on the Red Arrow express train to the northern capital where they were met by almost nine thousand people and five cameramen filming the occasion for a documentary. They were then whisked off to the Astoria Hotel. Days before the first tickets went on sale on June 25, Leningrad's Sports Committee had received fifty thousand requests for tickets.[9]

After the two defeats in Moscow, the honor of Soviet football and the nation's pride made a victory in Leningrad imperative. On instructions from the heads of the USSR's Sports Committee and the Komsomol, Leningrad's officials hatched plans to eviscerate their guests on the eve of the match. They took the Basques on a tiring excursion over Leningrad's worst and bumpiest thoroughfare, sat them down at a banquet to induce heavy drinking, and encouraged them afterward to enjoy the company of women. The plotters failed. Basques demanded an early end to the excursion, refused to drink excessively

Game of Basques and Lokomotiv, Moscow, Dinamo Stadium. *Fizkul'tura i Sport*, no. 14, July 1937, 3.

(despite numerous toasts in their honor), and ignored the advances of the women.[10]

On June 30, Leningrad matched the opening in Moscow a week before by dropping a bouquet of flowers from a low-flying plane that fell almost at the feet of the visitors' captain.[11] Perhaps overconfident, the Basques' coach did not field his best players in the first half. That and reportedly biased calls by the Soviet referee allowed the Soviet team to manage a 2–2 tie at game's end before a packed house of thirty thousand spectators.[12] Caught up in the excitement of the moment, *Leningradskaia pravda* reported that the tie was "unexpected, admirable, and well-deserved."[13] It would be small consolation. Six more games followed, all victories for the visitors with one exception. On July 8, in the fifth game overall, Moscow's Spartak, fortified by five players from other teams, overcame a fatigued Basque team that had played four games in the previous twelve days. Much to the delight of the ninety thousand in attendance at Dinamo's stadium, the game ended in Spartak's favor, 6–2. During the contest, the Basques bitterly and often complained of biased refereeing. At one point, they left the field in protest to return only forty minutes later.[14]

Pravda celebrated the victory with a large photo of one of Spartak's goals and the headline for an unsigned article, "Spartak's Big Win." The Soviet team, it declared, demonstrated "persistence and determination," its win "had not been an accidental success." The triumph had shown that Soviet football players "have all that it takes to enter the ranks of the world's best teams." Yet the preceding string of losses necessarily provoked a precautionary remark. The Basques' play had exposed the poor leadership provided by "our sports organizations," including, implicitly, the USSR's Sports Committee.[15] Perhaps the author or authors believed that Soviet administrators might do well to reinforce their squads, as Spartak had done, with additional players from other teams when engaged in international competition.

At the same time, Lev Abramovich Kassil', well-known novelist and author of the screenplay for *The Goalkeeper*, wrote of his delight with Spartak's win in *Izvestiia*, the daily organ of the Soviet state. The team had displayed outstanding skill and had thereby dismissed gloomy prophesies of defeat.[16] Nevertheless, Kassil' understood all too well for his own comfort the need to dramatically improve the quality of Soviet football. In its earlier contest with the Basques, Moscow's Dinamo had played an excessively aggressive physical game rather than a skillful one.[17] To successfully compete with the best foreign squads, the USSR needed to field not a Dinamo or Spartak team that was occasionally fortified with athletes from other squads but instead a team of the country's best athletes who trained together on a regular basis.[18]

Without explicitly saying so, *Pravda*'s contributors and Kassil' wanted the USSR's Sports Committee to create a national team of professionals of the highest rank who would be paid accordingly and given the opportunity over time to form a cohesive unit. *Krasnyi sport*'s correspondent, Mikhail Davidovich Romm, a former player, agreed. He also recommended that Soviet teams play first-class foreign teams on a consistent basis. Such contests were the "only means to achieve world class football."[19] Another Soviet correspondent agreed: Soviet football had much to learn from the Basques.[20] Yet another expressed the same sentiment more forcefully: for the sake of the future Soviet teams needed to play the West's strongest clubs.[21]

The chair of the USSR's Sports Committee, Ivan Ivanovich Kharchenko, and anyone else for that matter, could easily read the signals. On July 12, three days after the criticism in *Pravda* and Kassil's article, Kharchenko responded in *Izvestiia*. He began by proudly underscoring Soviet victories over foreign squads, including Spartak's recent win. But he acknowledged that the Basques' overall play had demonstrated that Soviet football had "serious problems." He did not, however, elaborate nor did he criticize his own committee's management of the sport.[22] Three weeks later, on July 31, he was arrested. On March 15, 1938, the Military Collegium of the USSR's Supreme Court found Kharchenko guilty of participation in a counterrevolutionary terrorist organization. His execution followed that very day.

Meanwhile, the Basques recovered well enough to convincingly win the next three games over Dinamo teams from Kiev and Tbilisi, both in the major league, and a Georgian national club. Soviet officials were not pleased. On August 5, *Pravda* featured an article, "Soviet Football Must Become Invincible," by sports journalist and former player Martyn Ivanovich Merzhanov.[23] Soviet football, he insisted, "should occupy first place in the world." And yet the recent competition with the Basques had revealed "that even our best teams are far from achieving such a highly skilled level of play." It was the case, Merzhanov insisted, despite the state's generous allocation of thousands of rubles a year to the nation's most prominent teams, including Moscow's Dinamo, Spartak, and Lokomotiv. Victory over foreign teams in the years before the Basques' arrival, Merzhanov added, had been achieved over weak and inexperienced clubs. His disappointment lingered. On August 8, the Basques played their ninth and final game in the USSR. They overwhelmed their opponent, Minsk's municipal squad, by the score of 6–1.

That month, the journal *Fizkul'tura i sport* published an article by Basque journalist Melchor Alegria, who had helped organize his team's European tour and traveled with it. There, he criticized Soviet clubs' timid play and, in his estimation, the USSR's poor refereeing. His Basques had demonstrated that their Soviet rivals should employ more headers and longer passes in order to drive the ball aggressively downfield. Referees should be more active in order to witness and call more fouls (implicitly to curb rough physical play).[24] The following month, Soviet journalist Boris Mikhailovich Chesnokov repeated Alegria's criticism of Soviet on-field tactics. Even now, play in the domestic league demonstrated that Soviet administrators, coaches, and players had yet to learn lessons taught by the Basques about the "manner and culture" of football.

"If we say that the only way to improve the quality of our game is by engaging the best foreign teams," Chesnokov concluded, "then we must be able to put to good use the lessons learned."[25]

In the meantime, Soviet football achieved little more than a modicum of self-respect when Moscow's Spartak, strengthened by the addition of several players from other teams, won all four of its contests over amateur squads at a Workers Olympiad in Antwerp, Belgium. It was an insignificant affair unlike football's World Cup, inaugurated in 1930, or the important but less prestigious Olympics. Spartak's victories occurred over four consecutive days from July 29 through August 1, an arrangement hardly conducive to the best any team could offer.[26] The Soviet team then journeyed to Paris to compete in the World Cup of amateur workers' teams, where it won both its games.

Three years later, Soviet teams seemed to demonstrate considerable skill in the international area and an ability to win. In August 1940, Moscow's Spartak, fortified with additional players, much to the surprise of the hosts, defeated two squads in Sofia, Bulgaria. The following October, first Spartak and then Dinamo vanquished a visiting Bulgarian crew in Moscow.[27] Aleksandr Petrovich Starostin, chair of the Section for Football of the USSR's Sports Committee, rushed to declare that "our huge victories" meant that now "Soviet football is highly regarded."[28] He knew better. The four games were easy victories, won by a combined score of 21–2.

On the Postwar International Stage

World War II delayed Soviet efforts to create an internationally competitive football organization. Months after the end of the war, Soviet football earned sudden international acclaim. In November 1945, Moscow's Dinamo, reinforced by several players from other teams, played four matches in Great Britain. "The spirit of friendship," Cold War historian David Caute has written, "was to be tested by sweat, mud, and fouls."[29] The contests drew huge crowds, one exceeding ninety thousand. As Merzhanov later recalled, the excellent play by the Soviet squad was for the host "like a bolt from the blue."[30] Two games ended with the guest's victory, one over the fabled Arsenal by the score of 4–3 and another over Cardiff City 10–1. Two, one with Chelsea and another with Glasgow's Rangers, finished in a tie.[31] David Downing, historian of the event, wrote that Dinamo "had all but destroyed the illusion of British supremacy."[32] The host nation had expected a slow and ponderous rival. Soviet coaches and athletes, however, demonstrated that they had finally learned much from the fiasco eight years earlier when competing with the touring Basques. In Great

Dinamo, 1945. *Ogonek*, nos. 46–47, November 30, 1945, 30.

Britain, Dinamo featured a sharp passing attack and a fluid game in which players changed positions on the field as the moment dictated. Back home, *Pravda* boasted that the Soviet Union's "pupils had become more like teachers" of the British.[33]

Dinamo's athletes also proved adept at matching the rough physical play of the host teams, a display that further soured the mood of British officials, players, and fans. That December, novelist George Orwell shared his dismay in the socialist newspaper *Tribune*. "Now that the brief visit of the Dynamo football team has come to an end, it is possible to say publicly what many thinking people were saying privately before the Dynamos ever arrived. That is, that sport is an unfailing cause of ill-will. . . . The result of the Dynamos' tour, in so far as it has had any result, will have been to create fresh animosity on both sides. . . . At the international level sport is frankly mimic warfare. . . . It is war minus the shooting."[34]

Mimicked warfare or not, Soviet officials and fans reacted to their team's performance with unfeigned enthusiasm. The tie with Chelsea demonstrated the "excellence of Soviet football."[35] The triumph over Cardiff City, *Pravda* reported, displayed "the excellence of Soviet football" and "the tenacity and extraordinary will to win" of its players. The defeat of Arsenal was "a huge victory for Soviet sports."[36] Millions in the USSR listened to broadcasts of the games (chiefly of taped delays) and watched films of the contests in the nation's movie theaters.[37] Soviet columnists and officials embraced their team's athletes unabashedly as professionals of the highest rank. Dinamo's players "had mastered the English professional way of playing." British observers had initially characterized Dinamo "as a team of 'amateurs,' but now they admit their mistake."[38] After the second game, Mikhail Davidovich Tovarorsky, who had coached Moscow's Dinamo from 1938 to 1939, observed that Dinamo had successfully engaged "highly skilled professional teams."[39] Izvestiia's correspondent, journalist and play-by-play announcer Vadim Sviatoslavovich Siniavsky, declared that Moscow's squad had prevailed in the face of local teams fortified with athletes from other clubs, often at great expense. British fans and the press marveled at the unexpected skill—the up-tempo game and sharp passing—displayed by their Soviet guests.[40] At the close of the match with Chelsea, thousands of fans descended onto the field to see the Soviet players up close, shake their hands, and lift several of them into the air.[41] The subsequent win over a heavily fortified Arsenal was, in fact, a victory over "an English national team."[42]

At the tour's end, Siniavsky embellished his tale by providing the cumulative score of the four games, 19–9 in Dinamo's favor. He then added, "Not one European team that has played in England has known such striking success."[43] Krasnyi sport editorialized that the "glorious Dinamo had valiantly defended the honor of Soviet sport." Its success was a "victory of our football school," of its reliance on collective rather than individual play, and on a will to win, characteristic qualities, it said, of the Soviet person.[44]

For the cover of its November 30 issue, popular weekly Ogonek presented a photograph of the head coach and twelve of Dinamo's players and in bold print: "19–9." The same issue featured the same score in its triumphant piece titled "19–9 in favor of Dinamo."[45] Fizkul'tura i sport proudly concluded that Soviet football "passed its graduate examination." "The school of Soviet football," it continued, "its training methods and game tactics had proven to be right and proper."[46] The young tennis star Nikolai Nikolaevich Ozerov later recalled, "That's when we tasted the joy of victory, when we believed in our strength and in the skill and strong character of our players."[47]

The team returned to Moscow in early December to a heroes' welcome at an airport festooned with the team's logo, a diamond-shaped emblem with a distinctive Cyrillic letter "D" within it. A delegation led by the head of the USSR's Sports Committee, Nikolai Nikolaevich Romanov, came to greet the champions. Dinamo's coach, Mikhail Iosifovich Iakushin, declared that the

Cover of *Ogonek*, nos. 46–47, November 30, 1945.

victories demonstrate that "we are able to defeat the strongest football teams in the world." The squad's athletes and coaches received cash payments for "having defended with honor the sports colors of the USSR." Eleven players received the title of Master of Sport or Meritorious Master of Sport, awards that guaranteed a supplement to their monthly salary.[48]

Tovarovsky thought Dinamo's performance could have been even more decisively victorious. If given a second chance, it could have defeated Chelsea. Similarly, player Vsevolod Mikhailovich Bobrov believed Dinamo could have won over Glasgow's Rangers if his teammates had not been so tired and if several of them had not been injured.[49] Their prideful imagination probably had gotten the best of them. With the advantage of hindsight, Edelman pointed out that in their enthusiasm over the British tour, Soviet officials and fandom inappropriately leaped to the conclusion that Dinamo's performance in Great Britain was a sign of the "global superiority of Soviet soccer."[50] In fact, glory in the international arena proved fleeting. Less than a year later, in August 1946, Romanov acknowledged the poor state of Soviet football in a letter to the party's Central Committee. In the previous month, several Soviet squads had hosted two club teams from Yugoslavia and Bulgaria. They had managed only four wins in eight games (one ended in a tie). As if on cue, Romanov admitted that he and his committee had failed to instill a proper understanding of the political gravity of the matches among coaches and athletes. Soviet personnel had accordingly approached the games as a get-together with "their Slavic brothers and not as crucial international contests. The results have adversely affected the Soviet Union's international prestige."[51] The Central Committee's Secretariat summoned Romanov to explain the poor showing.[52]

In 1947, Moscow's Dinamo won several matches in Sweden and Norway, admittedly against relatively weak clubs. Moscow's Red Army team lost two of its three games in Czechoslovakia.[53] The party's Central Committee was not pleased. The Cold War, now well underway, required impressive victories abroad. The following year, on December 27, the committee expressed this sentiment in no uncertain terms, demanding "world dominance by Soviet athletes in all major sports."[54] A month later, the USSR's Sports Committee and the Eleventh Congress of the Young Communist League used similar language to demand of Soviet athletes "world dominance in all major sports."[55] At the same time, Romanov was told to guarantee victory when and if Soviet squads in any sport were permitted to compete internationally.[56] In 1950, Spartak, fortified with athletes from other teams in Moscow, journeyed to Norway. Its three victories there, by the cumulative score of 18–1, were necessarily predictable over far weaker amateur workers squads.[57]

In the decade that followed, the USSR struggled to convert its hopes for football dominance into reality. In 1952, its national squad competed in Helsinki in the first Olympics in which the USSR participated. In sharp contrast to the claims that had accompanied Dinamo's play in Great Britain seven years before, Soviet officials now rhetorically bowed to Olympic rules by insisting on their players' amateur rather than professional status. They hoped that their entry would win the gold medal. It did not happen. In the knockout preliminary round, the USSR defeated Bulgaria and tied Yugoslavia after storming back from a 5–1 deficit. Yugoslavia then won the playoff. The loss had huge political implications.

Seven years earlier, at a reception following four games played by Moscow's Red Army team in Yugoslavia, the country's leader, Marshal Tito, shared his belief that contact between athletes of the two countries strengthened friendship between their respective nations.[58] But in 1952, Tito led a country that had rejected Soviet domination. Before the second playoff game on July 22, Romanov met with the Soviet team to read a telegram from Stalin demanding victory. The message, as Romanov recalled it, "made the players nervous."[59] It may have adversely affected their play. After scoring first, the Soviet team played defensively and poorly, losing 3–1. The team was sent home a day later.

In its extensive reports about the USSR's multiple achievements at these Olympic Games, in which it tied the United States for the total number of points, the Soviet press barely mentioned the tie then the loss to Yugoslavia.[60] *Fizkul'tura i sport* commented only that "our football team has performed poorly at the XV Olympic Games."[61] The defeat, however, hardly escaped the attention of higher authorities. After his return to Moscow, Romanov received a late-night telephone call from Grigorii Maksimilionovich Malenkov, a member of the Central Committee's Politburo. Malenkov wanted to verify that the losing national team consisted primarily of members of the Red Army's squad. Malenkov then insisted over Romanov's objections on the disbandment of that team, which had won the nation's major football league championship the preceding two years.[62] Romanov and his committee duly obeyed, declaring that the team's loss abroad "had damaged the prestige of our country."[63] In an interview published on August 6 in *Izvestiia*, Romanov laconically confessed that the football squad had performed "noticeably below its capabilities."[64] All of the results of the Red Army's previous games in the domestic league that year were annulled, and its upcoming matches were canceled without explanation. *Sovetskii sport*, successor to *Krasnyi sport*, and other media outlets dropped all mention of the squad "as if it had never existed."[65] The Red Army club regrouped only a year later, after Stalin's death. Soviet payback came in the 1956 Olympics. There the Soviet Union defeated Yugoslavia in the gold medal game in Melbourne, Australia, before one hundred thousand spectators. The Soviet press, however, did not present the victory as sweet revenge.[66] Relations between the USSR and Yugoslavia had improved considerably since Nikita Khrushchev's dramatic trip to Belgrade in 1955. *Sovetskii sport* duly pointed out that the players of the two "football powerhouses" embraced at the game's end.[67]

In 1958, in the World Cup, a quadrennial event like the Olympics, the USSR's entry reached the quarterfinals, where it lost on June 19 to Sweden, the host team. Disappointed at the failure to advance further, Merzhanov in *Ogonek* attributed the loss to his team's fatigue after a hard-fought win over England two days before, as did a report published in *Sovetskii sport*.[68] In a departure from criticism of anything less than total victory, *Fizkul'tura i sport* parried disappointment at the loss with considerable praise for the Soviet squad. The best team, Sweden, had won, but throughout the tourney, "our players courageously fought for a victory." Foreign correspondents had commented that Soviet players had "shown themselves to be strong-willed athletes."[69]

Better fortune followed two years later in France when the USSR's entry won the first-ever quadrennial European Football Championship (then known as the European Nations' Cup). It defeated Czechoslovakia on July 6 and four days later beat Yugoslavia in overtime in the finals. The next day, *Pravda* declared in its banner headline: "The Soviet Football Team Wins the European Cup," accompanied by a photograph of the team, its members identified by name.[70] The following day, the newspaper spoke of the "brilliant victory of Soviet football," made all the more glorious by the praise from French news agency France-Presse of Soviet athletes' "stamina and perseverance."[71] At the tournament's end, *Sovetskii sport*'s correspondent, Lev Filatov, reported that the Soviet team, now "the strongest on the continent," had achieved "a prize whose prominence and significance no Soviet squad had attained before."[72]

Back home, Grigorii Markovich Pinaichev, a member of the presidium of the USSR's Football Federation, greeted the win "as a great victory of Soviet football and a great success for our glorious athletes!"[73] The chair of the federation, Valentin Aleksandrovich Granatkin, declared that the Soviet national team had "answered all those who had doubted the strengths and potential of Soviet football. Our team proved that our nation's football is progressing in a proper fashion."[74] On July 12, the USSR's embassy in Paris hosted the team for an event attended by French journalists and officials, including one or more from the Ministry of Foreign Affairs. Upon their arrival home, impatient fans crowded Moscow's Sheremet'evo airport, and a reported one hundred thousand waited at Moscow's Lenin Stadium to welcome their heroes. Granatkin spoke, while Andrei Starostin, the national team's general manager and secretary of the USSR's Football Federation held aloft the trophy.[75] The Soviet play-by-play announcer for the game, former tennis star Ozerov, recalled that "the whole country rejoiced [at] the greatest success [in the history] of our football."[76]

The team's head coach, Gavriil Dmitrievich Kachalin, initially attributed his squad's performance to its "perseverance, diligence, dedication, discipline, and physical conditioning."[77] But he and other Soviet commentators put it more triumphantly when discussing the team's victory for the weekly *Futbol*. There they insisted on the superior skills of Soviet coaches and athletes. Kachalin and the retired star, Nikita Simonian, published two articles under the same title: "Athleticism but also Tactics," declaring that players had demonstrated not only considerable skill and determination but also superior tactics and technique.[78] The captain, Igor' Netto, agreed. Not just conditioning but also technique accounted for Soviet success.[79] Andrei Starostin contemptuously dismissed the opinions of many foreign specialists, who "understand in a vulgar fashion the Soviet school of football as only athleticism and the will to win."[80]

As had been the case after Dinamo's successful tour of Great Britain, Soviet coaches, players, and columnists exaggerated the quality of Soviet play in the international arena. Many football powerhouses, including England, Italy, Sweden, the Netherlands, and West Germany, had not sent a team to the inaugural European Championship, preferring instead to rest players for league play. In the quarterfinals, Spain's dictator, Francisco Franco, prevented his country's entry from going to the communist capital of the world, Moscow, to play the USSR.[81] The Soviet team thereby had advanced by forfeit to the semifinals.

For all of his bluster in 1960 about the misguided opinions of foreign specialists, Andrei Starostin understood to his dismay that coaches in the USSR's major league remained allergic to innovation. Their aversion to change did not bode well for the nation's national entry in future competition.[82] Starostin was more of a prophet than he wished to be. The Soviet Union's national team failed to advance to the final group of sixteen in the Olympic Games in Rome in September 1960. In the World Cup of 1962, the USSR's squad lost on June 10 in the quarterfinals to Chile, the host team. Soviet columnists had only subdued praise, at best, for their entry, which had, as one of them put it, reached a "fatal frontier" beyond which it could not advance.[83]

The Soviet Union's entry in the 1964 Olympic Games once again failed to qualify for the final round of sixteen teams. On a more hopeful note, the USSR's team had earlier that year defeated Denmark 3–0 in the European Championship to advance to the finals in Madrid against Spain. Fans back home and reporters on site embraced the fondest hopes for their team, hyping in the process its success on and off the field. *Izvestiia*'s special correspondent, Leonid Ivanovich Kamynin, reported from Barcelona of the local press's great interest in the Soviet squad and of fans greeting the club's players at the hotel where they asked for autographs.[84] *Sovetskii sport* informed its readers that Barcelona's citizens had bought all the tickets for the game. Over seventy thousand of them attended the match to see the Soviet flag raised in the city for the first time in twenty-five years, to hear the Soviet national anthem, and to support the team.[85] In response to the USSR's subsequent play and victory over Denmark, they expressed "exclusively warm and friendly feelings."[86] However, on June 21, the USSR lost in Madrid to the host 2–1 before 120,000 spectators. The defeat might have been easily endured because the USSR had reached the finals, but weeks earlier, the USSR's Sports Committee had informed the Central

Committee of the "political significance" of the match.[87] Nothing short of a first-place finish was acceptable.

Kamynin initially spun the defeat in a positive way. The victorious Spanish coach called the game a "great football battle." The host had exhibited considerable technique and speed. But then Kamynin vented his great disappointment. He singled out two players for criticism, complained that the Soviet attack frequently petered out, and admitted that the defense was not the best.[88] *Pravda*'s reporter Aleksei Ivanovich Leont'ev expressed his bitterness by attributing the loss in part to the unsportsmanlike play of the Spaniards. The opponents had been overly physical with the Soviet goalie and frequently faked injury when they needed a breather.[89] The defeat was all the more painful because Soviet television broadcast the game live. Viewers witnessed not only the loss but also, at game's end, the delighted Spanish dictator Franco, long a Soviet bête noire, applauding his victorious countrymen. According to historian Mikhail Iur'evich Prozumenshchikov, who cites unnamed witnesses, Khrushchev was especially incensed.[90] A team that had played so well in the tournament became the object of official criticism back home and its coaches were dismissed.[91]

Over the next two decades, the Soviet national team performed reasonably well by the standards of most sports aficionados. In the World Cup from 1966 to 1984, it played in the quarterfinals twice and finished fourth in 1966. In the European Championship, the team made it to the semifinals in 1968 (where after a tie in regulation time to Italy it lost by a coin toss) and then to England in a game for third place. Four years later, the USSR lost in Brussels to West Germany in the finals of the World Cup. It won the bronze in three consecutive Olympics from 1972 to 1980.

A traditional football powerhouse might have occasion to bemoan such a performance, but the USSR was hardly that. However, the national team's relative success was not good enough for a state that claimed ideological and political preeminence on a global scale and therefore demanded victory in international play. Soviet commentators accordingly responded to their national team's play with a mixture of subdued pride and bitter disappointment. *Izvestiia*'s correspondents greeted the USSR's defeat of Hungary in the quarterfinals of the 1966 World Cup as "a great victory and achievement."[92] But after the loss to West Germany in the semifinals, *Fizkul'tura i sport* laconically reported, "We have our strengths, but we also have our problems."[93] *Izvestiia* admitted that both Germany and the USSR had played a rough physical game, but it lightened the burden of defeat by insisting that the former's players had "theatrically flopped" so often that they earned the derision of their own fans.[94] The USSR then lost to Portugal to finish fourth in the tournament. Two years later, *Pravda* declared in its headline "Again Only Fourth Place" after the team's loss to England in the 1968 European Championship. Soviet players, it reported, had quickly tired and had then "ceased to fight for the ball. In the middle of the second half they had accepted defeat." The game's final fifteen minutes had not been worth watching.[95] "Our forwards toyed with the ball," *Izvestiia* lamented, "failing to move it promptly downfield."[96]

After yet another two years, the USSR lost to Uruguay in the World Cup quarterfinal in 1970 despite best wishes sent earlier from space by two Soviet cosmonauts. A slow-motion television replay, one seen only after the game's end, showed that the ball had been out-of-bounds just before Uruguay's winning kick.[97] Now editor of the weekly *Futbol*, Filatov bitterly remarked that at the time, Soviet players correctly thought the ball had left the field and they had ceased to play. The chief arbiter, however, had not blown his whistle.[98] The USSR lodged a protest, which was subsequently denied on the grounds that the on-field decision could not be appealed. *Izvestiia* underscored the injustice of it all by sharing the Soviet captain's complaint about refereeing throughout the tournament.[99] *Pravda* bitterly reported that no one had expected the defeat and, the arbiter's decision notwithstanding, the Soviet squad had played far too defensively.[100]

Despite the national team's appearance in the finals in the 1972 European Championship, *Ogonek* commented that its play "did not bring joy to its fans."[101] In a striking departure from an obsession with nothing short of victory, *Sovetskii sport*'s reporter Oleg Kucherenko allowed that although disappointing, the silver medal was "well-deserved and an honorable achievement."[102] However, *Pravda* could manage only to say, as if to blame outside forces, that in the semifinal game with the Federal Republic of Germany, half of the seventy thousand fans in attendance came from West Germany and some of them had stormed the field five minutes before the game's end. They were removed with the aid of the police.[103] For *Izvestiia*'s veteran sports reporter Boris Aleksandrovich Fedosov, second place was not nearly good enough. He criticized several Soviet athletes by name, blamed coaches and administrators for a poor selection of players for the team, and lamented the absence of a passionate attacking game.[104]

That September, after the USSR shared the Olympic bronze medal with East Germany, Filatov despondently wrote that for the Soviet entry, the favorite before the tournament, "things had not worked out."[105] *Izvestiia*'s reporters, Fedosov among them, had looked forward to the team's play in these Olympics with "excitement and hope." They had nothing to say about the disappointing third-place finish.[106] After another bronze in the 1976 Olympics, Kucherenko, writing for *Sovetskii sport*, thought that at least the medal brought the team (and implicitly its supporters) some comfort. But he concluded in a pessimistic and understated fashion: "And again four years of waiting, four more years of hoping."[107] *Izvestiia*'s reporters allowed only that "our players and coaches are hardly satisfied with third place; they were preparing for and counting on something more."[108] In the 1980 Olympics held in Moscow, the USSR's football entry managed no better than the bronze medal. *Ogonek*'s sports journalist, Viktor Iakovlevich Viktorov, reported that many people believed that the Soviet Union's team would win the gold medal in an Olympics staged at home and boycotted by thirty-six nations. "Alas, it did not happen."[109] Gennadii Radchuk, a veteran sports journalist and member of the editorial board of *Futbol-Khokkei*, wistfully observed, "Yes, we had hopes. They were not justified."[110] Four years earlier, Kucherenko found at best disappointing comfort in a third-place finish.[111] Upon the Soviet team's failure to advance to the semifinals in the 1982 World Cup after a tie in a game with Poland, *Izvestiia*'s correspondents Kamynin and Fedosov lamented that "it is difficult to write about it, there aren't words, it's painful."[112]

Prose and Poetry: Assessment of Defeat

Disappointed with less than dominance of their national football team, Soviet columnists allowed only the compliment that their entry had "fought the good fight." After losing to West Germany in the semifinals of the 1966 World Cup, Radchuk wrote that the opponent had failed to "break the fighting spirit of our Soviet players."[113] Merzhanov commented that in the loss that followed to Portugal for the bronze, the Soviet squad played "courageously."[114] After finishing fourth in the 1968 European Championship, the editors of *Futbol-Khokkei* mused that "our athletes again demonstrated a fighting spirit." *Ogonek* acknowledged that our players exhibited a "strong-will and perseverance."[115] This recognition of the team's toughness did not, however, comfort columnists who repeatedly attributed the Soviet team's failure to take the top prize to the absence of an aggressive and attacking style of play.[116] After the national team's loss in the quarterfinals in the 1982 World Cup, Filatov attributed the absence of an attacking style by Soviet teams in international tournaments to the conservative approach dominant throughout the nation's domestic leagues. When on the road, teams played defensively, hoping for a tie, 0–0 or 1–1, which would gain them a point in the league's standings. The tactic, Filatov surmised, might well have led to the national squad's tentative play in international competition that placed a premium on victories in order to advance to the next round.[117]

Occasionally, the Soviet press printed more poetic and probing analyses of a failure to win it all. In 1958, *Fizkul'tura i sport* published an anonymous piece based almost entirely on reasons set forth by foreign correspondents for the Soviet team's unexpected failure to reach the quarterfinals in that year's World Cup. The nation's athletes had repeatedly demonstrated their physical fitness and will to win. But coaches and players had relied on an "out-of-date style of play," on stratagems that precluded innovation and "a display of individual talent" on the field. They had not yet learned that "good football requires not only strong and fast legs, powerful lungs, a strong heart, and set plays, but also a collective effort in which players as individuals perform well."[118] It was surely not lost on the editors of *Fizkul'tura i sport* that this foreign critique of the USSR's national team paralleled that abroad of the Soviet government and society.

Trud's chief sports correspondent since 1950, Iurii Il'ich Van'iat, largely avoided emotional accounts of his national team's victories and defeats. That changed with the USSR's fourth-place finish in the 1968 European Championship. After finishing first in the 1960 European Championship and then second in 1964, the USSR "had now plummeted downward in the hierarchical ranks of European football."[119] Van'iat blamed not so much the players or coaches but rather the country's governing apparatus for football, specifically, the USSR's Football Federation. The newly installed leadership there, he insisted, must now critically analyze the reasons for the national team's relatively poor play. Only then might it "restore the good name of the USSR's national team in which we still believe and which we see as one of the most powerful football squads of our planet."[120] Four years later, a somewhat mollified Van'iat regarded the USSR's second-place finish in the European Championship as a major victory but one that nevertheless was unsatisfactory. A failure to win it all required that the country's top administrators for the sport undertake "a serious discussion about the direction taken in the development of our football."[121]

Van'iat took the disappointing occasion of the bronze in the 1976 Olympics to once again blame the governing organs of Soviet football. They were responsible, he said, for a team that was poorly prepared and worn down by far too many games abroad. Defeats can happen, he acknowledged, they were part of the sporting scene, but the Soviet team had performed in a "dull and indifferent fashion." Van'iat called on the USSR's Sports Committee to undertake a thorough review of the recruitment and training of the national squad.[122]

Van'iat wanted not only improvement but also more control over football by Moscow. By contrast, the Starostin brothers wanted less control and not just from the center. To be sure, after the Soviet team's loss to Portugal in the 1966 World Cup match for the bronze, Andrei Starostin, general manager of the USSR's national team from 1960 to 1964, predictably expressed in *Futbol-Khokkei* the usual combination of hope and disappointment.[123] But he and his brother, Nikolai, general manager of Moscow's Spartak, followed this up with a slashing appraisal of the Soviet system of football in *Ogonek*, which, in their estimation, accounted for the dismal performance of the nation's play internationally. Coaches in the Soviet Union's domestic leagues, Nikolai insisted, were dictators on and off the field. They demanded of their players a slavish adherence to their, the coaches' pet tactics. Soviet athletes thereby performed without initiative and imagination, displaying "a weakness of spirit incompatible with football," a game, Nikolai insisted, that required "boldness and risk."[124] The brothers wanted a reordering of Soviet football from its youth programs below to the national squad above. They insisted that the system (and perhaps Soviet society generally?) nurture players and coaches capable of creative and innovative play. We need, Andrei concluded, "to give our teams, [sports] schools, and athletes creative freedom."[125]

At about the same time in 1966, an anonymous author, identified only as a "Commentator"—likely Andrei Starostin or Merzhanov—criticized Soviet tactics that had contributed to the disappointing fourth-place finish in the World Cup in *Sovetskii sport*. They insisted that coaches, players, and referees in the USSR's domestic leagues introduce changes that would improve the performance of the national squad. On the field, athletes would have to employ new schemes so evident now in the play of teams abroad. Of particular importance, foreign squads relied on a fluid interchange of attackers and defenders (a style of play that, ironically, Dinamo had exhibited in Great Britain in 1945, a style that would become known in the 1970s as "total football"). The division between offensive and defensive players had thereby become an anachronism. Moreover, Soviet athletes needed to adopt a more physical game that was so dominant among foreign teams in international competition. Soviet referees in the USSR's domestic leagues would accordingly have to adjust their interpretation of the rules to encourage a more aggressive style by future members of the national team.[126]

After the disappointing loss to West Germany in the finals of the 1972 European Cup, Kucherenko complained that the Soviet team lacked skillful players able to engage in attacking football. "We need," he continued, "to develop a 'super class' of athlete."[127] Radchuk expressed a similar, albeit understated, opinion after the national team had managed only to take the bronze in Moscow's 1980 Olympics. He approvingly reported its coach's appeal that Soviet football prepare its athletes to play in a less stereotypical and predictable way.[128]

After the Soviet entry failed to reach the semifinals in the 1982 World Cup, Vladimir Vladimirovich Ponedel'nik, sports journalist and past chair of the Russian Republic's Football Federation from 1972 to 1976, agreed with the conclusions of a roundtable of foreign correspondents. Administrators, coaches, and players should embrace the need for "innovative football." "Is it not an urgent subject for our football?" Ponedel'nik rhetorically asked. "Is it not so?"[129] Perhaps Ponedel'nik had in mind a need for innovation in more than just Soviet football.

In stark contrast to the assessment of these sports journalists, prominent state and party officials provided a far different explanation for the USSR's alleged poor record. They attributed much of the national team's disappointing play to the coddling of its players at home. In June 1970, following the USSR's loss in the quarterfinals to Uruguay in the World Cup, Sergei Pavlovich Pavlov, chair of the USSR's Sports Committee, put the blame squarely on the nation's athletes in his report to the party's Central Committee. In their recruitment of athletes, professional teams in the nation's major and minor leagues offered all manner of benefits to players (and coaches) among whom, Pavlov noted, were not a few jerks, slackers, and drunks. The resulting poor play throughout the Soviet Union had contributed to the nation's poor performance abroad.[130] After the national team's failure to reach the semifinals in football's 1982 World Cup, the Central Committee's Propaganda Department declared at the end of July that excessive remuneration, including cars, apartments, bonuses, fictional jobs, and "other benefits," had produced players driven by "greed and a sense of impunity and entitlement," who were unwilling and unable to put forth the effort to win in international competition.[131] Two weeks later, at a session of the Central Committee's Secretariat, Iurii Andropov, until May head of the USSR's Committee for State Security, agreed. The Soviet Union lacked, he allowed, "proper procedures in the pay and remuneration of its football players. Why in the West do professional athletes fight [to win] each match? They want to do so. But for our players, it's all the same whether they win [or not]. [Win or lose] they have everything."[132]

Competing Demands

Less than victory on the international stage fueled a continuing debate over the apparent conflicting virtues of physical culture and sport. In 1972, higher educational institutions specializing in physical education introduced a course in the history of sport. Many members of the faculty objected. They insisted that the new subject privileged study of competitive sports, something designed for the few, at the expense of efforts promoting the physical fitness of the public at large. Georgii Stepanovich Demeter, professor at the Moscow region branch of the Smolensk Institute of Physical Culture, dismissed the new course as "contrived and artificial." Sport should be taught, he declared, only as a fundamental part of the history of physical culture. The mastery of skills in any particular sport was significant only in so far as it was part of the larger Soviet program to develop the nation's health and physical well-being.[133]

In 1979, Pavlov published a book on physical exercise and sport in which he emphasized the importance of physical activity to the formation of a harmonious personality. Sport played by professionals on the global stage, he said almost in passing, proved beneficial primarily as a means to bring about international friendship and an end to racial discrimination.[134] Shortly thereafter, Demeter, his branch university having now become the Moscow Regional Institute of Physical Culture, published two volumes on the history of physical culture and sport.[135] There he insisted that sports, especially professional sports, had no separate and intrinsic value of their own. Victories by the USSR's national teams and records set by its individual athletes were meaningful primarily as manifestations of the larger effort to promote the nation's spiritual and physical fitness and form a citizenry capable of contributing to the country's economic growth and defense against foreign enemies. By contrast, a bourgeois West's obsession with sports and victory for their own sake had inevitably led to the crass commercialization of sporting events (including the Olympics), doping, violent behavior by players and fans alike, athletes' drug addiction and alcoholism, and encouragement of racism and militarism.[136]

On September 11, 1981, the party's Central Committee and the USSR's Council of Ministers threw their rhetorical support behind the promotion of the nation's physical fitness and not of professional sport. They gave all the usual reasons: sustained physical activity developed individuals who were healthy in body, mind, and spirit and fit for productive labor and the defense of the country. By contrast, professional sport was worth no more than a mention. In brief comments about it, they suggested a reduction of expenditures on it by, implicitly, fewer games and less travel.[137]

In the rush to present Soviet physical culture and sport as part of an indivisible whole, critics of an allegedly undue emphasis on the latter failed to recognize the obvious. Professional sport in the USSR, football most prominently, had a long life and an ethos of its own. As we will see in part 2, Kirov's municipal and regional authorities knew it well. In the early 1980s, they had to decide how best to apportion funds among an advancement of the public's physical fitness, amateur athletics, and professional football. They would have to choose if, in the case of their club Dinamo, "winning was everything." And contrary to the center's suggestion in January 1981, although it was vague, to reduce expenditures on professional teams, Kirov proceeded in the opposite direction.

Soviet fixation on victory in international competition stood in sharp contradiction to the focus on the spirit of mass participation and physical fitness embodied in the Soviet focus on physical culture. The demand for victory on an international stage initially meant games with far inferior, often amateur squads or a frequent avoidance altogether of play in the international arena. This chapter underscores the significance of victories by a touring Basque team over Soviet clubs in 1937, hyperbolic praise of Soviet football after the tour of Great Britain by Moscow's Dinamo in 1945, the punishment of the national squad after its failure in the Olympics in 1952, and exaggerated pride with the national team's first place in the inaugural European Football Championship in 1960 in pushing the Soviet football team onto an international stage. Over the next quarter of a century, the national team performed admirably well with multiple finishes in the top four in European and world tournaments. Yet as this chapter shows in detail, high-ranking state officials, sports administrators, and the press responded with disappointment, even anger, at the failure to win it all. Nothing short of victory would do for a USSR that insisted on its ideological and political superiority. The national team's unsatisfactory play prompted several Soviet commentators to boldly insist on the need for initiative and imagination on the part of administrators, coaches, and players.

NOTES

1. On intense pressure on Soviet teams from the 1930s to the 1970s to win when abroad, see documents in N. G. Tomilina and M. Iu. Prozumenshchikov, *Igra millionov pod partiinym kontrolem: Sovetskii futbol po dokumentam TsK KPSS* (Moscow: Mezhdunarodnyi fond "Demokratiia," 2017), 470–577. On difficulties experienced by returning players, see M. Iu. Prozumenshchikov, "Za partiinymi kulasami velikoi sportivnoi derzhavy," *Neprikosnovennyi zapas*, no. 3 (2004), https://magazines.gorky.media/nz/2004/3/za-partijnymi-kulisami-velikoj-sportivnoj-derzhavy.html. Mikhail Prozumenshchikov also discusses the political imperative, especially during the 1950s, for the USSR's athletes in a variety of sports to win any and all competitions abroad. See also Mike O'Mahony, *Sport in the USSR: Physical Culture-Visual Culture* (London: Reaktion Books, 2006), chap. 6, "Aiming for World Supremacy," 151–175.

2. Robert Edelman, *Spartak Moscow: A History of the People's Team in the Workers' State* (Ithaca, NY: Cornell University Press, 2009), 192. On the Basque squad, see also Paul Dietschy, "Football Players' Migrations: A Political Stake,"

Historical Social Research 35, no. 1 (115) (January 2006): 35–36. Dietschy reports that the players were essentially stateless, that only two of about thirty players returned to Spain (36). For a history of Basque football, see Rober Györi Szabó, "Basque Identity and Soccer," *Soccer & Society* 14, no. 4 (July 2013): 525–547 and Ekain Rojo-Labaien, "Football and the Representation of Basque Identity in the Contemporary Age," *Soccer & Society* 18, no. 1 (January 2017): 63–80.

3. E. Fram, "Baskskie futbolisty v Moskve," *Izvestiia*, June 17, 1937, 4; *Krasnyi sport*, June 17, 1937, 1.

4. M. Nemov, "Ispanskie futbolisty edut v SSSR," *Pravda*, June 11, 1937, 6; M. Poliak, "Komanda vysokogo klassa," *Krasnyi sport*, June 11, 1937, 3; K. Oganesov, "Podlinnyi Ispanskii futbol," *Krasnyi sport*, June 15, 1937, 3. It seemed to matter little that the Basques had lost two games in Czechoslovakia.

5. "Segodnia—Vstrecha s ispanskimi futbolistami," *Pravda*, June 24, 1937, 6; *Trud*, June 24, 1937, 4. The Basques played several other games before their arrival in the USSR. See M. Nemov, "Ispanskie futbolisty edut v SSSR," *Pravda*, June 11, 1937, 6. See also *Leningradskaia pravda*, June 12, 1937, 4.

6. See plans for and reports about the first two contests in *Pravda*, June 23, 24, 25, 26, 27, and 28, 1937, all on page 6 and "Po povodu igry," *Krasnyi sport*, June 25, 1937, 3. See also reports on the first two games in *Fizkul'tura i sport*, no. 14, July 1937, 6–7. For a colorful account of the festivities preceding the first game, see the report by Soviet writer and journalist Tat'iana Tess, "Pervaia vstrecha," *Ogonek*, no. 19, July 10, 1937, 9–11.

7. "24 iiunia futbol'nyi match s baskami," *Izvestiia*, June 22, 1937, 4.

8. Tat'iana Tess, "Pervaia vstrecha," *Ogonek*, no. 10, July 10, 1937, 11. For football's aficionados, sports journalist Martyn Merzhanov has pointed out that the Basques employed superior tactics. They used the W-M formation, a 3-2-2-3 placement of players on the field that improved defense even as it allowed three forwards and two midfielders to launch numerous counterattacks on the opponent's goal: Martyn Merzhanov, *Igraet "Spartak"* (Moscow: Fizkul'tura i sport, 1963), 12–13.

9. *Leningradskaia pravda*, June 21, 1937, 4. See also several reports on the reception in Leningrad in *Leningradskaia pravda*, June 30, 1937, 4.

10. See documents in Tomilina and Prozumenshchikov, *Igra millionov*, 268–272 and 340n2. See a description of the game in V. Solov'ev, "Futbol'nyi match. Strana Baskov-Leningrad," *Pravda*, July 1, 1937, 6. All of the officials involved in this scandal (Utkin, Kosarev, Vershkov, Kharchenko, Tumchenok, and Poliak) were arrested in 1937 or 1938, albeit for other alleged activity, and subsequently shot with one exception (Utkin).

11. A. Sadovskii, "Futbol'nyi match, Strana baskov-Leningrad," *Leningradskaia pravda*, July 2, 1937, 4.

12. A report by a professional Soviet football referee, Georgii Il'ich Feponov, written shortly after the match, noted that the Basques had not fielded their best

players in the first half. In the second half, they did so and thereby dominated the game for the remaining forty-five minutes. See G. Feponov, "Baski v Leningrade," *Fizkul'tura i sport*, no. 14, July 1937, 10. Feponov also observed that the game featured rough physical play and had been poorly called by the referees. One of Leningrad's players, Dement'ev, recalled that at halftime, with the local team ahead 2–0, representatives of Leningrad's municipal party committee entered the squad's locker room. They reportedly had in mind something other than a victory by any means over the visitors. Rather, they insisted that the host play poorly in the second half so that the game would end, as it subsequently did, in a 2–2 tie: Petr Dement'ev, *Peka o sebe, ili Futbol nachinaetsia v detstve* (Moscow: Izvestiia, 1995), see the downloaded copy in Word format at https://royallib.com/book/dementev_petr/peka_o_sebe_ili_futbol_nachinaetsya_v_detstve.html. Butov suggests that the municipal party committee hoped thereby to neutralize the shenanigans that had preceded the contest and uphold the prestige of the Soviet state: Sergei Valer'evich Butov, "Razvitie sovetskogo futbola v 1921–1941 gg" (PhD diss., Sibirskii gosudarstvennyi tekhnologicheskii universitet, Krasnoiarsk, 2007), 113–114. But there are no documents to support such an account. And Dement'ev insists that the Basques were clearly superior to the Soviet team. On August 16, the acting head of the USSR's Sports Committee, Mark Vasil'evich Poliak, who earlier had been assigned to chaperone the Basques in Leningrad, wrote a lengthy condemnation of earlier efforts from on high to fix the game in favor of the Soviets and then told of his attempts to stop them. He said nothing about any lecture at halftime in the host's locker room. For Poliak's account, see Tomilina and Prozumenshchikov, *Igra millionov*, 270–272.

13. Sadovskii, "Futbol'nyi match," 4.

14. Butov commented that the chief referee called the game in a way favorable to the host: Butov, "Razvitie sovetskogo futbola," 115–116. The chief referee was an official in the Spartak sports club. Basques had earlier complained that Soviet referees inappropriately allowed rough physical play. On reports in the Soviet press of biased refereeing on July 8, see https://moslenta.ru/istoriya/futbolibaski.htm, accessed February 9, 2021. On Basques leaving the field, see Tomilina and Prozumenshchikov, *Igra millionov*, 340n1. Soviet novelist Lev Kassil' observed that both teams played a rough, aggressive game, which the chief arbiter failed to control: L. Kassil' and E. Fram, "Oproverzhenie miachom," *Izvestiia*, July 9, 1937, 4. *Krasnyi sport* reported that the Basques demonstrated, presumably in response to Dinamo's play, that they "knew how to play a tough physical game": *Krasnyi sport*, July 7, 1937, 3. Merzhanov noted that Spartak's victory occurred because of its choice to employ the W-M formation: Merzhanov, *Igraet "Spartak,"* 13. On the eve of the Basques' arrival in the USSR, *Krasnyi sport*'s reporter K. Oganesov had expressed doubts about the wisdom of the formation: *Krasnyi sport*, June 15, 1937, 3. Mikhail Romm has pointed out that the Soviet Union first encountered the W-M

in the game with Racing in 1936. But Soviet football needed another lesson in the formation's superiority, and the Basques delivered it. In its victory over the Basques, Spartak used the W-M, albeit "hesitantly and self-consciously." Mikhail Romm, *Ia boleiu za Spartak: Sport, puteshestvie, voskhozhdenia* (Alma-Ata: Zhazushy,1965), 92–93, 105.

15. "Krupnaia pobeda komandy 'Spartak,'" *Pravda*, July 9, 1937, 6.

16. Kassil' and Fram, "Oproverzhenie miachom," 4.

17. Lev Kassil' and E. Fram, "Khoziaeva polia i gosti," *Izvestiia*, June 28, 1937, 4.

18. Lev Kassil' and E. Fram, "Odinnadtsat'—v setke," *Izvestiia*, July 6, 1937, 4.

19. M. Romm, "Vtoraia vstrecha s Baskami," *Krasnyi sport*, June 29, 1937, 2 (the quote); *Krasnyi sport*, July 7, 1937, 3. Romm did add that in creating and supporting a national squad, sports authorities should not lose sight of the importance of individual Soviet clubs.

20. Iu. Van'iat, "Pervyi match s fubolistami Ispanii," *Krasnyi sport*, June 25, 1937, 1.

21. K. Oganesov, "Zametki o matche," *Krasnyi sport*, June 27, 1937, 3. After a loss to the Basques in Kiev, a game discussed below, a game poorly refereed, *Krasnyi sport*'s correspondent underscored the need for Soviet arbiters to acquire international experience: A. Vit., "Vyigrali v upornoi bor'be," *Krasnyi sport*, July 17, 1937, 3.

22. I. Kharchenko, "Sovetskii sport," *Izvestiia*, July 12, 1937, 3.

23. M. Merzhanov, "Sovetskie futbolisty dolzhny stat' nepobedimymi," *Pravda*, August 5, 1937, 4. Following Dinamo's loss on June 27, Soviet journalist M. Romm observed that the Basques had demonstrated to the Soviet side the need to reevaluate its style and tactics of play: *Fizkul'tura i sport*, no. 14, July 1937, 7.

24. M. Alegriia, "Neskol'ko zamechanii o sovetskom futbole," *Fizkul'tura i sport*, no. 16, August 1937, 5. Alegria began his article on a formally polite note, remarking that Soviet athletes had displayed more skills than expected. He attributed Spartak's recent victory primarily to the Basques' fatigue.

25. B. Chesnokov, "Ispol'zovat' uroki igry Baskov," *Fizkul'tura i sport*, no. 18, September 1937, 2.

26. See a report on the games in Ia. Konstantinov, "Sovetskie sportsmeny v Antverpene," *Fizkul'tura i sport*, no. 16, August 1937, 4. With the exception of Spartak, teams were amateur squads. Thus Konstantinov felt compelled to remark that in the third match, one played with a team representing Spain, the opponent included several players from a "Barcelona professional club." Merzhanov has pointed out that the final two games, the first with Spaniards (from Catalonia) and the second with a team representing Norway were contested affairs in part because of the opponents' reliance on the W-M formation, which Spartak also employed: Merzhanov, *Igraet "Spartak,"* 20. Spartak won the games 2–1 and 2–0.

27. Butov, "Razvitie sovetskogo futbola," 118, 120–122. Merzhanov later recalled that the initial win was a major victory, which at that time made a strong impression: Merzhanov, *Eshche raz pro futbol*, 37. A game with Leningrad's Dinamo team ended in a 2–2 tie. See Merzhanov's descriptions of the games in Merzhanov, *Igraet "Spartak,"* 34.

28. Aleksandr Starostin, "Sovetskii stil' pobezhdaet," *Fizkul'tura i sport*, no. 21, November 1940, 8. At the time, the section was also responsible for bandy, a sport discussed in chap. 6.

29. David Caute, *The Dancer Defects: The Struggle for Cultural Supremacy during the Cold War* (Oxford: Oxford University Press, 2003), 20.

30. Merzhanov, *Eshche raz pro futbol*, 42.

31. See reports on the games in *Pravda*, November 14, 1945, 3; November 18, 1945, 3; November 22, 1945, 3; and November 29, 1945, 2. N. N. Romanov, *Trudnye dorogi k Olimpu* (Moscow: Fizkul'tura i sport, 1987), 49–54; Ronald Kowalski and Dilwyn Porter, "Political Football: Moscow Dynamo in Britain," *International Journal of the History of Sport* 14, no. 2 (August 1997): 100–121. Goldblatt regards Dinamo's good showing as a sign of a decline in the quality of English football: David Goldblatt, *The Ball Is Round: A Global History of Soccer* (New York: Riverhead Books, 2008), 335. The games attracted crowds of 74,000, 45,000, 55,000, and 90,000.

32. David Downing, *Passovotchka: Moscow Dynamo in Britain 1945* (London: Bloomsbury, 1999), 155.

33. "Segodnia igraiut 'Dinamo' i 'Arsenal,'" *Pravda*, November 21, 1945, 3.

34. G. Orwell, "The Sporting Spirit," *Tribune*, December 14, 1945, 10–11, https://www.orwell.ru/library/articles/spirit/english/e_spirit. For an idiosyncratic argument that Orwell's article was less a critique of the games than of the Stalinist regime epitomized by Beria's favorite squad, Moscow's Dinamo, see Peter J. Beck, "'War Minus the Shooting': George Orwell on International Sport and the Olympics," *Sport in History* 33, no. 1 (2013): 86. Orwell attended none of the games. Although pleased with the results on the field, Soviet authorities in Moscow were concerned that the games "had stirred up a lot of anger": Downing, *Passovotchka*, 252.

35. *Trud*, November 14, 1945, 4.

36. "Blestiashchaia pobeda sovetskikh futbolistov," *Pravda*, November 18, 1945, 3. "Novaia pobeda sovetskikh futbolistov," *Pravda*, November 22, 1945, 3.

37. On radio transmissions, see *Pravda*, November 17, 1945, 3. On films, *Pravda*, November 23, 1945, 4 and December 28, 1945, 6; P. Podliashuk, "'Dinamo'-'Chelsi,'" *Trud*, November 24, 1945, 2.

38. "'Dinanmo'-'Chelsi'—3:3," *Pravda*, November 14, 1945, 3; "Segodnia igraiut 'Dinamo' i 'Arsenal,'" *Pravda*, November 21, 1945, 3.

39. M. Tovarovsky, "Uspekh 'Dinamo,'" *Krasnyi sport*, November 20, 1945, 4.

40. Siniavsky's reports in *Izvestiia*, November 7, 1945, 6; November 13, 1945, 2; November 14, 1945, 3; November 15, 1945, 3; November 20, 1945, 3; November 21, 1945, 3; November 22, 1945, 3; November 24, 1945, 2; November 28, 1945, 3; November 29, 1945, 3.

41. *Izvestiia*, November 14, 1945, 3; *Trud*, November 18, 1945, 2.

42. V. Siniavsky, "Dinamovtsy pobedili sbornuiu angliiskuiu komandu," *Izvestiia*, November 22, 1945, 3. On this page, *Izvestiia* displayed photographs of Dinamo's coach and several of its players.

43. Vadim Siniavsky, "Dinamo-Rendzhers," *Izvestiia*, November 29, 1945, 2.

44. "K novym uspekham sovetskogo sporta," *Krasnyi sport*, December 4, 1945, 1.

45. M. Martynov, "19:9 v pol'zu 'Dinamo,'" *Ogonek*, no. 46–47, November 30, 1945, 30. This issue was sent to the printer on November 28, following receipt of information about Dinamo's final game in Great Britain that day with Glasgow's Rangers. The following issue featured a short unsigned piece, "A Remarkable Victory," with the declaration that Dinamo's "success was truly extraordinary": "Zamechatel'naia pobeda," *Ogonek*, no. 48–49, December 9, 1945, 30.

46. "Spasibo vam, mastera futbola," *Fizkul'tura i sport*, no. 2, January–February, 1946, 4.

47. N. N. Ozerov, *Vsiu zhizn' za sinei ptitsei* (Moscow: Nauka, 1995), 195.

48. Iakushin's remarks in "Snova v rodnoi Moskve." *Krasnyi sport*, December 11, 1945, 2.

On the reception at the airport, see "Futbolisty 'Dinamo' vernulis' v Moskvu," *Pravda*, December 9, 1945, 2 and on the titles and monetary awards, "Nagrada futbolistam 'Dinamo,'" *Pravda*, December 19, 1945, 2. In November and December 1945, three clubs from the USSR's major football league, the Red Army team, Torpedo, and Tbilisi's Dinamo, which had finished second, third, and fourth, respectively, in the league's standings in 1945, toured Yugoslavia, Bulgaria, and Romania, respectively, winning ten and tying one. In contrast to its reports on Dinamo's visit abroad, *Pravda*'s commentary on these trips lacked enthusiasm. See articles in *Pravda*, November 28, 1945, 1; November 30, 1945, 4; December 3, 1945, 2; December 7, 1945, 3; December 17, 1945, 2; December 20, 1945, 2; December 21, 1945, 4; December 24, 1945, 3; December 26, 1945, 6; December 28, 1945, 5. For the most part, *Izvestiia* ignored the contests. Yet *Fizkul'tura i sport* took the results from these games and from those in Great Britain for the self-aggrandizing headline "The Score of Victories 68–25," the cumulative score of all fifteen contests: "Schet pobed 68:25," *Fizkul'tura i sport*, no. 2, January–February, 1946, 5. *Krasnyi sport* responded to these games in similar fashion: see reports in its issues of December 4, 1945, 3; December 11, 1945, 3; December 18, 1945, 3; December 25, 1945, 3; January 1, 1946, 1; and January 8, 1946, 3.

49. Tovarovsky, "Uspekh 'Dinamo,'" 4. V. Bobrov, "Dinamovtsy vozvrashchaiutsia domoi," *Krasnyi sport*, December 4, 1945, 3. The Rangers had tied the game

with a penalty kick on a call by the referee that many observers questioned: *Trud*, December 1, 1945, 4.

50. Robert Edelman, "Stalin and His Soccer Soldiers," *History Today* 43, no. 2 (February 1993): 47.

51. Tomilina and Prozumenshchikov, *Igra millionov*, 488. Romanov also confessed that he and his committee could have picked better athletes to place on the Soviet teams before the matches. He promised to take measures to prevent any such failure in the future.

52. Romanov, *Trudnye dorogi*, 137.

53. Romanov, *Trudnye dorogi*, 56, 139.

54. I. D. Chudinov, *Osnovnye postanovleniia, prikazy i instruktsii po voprosam fizicheskoi kul'tury i sporta, 1917–1957* (Moscow: Fizkul'tura i sport, 1959), 35. The decree did emphasize the importance of physical activity by the public at large but placed that development in the larger—and for it, the more significant—realm of training athletes to win in foreign competitions.

55. See the committee's instructions, February 1, 1949, and resolutions adopted by the Komsomol Congress, April 1949, in Chudinov, *Osnovnye postanovleniia*, 105, 112.

56. Romanov, *Trudnye dorogi*, 57.

57. Merzhanov, *Igraet "Spartak,"* 44–45.

58. "Sovetskaia sportivnaia delegatsiia na prieme u Marshala Tito," *Pravda*, December 26, 1945, 6; Lev Kassil', "Puteshestvie miacha," *Krasnyi sport*, January 1, 1946, 4.

59. Romanov, *Trudnye dorogi*, 201.

60. See, for example, mention of the games and scores in *Pravda*, July 23, 1952, 4 and in *Ogonek*, no. 31, July 27, 1952, 13. The daily *Sovetskii sport* had nothing to say about the defeat to Yugoslavia in its reports on the Olympics: see its issues of July 24, 1952, 4 and July 26, 1952, 3. After providing a detailed description of the initial contest with Yugoslavia, *Izvestiia* managed only to provide the score of the second: *Izvestiia*, July 22, 1952, 4 and July 23, 1952, 4.

61. *Fizkul'tura i sport*, no. 8, August 1952, 6.

62. Romanov, *Trudnye dorogi*, 282.

63. Romanov, *Trudnye dorogi*, 203.

64. "Ob itogakh piatnadtsatykh mezdunarodnykh igr," *Izvestiia*, August 6, 1952, 4.

65. M. Iu. Prozumenshchikov, *Bol'shoi sport i bol'shaia politika* (Moscow: ROSSPEN, 2004).

66. See, for example, the report on the win over Yugoslavia in *Pravda*, December 9, 1956, 6, *Izvestiia*, December 9, 1956, 4; *Trud*, December 9, 1956, 4; and *Ogonek*, no. 51, December 16, 1956, 3. The Soviet press and government, however, did lavishly celebrate the USSR's victory in the overall medal count

at Melbourne. See Barbara Keys, "The 1956 Melbourne Olympic Games and the Postwar International Order," in *1956: European and Global Perspectives*, ed. Carole Fink, Frank Hadler, and Tomasz Schramm (Leipzig: Leipziger Universitätsverlag, 2006), 293–294.

67. "Futbol: Final," *Sovetskii sport*, December 11, 1956, 7. The initial page of this issue displayed photographs of the eighteen Soviet players.

68. M. Merzhanov, "Trudnyi put,'" *Ogonek*, no. 27, June 29, 1958, 7. "Na pervenstvo mira po futbolu," *Sovetskii sport*, June 20, 1958, 5. A number of Soviet players had suffered an injury in the game with England. *Pravda* reported the losing score without commentary or elaboration: *Pravda*, June 20, 1958, 6.

69. "Zolotoi kubok—u luchshei komandy," *Fizkul'tura i sport*, no. 8, August 1958, 28. *Izvestiia* had very little of substance to say about the key games: see issues of June 10, 1958, 4; June 13, 1958, 4. In the June 13 issue, *Izvestiia*'s reporter for the Scandinavian region did mention praise from foreign commentators of the Soviet team's play and especially that of its goalie, Iashin.

70. *Pravda*, July 11, 1960, 4.

71. *Pravda*, July 12, 1960, 4. The newspaper displayed a photograph of the team's captain, Igor' Aleksandrovich Netto, holding aloft the cup.

72. L. Filatov, "Komanda SSSR—sil'neishaia sbornaia kontingenta," *Sovetskii sport*, July 12, 1960, 4.

73. Grigorii Pinaichev, "Pochetnaia pobeda," *Futbol*, no. 8, July 17, 1960, 3.

74. "Slovo posle finala," *Sovetskii sport*, July 12, 1960, 5.

75. "Moskva vstrechaet pobeditelei," *Sovetskii sport*, July 14, 1960, 3.

76. Ozerov, *Vsiu zhizn'*, 202.

77. See Kachalin's report in *Fizkul'tura i sport*, no. 9, September 1960, 23.

78. Gavriil Kachalin, "Atletizm, no i taktika . . .," *Futbol*, no. 8, July 17, 1960, 6 and Nikita Simonian, "Atletizm, no i taktika . . .," no. 8, July 17, 1960, 7.

79. Igor' Netto, "V Parizh cherez Marsel,'" *Futbol*, no. 8, July 17, 1960, 4.

80. As reported in the article by Iu. Van'iat, "Bol'shoi razgovor o bol'shom futbole," *Futbol*, no. 9, July 24, 1960, 2. Starostin expressed his opinion at a meeting of Soviet coaches, officials, referees, team captains, and journalists.

81. Franco feared the possibility of defeat at the hands of the Soviet team, which would have been a severe blow to his regime's image: Juan Antonio Simón and Julian Rieck, "Football, Propaganda and International Relations under Francoism: The 1960 and 1964 European Nations Cup and Their Impact on the International Press," *International Journal of the History of Sport* 39, no. 5 (2022): 474.

82. Van'iat, "Bol'shoi razgovor," 2.

83. See the reports by writer Lev Kassil', "'Sukhoi list' i lavry," *Ogonek*, no. 25, June 17, 1962, 25, and sports journalist Konstantin Sergeevich Esenin, "'Rokovoi rubezh,'" *Fizkul'tura i sport*, no. 8, August 1962, 22–23. *Pravda* reported the loss

to Chile without elaboration or commentary: *Pravda*, June 12, 1962, 4. See also N. Kiselev, M. Merzhanov, and A. Starodub, "Kak chetyre goda nazad," *Sovetskii sport*, June 12, 1962. After an enthusiastic announcement of "Victory" after the defeat of Uruguay, Oleg Ignat'ev had little more to say about the subsequent defeat at the hands of Chile: *Izvestiia*, June 8, 1962, 6 and June 12, 4. However, *Trud*'s reporter, Iurii Il'ich Van'iat, could not hide his "bitter disappointment" (*ogorchenie*): Iur. Van'iat, "Proshchai Sant-Iago," *Trud*, no. 138, June 14, 1962, 4.

84. L. Kamynin, "Futbol'naia Evropa v ozhidanii," *Izvestiia*, June 17, 1964, 4.

85. *Sovetskii sport*, June 18, 1964, 5 and June 19, 1964, 3.

86. L. Kamynin, "Pobeda v Barselone—3:0. Vperedi Madridskii final," *Izvestiia*, June 19, 1964, 4.

87. See the note from the chair, Iurii Dmitrievich Mashin, of the USSR's Sports Committee, May 29, 1964, about the upcoming semifinals and finals: Tomilina and Prozumenshchikov, *Igra millionov*, 555.

88. L. Kamynin, "Final futbol'nogo marafona," *Izvestiia*, June 23, 1964, 4.

89. A. Leont'ev, "Final'nyi match," *Pravda*, June 22, 1964, 4. *Sovetskii sport* reported only that the Spanish squad had dominated the second half: "Final kubka Evropy," *Sovetskii sport*, June 23, 1964, 4.

90. Prozumenshchikov, *Bol'shoi sport*, 87. The USSR's State Committee for Radio and Television sent crews to Spain to transmit the games live on Soviet radio and television: Tomilina and Prozumenshchikov, *Igra Millionov*, 688–689. The victory over Denmark had been shown on Soviet television in the wee hours of the morning of June 18. On Soviet television and football, see chap. 4, "Soviet Couch Potatoes: Football Fans in Front of the Television, 1960s–1980s," in Manfred Zeller, *Sport and Society in the Soviet Union: The Politics of Football after Stalin*, trans. Nicki Challinger (New York: I. B. Tauris, 2018), 110–142.

91. See M. Iu. Prozumenshchikov, "Za partiinymi kulasami velikoi sportivnoi derzhavy," *Neprikosnovennyi zapas*, no. 3 (2004), https://magazines.gorky.media/nz/2004/3/za-partijnymi-kulisami-velikoj-sportivnoj-derzhavy.html. Many of the 120,000 in attendance cheered and applauded Franco as he left. *Futbol* reported objectively on the game with a reliance on the views expressed by foreign correspondents: "Posle finala," *Futbol*, no. 26, June 28, 1964, 4–5. That sense of equanimity was not the case on July 3 at the session of the presidium of the USSR's Football Federation: see the report in *Futbol*, no. 27, July 5, 1964, 7. *Fizkul'tura i sport* may have tried to mitigate their readers' pain at the loss with an article condemning Western football, especially its variant in Italy. Italian sport had become "big industry," its football teams guilty of widespread doping, the importation of foreign "stars," dishonorable tactics on the field, and promotion of sports idols. See Emilio Sakki, "Industriia sporta," *Fizkul'tura i sport*, no. 8, August 1964, 19, 36–37.

92. M. Sturua and B. Fedosov, "Nashi v polufinale," *Izvestiia*, July 24, 1966, 6.

93. K. Rostov, "Slabykh ne budet," no. 6, June 1966, *Fizkul'tura i sport*, 11.

94. M. Sturua and B. Fedosov, "Final bez nas no vperedi—London," *Izvestiia*, July 27, 1966, 4.

95. Report by V. Ermakov, *Pravda*, June 9, 1968, 6. Much of the same criticism followed in *Pravda*'s next issue, June 10, 1968, 6. Ermakov had bitterly complained earlier of the injustice of the coin toss: *Pravda*, June 7, 1968, 6. *Sovetskii sport* similarly complained. Anatolii Kachalov and Vitalii Popov, "Ekho polufinalov," *Sovietskii sport*, June 7, 1968, 6. In *Trud*, Van'iat remarked on the coin toss: "It's terrible, but what can we say": Iur. Van'iat, "0:0 v pol'zu Ital'iantsev," *Trud*, June 6, 1968, 4. On the loss to England, *Sovetskii sport* consoled its readers with the comment that the Soviet team had lost to an obviously superior team: "Chempiony mira okazalis' sil'nee: SSSR-Angliia—0:2," *Sovetskii sport*, June 9, 1968, 5.

96. L. Zamoiskii, "Marafon blizok k zaversheniiu," *Izvestiia*, June 11, 1968, 6.

97. See reports in *Pravda*, June 16, 1970, 6 and June 17, 1970, 8.

98. Lev Filatov, "Chuzhaia igra," *Sovetskii sport*, June 16, 1970, 3.

99. L. Kamynin, "My poluchili khoroshii urok," *Izvestiia*, June 17, 1970, 8.

100. V. Kucherov and L. Lebedev, "'Krasnyj svet' pered polufinalom," *Pravda*, June 16, 1970, 6.

101. See the unsigned article in *Ogonek*, no. 26, June 24, 1972, 7.

102. "I opiat' povtorenie poidennogo: Sbornaia FRG—chempion Evropy," *Sovetskii sport*, June 20, 972, 4.

103. See Iu. Kharlamov's report in *Pravda*, June 19, 1972, 4.

104. B. Fedosov, "Vtoroi ras vtorye," *Izvestiia*, June 20, 1972, 6. Fedotov had reported on sports first for the newspaper *Trud* from 1956 to 1965 and thereafter for *Izvestiia*.

105. Lev Filatov, "Marshrut nanasen na kartu," *Futbol-Khokkei*, no. 37, September 10, 1972, 2.

106. D. Mamleev, S. Tosunian, and B. Fedosov, "Segodniq prazdnik u devchat," *Izvestiia*, August 30, 1972, 4.

107. O. Kucherenko, "Bronzovoe uteshenie futbolistov," *Sovetskii sport*, July 31, 1976, 2.

108. D. Mamleev and V. Silant'ev, "Vse iarche sportivnyi nakal," *Izvestiia*, July 31, 1976, 6.

109. V. Viktorov, "Sport—eto mir!," *Ogonek*, no. 32, August 9, 1980, 31.

110. Gennadii Radchuk, "Vysshaia tsena gola," *Futbol-Khokkei*, no. 31, August 3, 1980, 6.

111. O Kucherenko, "Bronzovoe uteshenie," *Sovetskii sport*, August 2, 1980, 1.

112. L. Kamynin and B. Fedosov, "Vybyli vmeste s chempionom mira," *Izvestiia*, July 6, 1982, 6.

113. G. Radchuk, "Liverpul'skie kommentarii," *Sovetskii sport*, July 27, 1966, 5.

114. Martyn Merzhanov, "Pod zanaves," *Sovetskii sport*, July 30, 1966, 4.

115. *Futbol-Khokkei*, no. 23, June 9, 1968, 4; M. Aleksandrov, "Futbol—delo obshchee," *Ogonek*, no. 27, June 29, 1968, 26.

116. See articles on the national team's play in its loss to Spain in the 1964 European Championship, *Pravda*, July 24, 1966, 6; in its loss to England for third place in the 1968 European Championship, *Pravda*, June 10, 1968, 6; in the 1970 World Cup, where it lost in the quarterfinals to Uruguay in extra time, Lev Filatov, "Igraiut ne linii, igraet komanda," *Futbol-Khokkei*, no. 25, June 21, 1970, 3 and V. Gavrilin, "Brazil'tsy tsantsuiut sambu," *Ogonek*, no. 26, June 27, 1970, 7; and *Pravda*, June 16, 1970, 6. On the loss in the finals to West Germany in the 1972 European Championship, see an unsigned article in *Futbol-Khokkei*, no. 26, June 25, 1972, 3. On the 1972 Olympics, see Lev Filatov, "Final kak otpravnaia tochka," *Futbol-Khokkei*, no. 38, September 17, 1972, 3. On the 1976 Olympics, see Valerii Vinokurov, "Otritsatel'nyi otvet," *Futbol-Khokkei*, no. 31, August 1, 1976, 4; Valerii Vinokurov, "Promezhutochnyi shag k istine, ili o tom, kak sbornaia gotovila i igrala deleko ot doma," *Futbol-Khokkei*, no. 32, August 15, 1976, 7; and *Pravda*, July 29, 1976, 1; O. Kucherenko, "Bronzovoe uteshenie," *Sovetskii sport*, August 2, 1980, 1.

117. L. Filatov, "Nash kommentarii," *Ogonek*, no. 29 (2870), July 17, 1982, 31.

118. "Zolotoi kubok—u luchshei komandy," *Fizkul'tura i sport*, no. 8, August 1958, 28.

119. Iur. Van'iat, "U 'bronzy' ne poluchilos,'" *Trud*, June 9, 1968, 4.

120. Van'iat, "U 'bronzy,'" 4 and quote in Iur. Van'iat, "Voprosy, kotorye zhdut otveta," *Trud*, June 11, 1968, 4.

121. Iur. Van'iat, "Sovetskaia sbornaia vyshla v final," *Trud*, June 16, 1972, 4 and quote in Iur. Van'iat, "Serebriannye medali futbolistov SSSR," *Trud*, June 20, 1972, 4.

122. Iurii Van'iat, "Net predela rekordam," *Trud*, July 29, 1976, 4 (including the quotation), and Iurii Van'iat, "Lidiruet sbornaia SSSR," *Trud*, July 31, 1976, 4. Van'iat implied that favoritism had accounted for the team's lackluster performance. Eleven of the players on the squad came from Kiev's Dinamo club, coached by Valerii Vasil'evich Lobanovsky, also the national team's coach.

123. Andrei Starostin, "Chetvertaia vysota," *Futbol-Khokkei*, no. 32 (324), August 5, 1966, 10–12.

124. N. Starostin, "Vernut' futbolu muzhestvo," *Ogonek*, no. 33, August 14, 1966, 29.

125. A. Starostin, "Igrat' po-raznomu," *Ogonek*, no. 34, August 21, 1966, 27.

126. Obovrevatel', "Epilog i prolog!," *Sovetskii sport*, July 31, 1966, 4.

127. "I opiat' povtorenie proidennogo. Sbornaia FRG—chempion Evropy," *Sovietskii sport*, June 20, 1972, 4.

128. Gennadii Radchuk, "Match svoei sud'by," *Futbol-Khokkei*, no. 32, August 10, 1980, 7.

129. Viktor Ponedel'nik, "Podstraivaias' pod drugikh, nevozmozhno dostich' bol'shoi tseli," *Sovetskii sport*, July 9, 1982, 3. In 1972, in basketball and hockey, the Soviet Union reestablished itself as a preeminent force on the international sports scene. On September 10, 1972, thanks to three seconds put back on the clock on two consecutive occasions at game's end, the USSR won the Olympics' gold medal in basketball on a final shot against the USA's entry. On the theatrics at game's end and the questionable roles played by the referees and the head of the International Basketball Federation, see David A. F. Sweet, chap. 8, "Was the Fix In," in his book *Three Seconds in Munich: The Controversial 1972 Olympic Basketball Final* (Lincoln: University of Nebraska Press, 2019), 119–135, and Kevin B. Witherspoon, "'Fuzz Kids' and 'Musclemen': The U.S.–Soviet Basketball Rivalry, 1958–1975," in *Diplomatic Games: Sport, Statecraft, and International Relations since 1945*, ed. Heather L. Dichter and Andrew L. Johns, 297–326 (Lexington: University Press of Kentucky, 2014). From September 2 through 28, the USSR's hockey team performed far better than anyone in the West could have imagined against a Canadian squad in the so-called Summit Series. Three of the games concluded in a Soviet victory, one in a tie, and four in Canada's favor. Eight years later, however, in Lake Placid, New York, the Soviet Union's entry in the Olympics lost in a semifinal match to the US's squad 4–3. Until then, beginning in 1963, the Soviet Union had won nine consecutive world or Olympics championships. John Soares, "The Cold War on Ice," *Brown Journal of World Affairs* 14, no. 2 (Spring/Summer 2008): 77–87 and Mary G. McDonald, "'Miraculous' Masculinity Meets Militarization: Narrating the 1980 USSR-US Men's Olympic Ice Hockey and Cold War Politics," in *East Plays West: Sport and the Cold War*, ed. Stephen Wagg and David L. Andrews (New York: Routledge, 2007), 222–234. After the defeat in 1980, the Soviet Union resumed its international dominance in hockey.

130. Tomilina and Prozumenshchikov, *Igra millionov*, 454. Pavlov responded in part to information on June 14 from the Central Committee's Propaganda Department: 457.

131. Tomilina and Prozumenshchikov, *Igra millionov*, 458–460, quote on 459.

132. Tomilina and Prozumenshchikov, *Igra millionov*, 463.

133. G. S. Demeter, "Istoriia sporta ili istoriia fizicheskoi kul'tury," *Teoriia i praktika fizicheskoi kul'tury*, no. 5 (1976): 59–62, quote on 60. Demeter wanted a single course, "The History of Sport and Physical Culture" with its own single textbook. The course, it seems, had itself only a brief history. A Commission for the History of Physical Culture of the USSR's Sports Committee discussed the new discipline. A majority of its members disapproved: Demeter, "Istoriia sporta," 62. "The History of Sport and Physical Culture" and not a separate course on the history of sport remains the dominant if not only offering for the subject matter.

134. S. P. Pavlov, *Fizicheskaia kul'tura i sport v SSSR* (Moscow: Znanie, 1979).

135. G. S. Demeter, *Fizicheskaia kul'tura v sotsialisticheskom obshchestve (istoricheskii ocherk)* (Moscow: Znanie, 1987) and the second book, coauthored with sports journalist Viktor Vasil'evich Gorbunov, G. S. Demeter, and V. V. Gorbunov, *70 let sovetskogo sporta: Liudi, sobytiia, fakty* (Moscow: Fizkul'tura i sport, 1987).

136. Demeter emphasized the evils of bourgeois sport in his *Fizicheskaia kul'tura*, 69–70. He singled out for its violence American football. Years later, Demeter adopted a more tolerant and informative approach toward professional sport, perhaps best illustrated by his comment "Sport is sport": G. S. Demeter, *Ocherki po istorii otechestvennoi fizicheskoi kul'tury i olimpiiskogo divzheniia* (Moscow: Sovetskii sport, 2005), quote on 24.

137. See the decree in http://www.libussr.ru/doc_ussr/usr_10897.htm. On October 30, 1981, the Russian Republic's Council of Ministers adopted a piggyback resolution. It is at http://www.libussr.ru/doc_ussr/usr_10897.htm.

3

THE SYSTEM AND ITS FAULT LINES

As in almost every activity in the USSR, a complex bureaucracy governed professional sport. And, as elsewhere, it did so with mixed results as it undertook the Sisyphean task to simultaneously promote and regulate its sphere of responsibility. Something on the order of "organized chaos" resulted, which benefited victorious teams while punishing losers.

As mentioned previously, in 1936, the Soviet state created an All-Union Council of Physical Culture and Sport (the USSR's Sports Committee).[1] The Russian Republic had an analogous committee under its own Council of Ministers. Each of the republic's territorial units, including Kirov, had its own organization under the jurisdiction of the regional soviet. All of these committees reported to and received instructions from corresponding party organs. At the summit, the USSR's Sports Committee worked with the party's Central Committee—more precisely, with its Propaganda Department. The mundane administration of football, including the scheduling of games, fell to the Football Section founded in 1934, which was under the jurisdiction of the Supreme Council of Physical Culture. After 1959, the USSR's Football Federation, under the authority of the USSR's Sports Committee, took up these common chores.

Municipal and regional officials frequently appealed to the party's Central Committee when dissatisfied with the decisions of the sports committees. And, as historian Mikhail Prozumenshchikov has shown, until the 1970s, they more than occasionally won their case.[2] However, in the late 1970s and early 1980s, the party organ played a far less decisive role. The materials about football it now received were less an urgent request for intervention and more a routinized transmission of information with the sports committees or Football Federation left to make any final decision.[3] That development did not mean, as we will see repeatedly below, that Soviet football had become less troubled or politicized.

The Dinamo organization had its own bureaucratic hierarchy. The Dinamo society, sponsor of Kirov's Dinamo, existed under the ascending tutelage of the regional Dinamo soviet in Kirov, the Dinamo soviet of the Russian Republic, and the Central Dinamo soviet for the USSR. At every level of governance, these agencies, in turn, fell under the jurisdiction of the aforementioned sports committees and the Ministry of Internal Affairs.

Too Much of a Good Thing

And yet this elaborate bureaucracy regulated professional football haphazardly, its authority limited by countervailing local and regional interests. The Soviet Union was hardly unique in this respect. In Franco's Spain, Madrid cultivated a limited regionalism, including support for local football teams, to introduce an element of popular support for the central government. Nevertheless, Catalans and Basques employed the sport to advance their own alternative identities.[4] Likewise, in fascist Italy, Rome's campaign to use football to promote the "idealized Fascist national community" incited "strong city-based and regional identities" associated with "their" own team.[5] So it was in the USSR. Despite repeated efforts by the center to control the sport's growth, it could not prevent an explosion in the number of teams. Like a new toy (or weapon), everyone had to have one. Managers of industrial enterprises, party bosses, and state officials wanted a football club whatever the price, no doubt as an expression of their love of the sport. They also desired a team as a display of their personal power and to enhance the prestige of their enterprise, municipality, or province.[6] In November 1952, the head of the USSR's Sports Committee, Nikolai Nikolaevich Romanov, complained about the multiplication of clubs in a letter to Grigorii Malenkov, secretary of the Central Committee. Various institutions had organized professional teams without the approval of the USSR's Sports Committee. The defense ministry and naval ministry were especially guilty. They had recently organized fourteen and six squads, respectively.[7] Romanov's complaints were in vain.

The USSR's Council of Ministers had repeatedly hoped to end the problem by fiat. In 1954, it limited the number of teams in what was then the major league's first division to sixteen and in its second division to thirty-two. The diktat had little effect. By 1957, the number of teams in the second division had increased to sixty-four and in the following year to ninety-four.[8] In 1965, the first division, now arranged into several hierarchical tiers, consisted of fifty-three teams, the second of 165. Four years later, the first boasted 107 clubs (twenty of which were listed in yet a higher classification), the second 201.[9]

In 1970, the USSR's Sports Committee tried a different approach. It established three discrete leagues: a Higher League of sixteen clubs, a First League of twenty-two, and a second league with 125 divided into six geographical zones. The number of clubs soon increased. By 1980, the year Kirov's Dinamo began to show promise, eighteen teams comprised the Higher League, twenty-four the First League, and 142 a second league.[10]

Gross Wages

The huge number of teams and desire to field a winner triggered stiff competition not only for the best athletes but also for their mediocre brethren. Players benefited handsomely from what historian Karl Manuel Veth has called "a football shadow economy."[11] This had long been the case in the Soviet Union, official rhetoric notwithstanding. As previously discussed, during the 1920s and 1930s, football players had officially and unofficially received generous salaries and all manner of benefits. As the number of teams escalated, the scramble for players intensified. "If you ain't cheatin'," declared American basketball commentator Charles Barkley, "you ain't tryin'." Teams sent out buyers (*pokupateli*) to recruit their targets with offers of "golden mountains."[12] They did not have to search for long. At the end of the season, athletes rushed to offer their services to the highest bidder.

Players received ever-more handsome salaries and large monetary bonuses. They might also get an apartment, land with a residential home attached (more than the typical cottage or dacha), privileged access to deficit goods from furniture to baby strollers, paid vacations, and assorted gifts (including a car for a top performer). They might also benefit from an additional salary from one or more fictitious jobs at a factory, government agency, higher educational institution, or public school.[13] Or they could also receive full pay for the time spent at preseason training camp, whose length exceeded the period officially allowed. Permission to travel abroad, with or without their team, was especially desirable. Beyond the USSR, they could purchase consumer goods unavailable in stores at home for their own use or for resale back home at a handsome profit.

Enticing benefits left clubs, even at the center, victimized as key players were lured away. In December 1963, the administrators of Moscow's Lokomotiv team, sponsored by the Ministry of Transportation, complained to a secretary of the Central Committee, Leonid Fedorovich Il'ichev, about the loss of its key players, enticed away by several other teams in the capital (Spartak, Dinamo, and the Red Army team).[14]

Athletes on teams sponsored by the armed forces or the Ministry of Internal Affairs (the sponsor of multiple Dinamo teams) enjoyed many of the privileges enumerated above and more. They were given an officer's rank with its corresponding pay, "a sinecure of an army commission," as sports historian James Riordan has called it, but without any obligations beyond the playing field.[15] Occasionally, the USSR's civilian leadership complained about the practice. "It is impossible not to say," the Central Committee's Department for Ideology wrote in April 1963, "that the situation is normal when a significant number of individuals in the Armed Forces and in the troops for internal security do not in fact serve in a military capacity but instead are involved in sport."[16]

And yet the armed services doubled down on their misbehavior, determined that their teams not just win but dominate their respective leagues. They drafted other clubs' promising athletes with the intention that the draftees "serve" by playing for the military's own. In February 1974, the editors of *Sovetskii sport* responded to the multiple complaints their newspaper had received from fans of the offended clubs. In a letter to the Central Committee, they underscored the inappropriate use of the draft for the benefit of Moscow's Red Army team and Kiev's Dinamo club.[17] In June of the following year, a Spartak fan, Dmitriev, wrote the Central Committee to complain about the conscription of his team's star, Sergei Petrovich Ol'shansky, by the Red Army for its Moscow club. "The army's team," the fan sarcastically noted, "very easily resolves all issues in the compilation of its roster."[18] Local officials registered similar complaints.

In early 1980, the chair of the regional council of unions in Voroshilovgrad (Lugansk before 1935 and after 1990), Iu. A. Rokachev, wrote the Central Committee to complain about the recent poaching of members from his city's football team, Zaria. While Zaria refused to provide its athletes with illegal benefits, Rokachev declared, other teams had enticed its best players with offers of apartments, cars, and secretive cash payments. The recipients of such largesse had become like "birds in flight in search of the easy life." Rokachev was especially upset that the Red Army and Ministry of Internal Affairs had taken eight of Zaria's best for the teams they sponsored in Rostov-on-Don and Kiev. While the lure of illegal material benefits played a role in the players' departure, their draft into the armed forces, Rokachev hastened to add, compelled their transfer. Several of the individuals in question had been enrolled in the Voroshilov Pedagogical Institute and therefore had student deferments. One draftee, Sergei Vasil'evich Andreev, who now played for Rostov-on-Don's Red Army team, a bachelor no less, had received an apartment and an automobile for the trouble of his forced relocation.[19] As a result of the loss of its best athletes, the club had been relegated from the Higher League to the First League.

The Central Committee forwarded the complaint to the USSR's Sports Committee. In early April, its chair, Sergei Pavlov, responded with a letter to the Central Committee's Propaganda Department. He chose discretion over valor by dutifully acknowledging that the athletes in question had been legally drafted and broke no rules by playing for the military's teams.[20]

In mid-May, Mikhail Georgievich Sobolev, lieutenant general and deputy head of the Political Administration of the Soviet Union's Army and Navy, responded to Rokachev's grievance. The Sports Committee of the USSR's Ministry of Defense had investigated and found nothing to support his accusations. Andreev had voluntarily joined the Soviet Army. He had received an apartment and a car not so much as a player for Rostov-on-Don's army club but more so as a prospective member of the USSR's national team preparing for the upcoming Olympics. In the case of other draftees, Voroshilovgrad's pedagogical institute had suspended several of them for poor grades. Still others had graduated and had voluntarily enlisted. Sobolev knew full well, however, that his response dodged the central issue raised in the complaint—the armed forces had compelled athletes via the draft (or the threat of it) to leave Voroshilovgrad and play for their teams. He admitted as much when he concluded with the brutally antiseptic remark that the military's recruitment of Zaria's players was correct "from a formal, legal, and juridical point of view." Acknowledging that the armed forces' teams could do a better job in developing their own players locally, Sobolev then admitted that Voroshilovgrad's Zaria had been unfortunately, if correctly, victimized.[21]

To be sure, many players conscripted to play for the military's teams willingly accepted their fate, fully cognizant they would in all likelihood play for a winner and would reap many benefits, including an officer's rank and pay. They might not, however, always get their wish, but they were well compensated for it. An offended team might resist the recruitment of its stars by using the connections of local state and party chiefs to force a military deferment or assignment to the inactive reserves. In such a case, the local club usually had to pay the player a handsome sum in salary, bonuses, and other rewards to keep them safely at home.[22]

The allure of legitimate and illegitimate benefits created a free-for-all market in the land of socialism. "Soviet athletes," Edelman has observed, "actually had more freedom within the Soviet market than did contemporary Western players in theirs."[23] In this respect, the USSR resembled the madcap laissez-faire economy that had dominated English football throughout much of the late

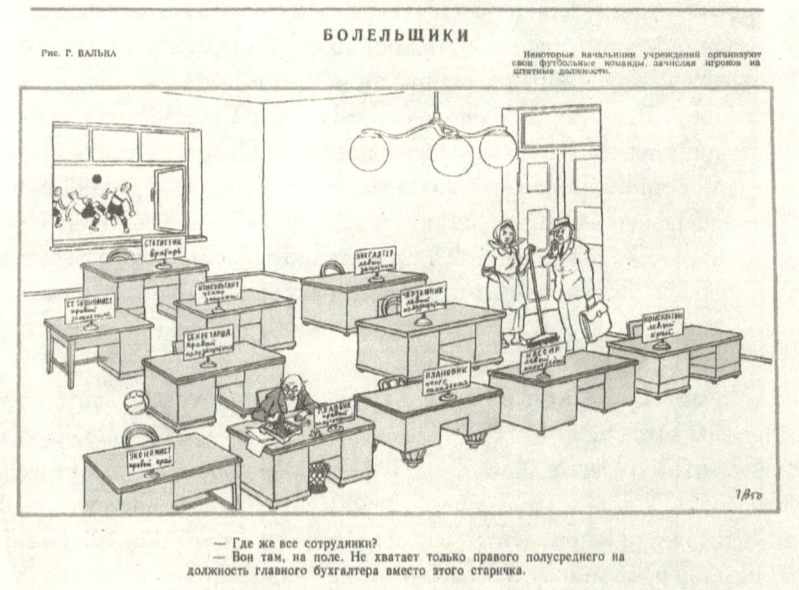

Cartoon, "Fans." Inscription in the upper-right-hand corner: Some heads of institutions form their own football teams, signing up players for full-time jobs. Conversation below: Question: "Where are all the workers?" Response: "There they are, on the football field. We still don't have a right-wing midfielder to replace this old geezer as chief bookkeeper." From the Soviet Union's satirical journal *Krokodil*, May 10, 1950, 13.

nineteenth century. England's (and Scotland's) best athletes performed for the highest bidder for their "amateur" services. Players might leave one team for another after a match. That changed with a legitimation of professionalism by England's Football Association in the mid-1880s. The formation of a league that followed compelled players to sign binding contracts. It also led to the adoption of regulations restricting transfers and wages, albeit sometimes at first honored in the breach.[24] In the USSR, however, the Soviet state and sponsors of professional teams largely failed to restrict inducements and the resulting movement of players. Until the end of the Soviet period, Veth has observed, players enjoyed essentially "permanent free agency."[25]

Moscow tried to limit direct monetary payments, if not benefits under the table, through a salary schedule. In March 1941, the USSR's Council of Peoples Commissars set monthly pay for players at 800–1,200 rubles.[26] These were handsome sums. At the time, the average salary per month in the USSR was 339 rubles. An industrial worker made 360 and midlevel administrators

390 rubles.[27] After several monetary reforms, in March 1966, the state limited salaries in redenominated rubles to 200 rubles a month for a head coach and 130–180 for players.[28] Albeit generous, these salaries were not officially out of the ordinary. That year, the average monthly pay in the USSR was about 100 rubles a month; a teacher made somewhat less, an industrial worker somewhat more, and a midlevel manager, engineer, and technician 50 percent more.[29] Eight years later, the Central Committee's Politburo limited pay in the Higher League to 150–250 rubles a month for players and a maximum for a head coach of 275 rubles.[30] These sums were unextraordinary as well. That year, the average income in the USSR was about 130 rubles a month.[31] However, the pay scales for football's professionals were not honored.

In November 1952, Romanov complained to Malenkov at the Central Committee that some teams (notably those sponsored by the military) paid not the 800–1,200 rubles as allowed but rather 1,000–3,000 a month (as well as offering sizable bonuses and other benefits).[32] Aleksandr Andreevich Keller, who had coached Kirov's Dinamo in the 1950s, was among those handsomely and illegally paid. In 1965, as coach of Alma-Ata's Kairov squad in the major league, he received 320 rubles a month up front, a sum considerably more than the legal maximum of 220.[33] That same year, the goalie for Moscow's Torpedo, Anzor Amberkovich Kavazashvili, a member of the USSR's national team from 1965 to 1970 and later a critic of Kirov's Dinamo received 1,820 rubles in illegal bonuses.[34]

Moscow periodically attempted to curb ubiquitous benefits that went well beyond even an illegally inflated annual salary. It did so in vain. In November 1952, the editor of the popular daily, *Sovetskii sport*, Nikolai Ivanovich Liubomirov, sent a lengthy letter to Malenkov to complain about improper perquisites and special payments. Some players regarded football, he caustically commented, "as a means of existence and personal enrichment."[35] Ten years later, the Ministry of Finance cataloged the full range of illegal benefits provided to players for the Central Committee. It listed items big and small: hefty bonuses, fictional jobs, paid vacations at the best resorts, meals in the finest restaurants, and free vodka and cigarettes.[36]

Several months later, in October 1965, the deputy head of the Central Committee's Department of Propaganda and Agitation, Aleksandr Nikolaevich Iakovlev, a future architect of Mikhail Gorbachev's perestroika, lodged a similar and lengthy complaint with the Central Committee. He began, "Gross violations of financial discipline as well as excesses and profligacy in the support of football teams occur everywhere." Iakovlev might have followed with an assessment of how such excessive and illegal benefits produced an uneven playing field. But he chose instead to denounce them in a way that might appeal to a socialist conscience. These forms of compensation, he said, "instill in players selfishness, dependency, conceit, fecklessness, and a sense of entitlement." In their pursuit of profit, players were like "birds in flight, flitting from one team to the next."[37] Seven years later, in early 1972, a report on professional football from the Central Committee's Committee for Party Control and the Propaganda Department spoke of an "unhealthy situation" and a "waste of state and society's resources." In June 1974, the USSR's Ministry of Finance complained to the Central Committee about the continued reliance by many teams on illegal benefits in cash or kind.[38]

Broke but Proud

The quest for victory exacted a hefty price. With payments "off the books," clubs incurred expenditures well beyond gate receipts and anything they could officially receive from their sponsors or government agencies. They survived by encouraging and, more often than not, coercing local party and state organs, factories, and collective farms to foot the bill. Some institutional patrons compelled their employees to purchase season tickets by withholding the cost from their pay.[39]

With so many expenditures "off the books," audits by state agencies grossly underestimated the number of clubs that lived far beyond their official means. While therefore far off the mark, these official numbers nevertheless made for a depressing tale. In 1965, an audit of 187 teams found that 118 operated at a total loss of 2 million rubles. It was a gigantic sum, considering the average industrial worker earned a little more than one hundred rubles a month.[40] Three years later, an examination of 256 professional teams found that only 123 lived within their official budgets.[41] In 1969, of fifty teams checked, thirty-four ran up a deficit of 1,263,300 rubles.[42] Five years later, the USSR's Sports Committee reported that in 1973, of 161 teams surveyed, 121 teams operated at a loss.[43]

Local and regional governing organs covered their debts by commandeering funds officially designated to promote the public's physical fitness and amateur sports.[44] In 1961, Romanov complained that they did so out of their "insane passion for football."[45] In February 1975, a report from the Central Committee's Propaganda Department and its Committee for Party Control focused on one such grievous example. The Ministry of Transportation had covered the deficit of 163,000 rubles incurred by its football team, Lokomotiv, by transferring funds to it initially allocated to support the public's physical exercise, nonprofessional sports, and the construction of housing.[46]

Make It Right

Repeated but ineffectual denunciations of financial shenanigans testified to their pervasiveness and cast the party's Central Committee, among other agencies, as a Don Quixote, as Prozumenshchikov has characterized them, fighting windmills.[47] Yet every now and then, rote condemnation gave way to far more radical assessments. As mentioned previously, in 1965, Iakovlev came close to condemning professional football as a fundamentally corrupt enterprise from top to bottom. Ten years later, at a session of the committee's secretariat, Andrei Pavlovich Kirilenko, a secretary of the Central Committee and member of its Politburo, condemned what he called football's "depraved system."[48] The same sentiment led other officials to propose a radical modification of the sport.

In late 1969, Vasilii Pavlovich Mzhavadze, first secretary of the Georgian Communist Party, recommended a major change if only to drop the pretense of teams operating within their budgets. In a letter to the Central Committee, he acknowledged that an audit of seventeen of his republic's teams had found, not unexpectedly, that over the last two seasons at least eight had operated at a deficit, the losses covered by subsidies from a variety of agencies and enterprises. Yet the cities with these teams wanted, Mzhavadze approvingly stated, to keep their clubs whatever the cost. He requested that the Central Committee allow the Georgian state (its Council of Ministers) to openly subsidize them all. If it was allowed to do so, Mzhavadze promised that inappropriate bonuses and salaries from fictional jobs would, by the stroke of a pen, become aboveboard and legal.[49]

Eleven years after Mzhavadze's proposal, in January 1980, Pavlov, head of USSR's Sports Committee, made an even more radical proposal. Collectively, teams in the second league received inappropriate subsidies of 4–5 million rubles. Pavlov suggested putting an end to the financial disaster by eliminating the second league altogether. For the upcoming season, the Higher League would continue to consist of eighteen teams. The First League would add to its existing twenty-four clubs thirty-six of their most financially sound brethren from the second league. The remainder of the teams in the second league would cease to exist or would survive strictly on an amateur basis.[50]

Then, just after the disastrous 1979 season when Kirov considered a redoubling of efforts to support its Dinamo football team (as will be discussed below), Pavlov suggested, in effect, the team's elimination. Pavlov's proposal went nowhere because, to put it colloquially, it gored too many local and regional oxen, Kirov's included. Three weeks later, he relented.[51] That season, the second league actually expanded from 142 to 154 teams. Then, at year's end, Boris

Nikolaevich Rogatin, an official in the Central Committee's Propaganda Department, expressed his and presumably his organization's frustration with the league. In a major report at a conference of the leadership of the USSR's Sports Committee, Rogatin chastised the league for poor play and an annual turnover of twenty-five to thirty coaches.[52] The criticism had little effect. The next year, it expanded again to include 165 teams.

Three years later, veteran sports journalist Viktor Asaulov renewed the call for a radical restructuring of football's lowest tier. The second league had far too many teams and featured on the whole inferior play. Asaulov proposed banishing most of the clubs to a new third league or to leagues organized in separate republics of the USSR. A "real second league" would remain with only two or three zones.[53] His proposal went nowhere; it, too, threatened the interests of too many people and institutions.

Players Victimized

Not everyone in the USSR thought the players held such a great advantage. In 1949, at only fifteen, future poet Evgenii Evtushenko published his first verses, "Two Sports," in *Sovetskii sport*. There Evtushenko complained that a beautiful and entertaining game was marred by the broken hands and ribs suffered by players and the scheming of operators who dragged the athletes to and fro.[54]

Evtushenko might have had in mind the famed case of the Starostin brothers. In the Soviet Union's professional football league formed in 1936, the team Spartak, led by Nikolai Petrovich Starostin (and his three brothers, Aleksandr, Andrei, and Petr) won the second, third, and fourth seasons. Its success galled Lavrentii Beria, since 1938 head of the Commissariat of Internal Affairs, the proud sponsor of Spartak's chief rival, Moscow's Dinamo. In 1939, Beria hoped to humiliate, if not arrest, Nikolai "for running a professional organization along bourgeois lines."[55] At the time, Viacheslav Mikhailovich Molotov, chair of the USSR's Soviet of Peoples Commissars, shielded the brothers. Beria finally succeeded in 1942 with the arrest of all four followed by their dispatch to labor camps. They did not return from confinement and exile until twelve years later following the deaths of Iosif Stalin and Beria.

Condemned by their football prowess, the brothers were also saved by it. Nikolai, in particular, survived reasonably well by coaching football teams in or near the camps of his imprisonment. In almost every case, the head of the camp, an official in Beria's commissariat, picked Starostin to coach the local Dinamo squad.[56] Starostin later explained the irony of it all. His imprisoners "were disposed favorably to anything that concerned football, their immense power over people was nothing compared to the power of football over them."⁵⁷

In the late 1940s, promising player Nikita Simonian, then playing for Moscow's Kryl'ia Sovetov (Wings of the Soviets), only with great difficulty repulsed efforts by the same commissariat to compel him to play for its Dinamo squad in Tbilisi. The attempt included the arrest of Simonian's father. The son resisted. His father was released after two days of detention.⁵⁸

In 1950, one of the stars of Moscow's Spartak club, Sergei Sal'nikov, was forced to transfer to the capital's Dinamo squad, the result, as Edelman recounts it, of "good old-fashioned blackmail."⁵⁹ Years earlier, Sal'nikov's stepfather had been convicted of economic crimes and sent to a camp above the Arctic Circle. Dinamo's patron, the Commissariat (now Ministry) of Internal Affairs, responsible for the camp, informed Sal'nikov that if he agreed to the transfer, his stepfather would be moved to a prison near Moscow. Sal'nikov acquiesced and played for Dinamo for the next five years. His forced exile to Dinamo, however, did not preclude criticism of the benefits he reaped there. In November 1952, in a letter to Malenkov, Liubomirov, the editor of *Sovetskii sport*, included Sal'nikov among those who allegedly used football as a means of personal enrichment.⁶⁰ In 1955, the newly freed Nikolai Starostin, now head of Spartak, pulled his own bureaucratic strings to move Sal'nikov back to Spartak.

Aleksandr Bubnov, a prominent player for Moscow's Dinamo from 1974 through 1982, discovered that he could not move about freely. He later recalled the obstacles when he wished to transfer to Moscow's Spartak. Dinamo's administrators had the connections to prevent the move. Iurii Chubanov, deputy minister of the USSR's Ministry of Internal Affairs and son-in-law of the Communist Party's first secretary Leonid Brezhnev, intervened. Dinamo forced Bubnov into active military service for the next one and a half years and then disqualified him from further play. With Brezhnev's passing in November 1982, however, Chubanov's authority waned (he would soon be arrested). The day after the first secretary's death, Dinamo released Bubnov. Spartak's administrator, none other than Nikolai Starostin, worked with the first secretary of the party's Moscow Municipal Committee, a Spartak fan, to annul Bubnov's disqualification. Bubnov subsequently played for Spartak from 1983 through 1989.⁶¹

Finally, the notorious case of Eduard Anatol'evich Strel'tsov bears mention. Unlike previous examples just discussed, Strel'tsov's problems arose primarily if not exclusively from his personal behavior off the field rather than from his athletic skill on it. A star player for Moscow's Torpedo since 1954 and a member of the Soviet national team, Strel'tsov was arrested in early 1958 and charged with the rape of a young woman. Following his confession and trial, the state sentenced Strel'tsov to twelve years in prison. Many commentators argued subsequently that whatever the facts of the matter, authorities promptly and vigorously prosecuted Strel'tsov at the behest of a member of the Central Committee's Politburo, Ekaterina Alekseevna Furtseva. Strel'tsov had purportedly rudely rejected her suggestion that he marry her teenage daughter. No doubt his readily verifiable bohemian behavior (drinking, carousing, womanizing) contributed to his vigorous prosecution. Strel'tsov spent five years in confinement, initially in the Kirov region's forced labor camp, Viatlag. In 1965, he resumed his career with Torpedo, then retired in 1970.[62]

Special Effects

We know a great deal, as previously mentioned, about the various ways players (and coaches) received illegal benefits. We know little, however, about the monetary worth of such compensation. Little is known as well about another source of income. Rumors circulated constantly about bribes paid to players and coaches (and to referees). Yet testimony from former athletes, coaches, referees, and sports correspondents has routinely ignored or minimized the practice.[63] During an interview in 1992, Valerii Ovchinnikov, who, as will be seen below, served as coach of Kirov's Dinamo from 1981 to 1983, confessed without prompting that he and other coaches bribed referees. "Do you think I'm the only coach who does?" Ovchinnikov asked.[64] That year, British sports journalist Simon Kuper discussed Ovchinnikov's remarks with Vladimir Nikolaevich Shinkarev, a fan of Moscow's Spartak and an anthropologist at the Russian Academy of Sciences. "Did this not cause a scandal?" he wanted to know. His interlocutor responded laconically, "We have so many scandals in Russia nowadays that it is very hard to get excited about any new one."[65] A few days later, Kuper brought up Ovchinnikov's testimony in a meeting with Viacheslav Ivanovich Koloskov, president of the Russian Football Federation. "It was a joke," Koloskov responded, "two weeks ago, Ovchinnikov stood on this very carpet and swore he was joking."[66]

Bribery, real or imagined, might be a joking matter. Or it could be no more significant than a host of other sins an athlete could commit. Iurii Nikolaevich Adzhem had played for Moscow's Red Army team since 1979 and held the rank of lieutenant in the armed forces. In the first half of the 1981 season, his coach and other officials complained of his poor conduct on and off the field. When the USSR Sports Committee deliberated his case in August, his coach added that Adzhem had taken a bribe. The committee approved his dismissal from the squad. Two weeks later, it banned Adzhem from professional football and deprived him of his title of Master of Sport. It did so without a direct mention of bribery but, perhaps euphemistically, for "a violation of moral and ethical norms." The committee simultaneously disqualified twelve others for assorted and, apparently, no less or more serious misdeeds: poor play, drunkenness at a team's training facility, reckless and dangerous behavior during matches, and persistent demands for excessive benefits. Adzhem would return to the field in the late spring of 1982 when the L'vov regional party committee asked the Central Committee to annul the ban. Adzhem was, it said, honorably fulfilling his duties as an officer in the armed forces. He was helping coach the local Red Army team and should now be allowed to play for it.[67] That September, after consultation with the Central Committee's Propaganda Department, the USSR's Sports Committee lifted Adzhem's suspension. He played, however, not for L'vov's but for Moscow's Red Army team.[68] This apparent trivialization of bribery in Adzhem's case from the initial charge against him until his return to football's good graces helps explain the relative silence about the practice in the public and archival record.

We know next to nothing about the extent and effect on visiting players and referees of exceptionally good transportation, meals, hotel rooms, and other benefits the home team might provide. We do learn, however, much about fixed matches from the memoir by Aleksandr Bubnov. As he described it in detail, players on two competing teams would agree to a prearranged outcome to allow a club to finish atop the standings; to avoid relegation; or, out of spite, to ruin a hated third team's chances of winning a championship.[69] Kuper was told that coaches of all eighteen clubs in Russia's Higher League had been asked, "Are there arranged matches in our league?" All eighteen replied, "Yes." To the question "Does your club play in these matches?" they all answered, "It does not."[70] In an interview in 2007, the aforementioned Ovchinnikov denied any involvement in a prearranged contest. He then admitted that some of his players had sometimes thrown a match. Ovchinnikov hastened to add, "But I have fought against any such effort."[71]

Soviet football was governed by an extensive bureaucracy extending from the center to local sports committees. Despite such widespread bureaucratic oversight, the USSR's Sports Committee and its affiliated organizations were not able to limit the proliferation of football clubs, which provided prestige to the enterprises and organizations they represented. They were equally unsuccessful at limiting the poaching of the best players, particularly by teams associated with the armed forces who frequently used the draft to secure the best players from other teams. Recruiting the best players did not simply rely on strong-arm tactics, though. A competitive market flourished where star players were offered a number of questionably legal incentives such as fictitious jobs or military ranks, access to scarce goods or apartments, cars, and country houses to play for clubs desperate to win. Despite multiple complaints to the Central Committee and other high-level party and state organs, the Soviet bureaucracy was unable to curb this practice. In some cases, not carrots but sticks were used to remove talented players who were playing for the "wrong" team or to try to force players to switch teams. Arresting competitors or threatening to arrest players to force them to play for one of the Dinamo organizations was something the Commissariat (and then later Ministry) of Internal Affairs, Dinamo's sponsor, resorted to on multiple occasions. Other issues, such as bribes and thrown matches, are less well understood but also highlight how willing teams were to win at all costs and how powerless the bureaucracy was to put a stop to such behaviors.

NOTES

1. The committee experienced several name changes and governing bodies. In 1953, it became the Chief Administration for Physical Culture and Sport of the USSR's Ministry of Health, then in 1954, the All-Union Committee for Physical Culture and Sport of the USSR's Council of Ministers; in 1959, the Union of Sport Societies and Organizations of the USSR; in 1968, the Committee for Physical Culture and Sport of the USSR's Council of Ministers; and in 1986, the State Committee for Physical Culture and Sport. I will consistently refer to it as the USSR's Sport Committee.

2. See many examples in M. Iu. Prozumenshchikov, *Bol'shoi sport i bol'shaia politika* (Moscow: ROSSPEN, 2004), 345–385; "Interv'iu s M. Iu. Prozumenshchikovym," *Sotsiologicheskoe obozrenie* 17, no. 2 (2018): 182–183, 186–187; and the collection of documents, N. G. Tomilina and M. Iu. Prozumenshchikov, *Igra millionov pod partiinym kontrolem: Sovetskii futbol po dokumentam TsK KPSS* (Moscow: Mezhdunarodnyi fond "Demokratiia"), 2017.

3. M. Iu. Prozumenshchikov, "Obratnaia storona sovetskogo futbola," in Tomilina and Prozumenshchikov, *Igra millionov pod partiinym kontrolev*, 24; Prozumenshchikov, *Bol'shoi sport*, 390. In the 1980s, the volume of material on football sent to the highest party organs (items available in the Russian State Archive of Modern History [RGANI]) sharply declined. The Central Committee now refused to support pleas from sponsors of teams doomed by poor play to relegation. There were exceptions. In 1967, Leningrad's squad, Zenit, finished in last place in the major league. It was, however, deemed impolitic to demote a squad representing Leningrad in the year of the fiftieth anniversary of the October revolution (see Prozumenshchikov, *Bol'shoi sport*, 354–355). In 1970,

however, the Central Committee ruled against an annulment of the relegation of Odessa's Chernomortez despite pleas from the region's regional party committee (Tomilina and Prozumenshchikov, *Igra millionov*, 108–112). The following year, the committee insisted on the demotion of Donetsk's Shakhter and Tashkent's Pakhtakor despite urgent requests from state and party officials not to do so (Tomilina and Prozumenshchikov, *Igra millionov*, 120–125). In 1976, despite pleas from the Russian Republic's Sports Committee and first secretary of Moscow's Municipal Party Committee, the Central Committee did not intervene to stop Moscow's Spartak from relegation from the Higher League (Prozumenshchikov, *Bol'shoi sport*, 360). In 1987, the committee refused to overrule the relegation of Moscow's famed Red Army club (Tomilina and Prozumenshchikov, *Igra millionov*, 137–140). For a description of the standard litany of requests for an annulment of relegation, see Prozumenshchikov, *Bol'shoi sport*, 350. During the early 1980s, in the field of literature, film, and the arts, the party's Central Committee, while still powerful, increasingly delegated to regional leaders the right to make decisions. See N. G. Tomilina and M. Iu. Prozumenshchikov, eds., *Apparat TsK KPSS i kul'tura, 1979–1984: Dokumenty* (Moscow: ROSSPEN, 2019), 7–8.

4. Alejandro Quiroga, "Spanish Fury: Football and National Identities under Franco," *European History Quarterly* 45, no. 3 (2015): 507–508. Alternative identities did not necessarily mean a rejection of the notion of a "Spain," especially one without Franco.

5. Simon Martin, *Football and Fascism: The National Game under Mussolini* (New York: Berg, 2004), 3, 76.

6. "Interv'iu s M. Iu. Prozumenshchikovym," 186. A letter of April 12, 1962, from Romanov, chair of the USSR's Sports Committee to the Central Committee, made the same point. Romanov spoke of "local attitudes" and of a special passion among local and regional leaders for football: Tomilina and Prozumenshchikov, *Igra millionov*, 158, 159. On especially intense efforts by the head of Ukraine's Communist Party to advance his republic's Dinamo team in Kiev in the 1970s, see Prozumenshchikov, *Bol'shoi sport*, 370–371.

7. See the report from Romanov, November 29, 1952, to Malenkov, Tomilina and Prozumenshchikov, *Igra millionov*, 153.

8. Prozumenshchikov, "Obratnaia storona," 10.

9. Tomilina and Prozumenshchikov, *Igra millionov*, 162 (for 1965), 104 (for 1969).

10. Tomilina and Prozumenshchikov, *Igra millionov*, 131.

11. K. Manuel Veth, "Selling the People's Game: Football's Transition from Communism to Capitalism in the Soviet Union and Its Successor State" (PhD diss., King's College, London, 2016), 17.

12. See the report of the Party Control Commission in early 1972, Tomilina and Prozumenshchikov, *Igra Millionov*, 211.

13. For players designated as a schoolteacher, see information provided by Kirov's regional Dinamo soviet, November 5, 1979, in the State Archive for the Social and Political History of the Kirov Region, f. R-6766, op. 1, d. 743, l. 87. The players were Vladimir Vasil'evich Darovskoi, Lev Nikolaevich Isupov, Sergei Vasil'evich Skobelkin, Sergei Ivanovich Erdiakov, and Sergei Arkad'evich Bubnov. For a frank discussion of players' salaries, including bonuses, and of other perquisites (an apartment and car, for example), see Aleksandr Bubnov, *Spartak: 7 let strogogo rezhima* (Moscow: Eksmo, 2015), 26, 32, 96, 103, 118–199. Spartak's administrator, Nikolai Starostin, had a good relationship with the party's Moscow municipal committee and thus could secure apartments for his team's athletes: 96, 103. Decades earlier, in Great Britain, players might receive payments under the table by "selling" their dog to a club director or "serving" as a club's assistant secretary: see a discussion of such benefits in Nicholas Fishwick, *English Football and Society, 1910–1950* (New York: Manchester University Press, 1989), 77 and Wray Vamplew, *Play Up and Play the Game: Professional Sport in Britain, 1875–1914* (New York: Cambridge University Press, 1988), 200.

14. Tomilina and Prozumenshchikov, *Igra millionov*, 83–84.

15. James Riordan, "Sport after the Cold War: Implications for Russia and Eastern Europe," in *East Plays West: Sport and the Cold War*, ed. Stephen Wagg and David L. Andrews (New York: Routledge, 2007), 281. In 1970, a major earned a base pay of 135 rubles a month, a lieutenant colonel 165: *Military Compensation in the Soviet Union* from the National Foreign Assessment Center, December 1980, 4, https://www.cia.gov/library/readingroom/docs/DOC_0000969802.pdf, accessed August 12, 2020. Officers would normally receive additional compensation based on their duties or assignment. In 1984, a captain received 140 rubles a month, a major 150, and a lieutenant colonel 160, https://zen.yandex.ru/media/id/5de553f835ca3100afdc3536/zarplata-leitenanta-v-sa-v-sssr-v-1984-godu-chto-s-nei-stalo--pacany-ne-veriat-5de92cfd43863f00b2046063, accessed August 13, 2020.

16. See the note from the department, April 28, 1963, in Tomilina and Prozumenshchikov, *Igra millionov*, 299. The department also complained of the enticement of players to move from one team to another by offering fictional jobs, apartments, and excessive and illegal monetary benefits: 299–300.

17. Tomilina and Prozumenshchikov, *Igra millionov*, 397. The military had even drafted players who had already served in the armed forces.

18. Tomilina and Prozumenshchikov, *Igral millionov*, 398. For earlier complaints in 1956, for example, for objections from the USSR's Ministry of Transportation, from workers at a factory concerning the loss of players of their Lokomotiv team, and from administrators at a Moscow factory that sponsored Torpedo, see Tomilina and Prozumenshchikov, *Igra millionov*, 358–360.

19. See Rokachev's letter of March 14, 1980, to Mikhail Vasil'evich Zimianin, a secretary of the party's Central Committee: RGANI, f. 5, op. 77, d. 149, ll. 28–30,

quote on l. 30. See a discussion of the case in Prozumenshchikov, *Bol'shoi sport*, 370 and documents published in Tomilina and Prozumenshchikov, *Igra millionov*, 401–405. Andreev had played for Zaria from 1973 through 1977. In 1978, he transferred to the army team in Rostov-on-Don. Andreev played for the Soviet Union's national team in the 1980 Olympics. Before drafting athletes, the military might move its draft registration district from Voroshilovgrad to a district where the targeted team played.

20. See Pavlov's memorandum, April 4, 1980, RGANI, f. 5, op. 77, d. 149, ll. 31–32.

21. RGANI, f. 5, op. 77, d. 149, ll. 33–34. The Central Committee's Propaganda Department summoned the chair of the Ministry of Defense's Sports Committee to tell him to improve the recruitment of his teams' rosters by the development of their own young players: ll. 35–36. Zaria remained in the First League until 1984 when it fell even farther by relegation to the second league. It returned to the First League in 1988.

22. See Prozumenshchikov, "Obratnaia storona," 14, 19 and Prozumenshchikov, *Bol'shoi sport*, 365. For multiple instances of the drafting of players by the armed services and requests for their deferment or assignment to the inactive reserve, see Tomilina and Prozumenshchikov, *Igra millionov*, 343–413.

23. Robert Edelman, *Serious Fun: A History of Spectator Sports in the USSR* (New York: Oxford University Press, 1993), 180. "Until the rules were clarified and a contract system was instituted the situation remained unclear and, no doubt, quite corrupt": 181.

24. For the best discussion of English football and the onset of professionalism, see Steven Tischler, *Footballers and Businessmen: The Origins of Professional Soccer in England* (New York: Holmes and Meier, 1981), especially chap. 2, "The Basis of Professionalism," 31–50 and chap. 3, "Toward a 'Sound Business Footing,'" 51–67. On financing of English football and remuneration of players, see Tony Mason, *Association Football and English Society, 1863–1915* (Atlantic Highlands, NJ: Humanities), 69–137. On the professionalization of football in other countries, see Bill Murray, *The World's Game: A History of Soccer* (Urbana: University of Illinois Press, 1996), 47. In England, even after the introduction of a maximum wage in 1900 and until its abolition in 1961, some teams provided both hidden and open inducements beyond the allowable wage for their very best players: David Goldblatt, *The Ball Is Round: A Global History of Soccer* (New York: Riverhead Books, 2008), 67; Matthew Taylor, "Beyond the Maximum Wage: The Earnings of Football Professionals in England, 1900–39," *Soccer & Society* 2, no. 3 (Autumn 2001): 101–118. Taylor observes, "The maximum wage seems to have increasingly come to represent a symbolic rather than a real ceiling on earnings": 115.

25. Veth, "Selling the People's Game," 279. With the collapse of the USSR, Veth noted that "football players were perhaps the only profession in the Soviet Union that had to give up rights."

26. Tomilina and Prozumenshchikov, *Igra millionov*, 153.
27. https://ihistorian.livejournal.com/412544.html, accessed August 12, 2020.
28. Tomilina and Prozumenshchikov, *Igra millionov*, 179. Fifteen players would receive 180 rubles; six 150, and six more 130.
29. http://skolko-poluchaet.ru/skolko-poluchayut/skolko-poluchali-v-sssr.html, accessed August 12, 2020; https://www.liveinternet.ru/users/sem_9011/post197942481, accessed August 12, 2020.
30. Tomilina and Prozumenshchikov, *Igra millionov*, 216–218. The Politburo approved a draft resolution for the USSR's Council of Ministers. On a given squad, fifteen players could receive 250 rubles a month, six 200, and six others 150. Any athlete with the title Master of Sport would receive ten additional rubles a month, those with the title Meritorious Master of Sport twenty more.
31. http://skolko-poluchaet.ru/skolko-poluchayut/skolko-poluchali-v-sssr.html, accessed August 12, 2020; https://www.liveinternet.ru/users/sem_9011/post197942481, accessed August 12, 2020.
32. See Romanov's report to Malenkov, November 29, 1952, Tomilina and Prozumenshchikov, *Igra millionov*, 153–154, 156. All this was detailed in an appended draft resolution for the USSR's Council of Ministers. Romanov had a history of both criticism and support of professional athletes. In 1946, he sternly reproached the Dinamo society for providing its best athletes with fictional jobs and illegal pay. Yet that same year and again in 1955, he called for a legalization, as it were, of special benefits for the nation's top performers so they could successfully compete on the international stage. See Elena Zubkova and Aleksandr Kupriianov, "Professionalizatsiia sovetskogo sporta v usloviiakh kholodnoi voiny (1946–1959)," *Rossiiskaia istoria*, no. 1 (February 2020): 146–148, 150.
33. See the letter from deputy minister of finance V. Sitkin, July 30, 1965, to the Central Committee, Tomilina and Prozumenshchikov, *Igra millionov*, 169.
34. Tomilina and Prozumenshchikov, *Igra millionov*, 171.
35. Letter in Tomilina and Prozumenshchikov, *Igra millionov*, 147–152, see especially 148, quote on 151. Liubomirov noted the awarding of fictional jobs, apartments, and military ranks. On unsuccessful attempts by the center to limit if not eliminate illegal benefits provided to football players, see Sylvain Dufraisse, "Struggling against the Caste System, Patronage and Unhealthy Payments: Attempts at Regulation of Football Players' Remunerations from the 1950s to the 1970s in the Soviet Union," *Soccer & Society* 21, no. 6 (2020): 648–656.
36. Tomilina and Prozumenshchikov, *Igra millionov*, 166, 170, 172–173.
37. Tomilina and Prozumenshchikov, *Igra millionov*, 160, 163. At this time, Iakovlev's attitude toward sports was formed primarily out of ideological considerations: Mikhail Prozumenshchikov, "Action in the Era of Stagnation: Leonid Brezhnev and the Soviet Olympic Dream," in *The Whole World Was Watching:*

Sport in the Cold War, ed. Robert Edelman and Christopher Young (Stanford, CA: Stanford University Press, 2020), 78.

38. Tomilina and Prozumenshchikov, *Igra millionov*, 229–231. Complaints of a continued reliance by many teams on such illegal benefits followed in the ensuing years. See the report of the Central Committee's Propaganda Department, February 11, 1975, and Party Control Commission, Tomilina and Prozumenshchikov, *Igra millionov*, 247–248.

39. See the report of the Central Committee's Party Control Commission and Propaganda Department, early 1972, Tomilina and Prozumenshchikov, *Igra millionov*, 209. A collective farm in the Lipetsk region levied fees on its members in support of the region's Metallurg: Prozumenshchikov, *Bol'shoi sport*, 382.

40. See the report of deputy minister of finance V. Sitkin, July 30, 1965, to the Central Committee, Tomilina and Prozumenshchikov, *Igra millionov*, 167. On a worker's income, see http://skolko-poluchaet.ru/skolko-poluchayut/skolko-poluchali-v-sssr.html.

41. Prozumenshchikov, *Bol'shoi sport*, 380.

42. See the report of the Central Committee's Party Control Commission, November 2, 1965, in Tomilina and Prozumenshchikov, *Igra millionov*, 181–183.

43. See the report of the USSR's Sports Committee to the Central Committee, May 28, 1974, in Tomilina and Prozumenshchikov, *Igra millionov*, 255. A few months later, the committee reported that teams in the Higher League and First League, clubs chiefly in cities that might conceivably cover expenses through gate receipts, lost collectively a total of 900,000 rubles a year. See the report submitted by the USSR's Sports Committee, July 8, 1974, to the Central Committee's Propaganda Department, in Tomilina and Prozumenshchikov, *Igra millionov*, 237.

44. See, for example, the complaint by Romanov to the Central Committee in a report of April 12, 1962: Tomilina and Prozumenshchikov, *Igra millionov*, 158.

45. See the report of April 12, 1961, from Romanov to the Central Committee, in Tomilina and Prozumenshchikov, *Igra millionov*, 157.

46. Tomilina and Prozumenshchikov, *Igra millionov*, 247.

47. Prozumenshchikov, *Bol'shoi sport*, 383.

48. Tomilina and Prozumenshchikov, *Igra millionov*, 243.

49. See the report of November 19, 1969, to the Central Committee, Tomilina and Prozumenshchikov, *Igra millionov*, 107.

50. See Pavlov's report, January 2, 1980, in Tomilina and Prozumenshchikov, *Igra millionov*, 132.

51. Prozumenshchikov, *Bol'shoi sport*, 387. The weekly *Futbol-Khokkei* did not discuss Pavlov's proposal, nor was it on the agenda of a conference of football coaches that met in Moscow from January 17–19, 1980, where the head of the Governing Board of Football, Viacheslav Koloskov, and the deputy chair of the

USSR's Sports Committee, Valentin Lukich Sych, spoke. See *Futbol-Khokkei*, no. 3, January 20, 1980, 2 and no. 4, January 27, 1980, 2–3. Koloskov mentioned without commentary that 184 professional football teams existed in the Soviet Union (issue of January 27, 1980, 2).

52. State Archive of the Russian Federation (GARF), f. R-7576, op. 31, d. 5635, l. 92.

53. Viktor Asaulov, "... I pozabotimsia o budushchem," *Futbol-Khokkei*, no. 42, October 16, 1983, 10–11. Asaulov had reported for *Futbol-Khokkei* since 1968. He did allow for the possible creation of a few leagues (or zones, as he called them) that included teams from more than one republic.

54. Ev. Evtushenko, "Dva sporta," *Sovetskii sport*, June 2, 1949, 4. A self-admitted football fanatic, Evtushenko once dreamed of a career as a goalie. In 2009, he published his thoughts on the game: Evgenii Evtushenko, *Moia futboliada: Poeziia, proza* (Poltava: ASMI, 2009).

55. Edelman, *Serious Fun*, 65.

56. Jim Riordan, "The Strange Story of Nikolai Starostin: Football and Lavrentii Beria," *Europe-Asia Studies* 46, no. 4 (1994): 681–690. See also a discussion of the Starostins in Robert Edelman, *Spartak Moscow: A History of the People's Team in the Workers' State* (Ithaca, NY: Cornell University Press, 2009). Starostin coached teams in Ukhta, Komsomol'sk-na-Amur, Ul'ianovsk, and Alma-Ata. For him, football was "the means of survival": 81. For the arrest, interrogation, torture, and subsequent "careers" in prison of the four Starostin brothers, see Boris Dukhon and Georgii Morozov, *Brat'ia Starostiny* (Moscow: Molodaia gvardiia, 2012), 78–180. See also Steven Maddox, "Gulag Football: Competitive and Recreational Sport in Stalin's System of Forced Labor," *Kritika* 19, no. 3 (Summer 2018): 509–536.

57. Nikolai Petrovich Starostin, *Futbol skvoz' gody* (Moscow: Molodaia gvardiia, 1989), 80–81.

58. Nikitia Simonian, *Futbol—tol'ko lli igra?* (Moscow: Agenstvo "FAIR," 1998), 50–54. For similar pressure decades later on a young Georgian goalkeeper, Anzor Kavazashvili, a figure of some importance in subsequent chapters in this book, to play for Dinamo's Tbilisi rather than in Russia, see Erik R. Scott, "Soccer Artistry and the Secret Police: Georgian Football in the Multiethnic Soviet Empire," in *The Whole World Was Watching: Sport in the Cold War*, ed. Robert Edelman and Christopher Young (Stanford, CA: Stanford University Press, 2020), 95–96.

59. Robert Edelman, "Romantic Underdogs: *Spartak* in the Golden Age of Soviet Soccer, 1945–1952," in *Euphoria and Exhaustion: Modern Sport in Soviet Culture and Society*, ed. Nikolaus Katzer, Sandra Budy, Alexandra Köhring, and Manfred Zeller (New York: Campus, 2010), 241.

60. Tomilina and Prozumenshchikov, *Igra millionov*, 150.

61. See Bubnov's discussion of his transfer in Bubnov, *Spartak*, 16–19, 24. Decades earlier, in the 1930s, Petr Dement'ev, a player for Leningrad's Dinamo, had a similar experience when he wanted to accept an invitation to play for Kiev's Dinamo. It seemed possible until Leningrad's party boss, Andrei Aleksandrovich Zhdanov, intervened to stop the transfer: Petr Dement'ev, *Peka o sebe, ili Futbol nachinaetsia v detstve* (Moscow: Izvestiia, 1995, 31), see the downloaded copy in Word format at https://royallib.com/book/dementev_petr/peka_o_sebe_ili _futbol_nachinaetsya_v_detstve.html.

62. Much of the literature on the case is quick to absolve Strel'tsov of rape while acknowledging his so-called youthful indiscretions. One of the better, more objective accounts is A. T. Vartanian, *Eduard Strel'tsov—nasil'nik ili zhertva?* (Moscow: TERRA-Sport, 2001), 45–62. It was rumored that Strel'tsov wished to play professionally abroad and thereby provoked the ire of governing organs of football and, on a higher plane, of the Kremlin.

63. At the end of the 1970s, Kirov's sport correspondent Viktor Chudinovskikh wanted to know why the city's Dinamo so frequently lost when on the road. He traveled with the team to Georgia where he discovered that local officials and the public bribed referees and opponents. It could take an openly brazen form. In the middle of a game, someone approached Dinamo's goalie, Bubnov, offering payment in return for poor play. See V. A. Chudinovskikh, *Ispoved' "perevertysha": Iz zhizni reportera* (Kirov: Avtor, 2008), 35. See in chap. 6 a discussion of charges of bribery made in 1981 against the club Kryl'ia sovetov from the city of Kuibyshev.

64. As reported in Simon Kuper, *Soccer against the Enemy*, 2nd ed. (New York: Nation Books, 2006), 41, 61. At the time, Ovchinnikov was coach of Nizhnii Novgorod's Lokomotiv.

65. Kuper, *Soccer*, 41.

66. Kuper, *Soccer*, 61.

67. For deliberations of the USSR's Sports Committee on August 20, 1981, and its subsequent disqualification of Adzhem and others on September 24, see RGANI, f. 5, op. 88, d. 140, ll. 23–24, 26. For the request from the L'vov regional party committee, l. 22. The coach charged that Adzhem had taken a bribe before a game with the city of Dnepropetrovsk's Dnepr, though he did not say which of the two games played that year. Moscow's Red Army team played Dnepr at home on April 19 (a 1–1 tie) and on the road August 13 (a 2–1 loss). Curiously, Adzhem played in both games.

68. GARF, f. R-7576, op. 31, d. 7511, l. 12 and RGANI, f. 5, op. 88, d. 140, l. 27. In 1981, Adzhem played in seventeen games for Moscow's Red Army team, presumably before his disqualification; in 1982, for six, probably after removal of the suspension; and in 1983, now free and clear, for thirty.

69. Bubnov, *Spartak*, 65–67, 188–195, 254–256. Simonian discusses an attempt at a prearranged match in Simonian, *Futbol*, 193. For a frankly depressing

discussion of the extent and variety of prearranged matches (and shady business deals) in the recent history of Russian football, see Aleksei Matveev, *Dogovorniak-2: Kak pokupaiut i prodaiut matchi v rossiiskom futbole* (Moscow: Eksmo, 2011), especially information provided by Aleksandr Bubnov, 131–153; Matveev, *Kriminal'nyi futbol: Ot Koloskova do Mutko. Rassledovanie s riskom dlia zhizni* (Moscow: Eksmo, 2009); and Nikolai Iaremenko, *Futbol ub'et Rossiiu: Narodnaia igra v rubliakh, dogovorniakakh i vziatkakh* (Moscow: Astrel', 2011). Iaremenko concluded, "When budgets are not transparent, when business relationships are beyond understanding, there can't be [real] football," 70. See also a discussion of such matches in N. N. Ozerov, *Vsiu zhizn' za sinei ptitsei* (Moscow: Nauka, 1995), 84–86.

70. Kuper, *Soccer*, 41–42.

71. Interview in *Futbol*, April 13, 2007, https://lokomotiv.info/blogs/130407/2276/.

PART II

FOOTBALL IN RUSSIA'S DEPTHS, 1979–1985

4

KIROV'S DINAMO

As with all other professional football teams in the USSR, the sources and magnitude of the financing of Kirov's Dinamo remain largely unknown. If such a fate were to be avoided in the future, the club's miserable showing in the 1970s and especially in 1979 required far greater backing to enable it to recruit better athletes and coaches.

The Mystery of Funding

Kirov's archives contain the annual budgets of the region's government and the specific sums it allocated for the promotion of physical fitness and amateur sport.[1] They also provide a wealth of information about the Dinamo society's overall administrative costs and its expenditures on amateur athletics. In 1979, the society had a total budget of 336,800 rubles, over 300,000 of which was designated for salaries. It employed 180 people, 179 of whom (80 men and 99 women) worked in urban areas, almost exclusively in the city of Kirov. Twenty-two of the total coached youths and adults in sambo, judo, skiing, ice-skating, wrestling, and football. Coaches were poorly paid, receiving 120–145 rubles per month. The director of Dinamo's stadium received 135 rubles monthly, its janitor a mere 70.[2] The regional Dinamo soviet's deputy chair, Mikhail Nikolaevich Sergeev, received 362.50 rubles a month and another deputy chair, Evgenii Petrovich Kolchanov, 310.50.[3] By comparison, in 1979, the average monthly salary in the USSR was 146 rubles.[4]

The available record tells us little about the level of support of Kirov's professional football team beyond indications that it was considerable. More precisely, it is silent about what the regional Dinamo society, the regional soviet, or the regional branch of the Ministry of Internal Affairs allocated to the team. Because of the expense and illegalities involved, that information, if preserved, remains classified. Almost by accident, we learn that in 1984, 70 percent of the club's players served in the armed forces of the Ministry of Internal Affairs. That year, Dinamo protested the unprecedented plan to call its athletes into active service during the period usually set aside for preseason training. We do not know, however, their rank and corresponding base salary.[5] In its successful years, Dinamo awarded its players publicly announced bonuses. But at the same time, it provided other, unpublicized awards, guaranteed regardless of performance. These sums were essentially a second salary that was then (and is still) off the books.[6]

We also know little about gate receipts. The club set prices that varied according to the desirability of the location. But we rarely can be certain about the number of fans at a game and the sale of tickets. When attendance is known, it is almost always a rough estimate provided not by Dinamo but by sports correspondents.[7]

In an interview, Kolchanov acknowledged that each year, Kirov's Dinamo received 110,000 rubles for its football team from the Russian Republic's Dinamo soviet.[8] As we will see below, when the club was at its most successful and costly, it repeatedly turned to that soviet for far more (often to be transferred from the immense profits of Kirov's own Dinamo Sports Factory). Kirov's Dinamo also passed the hat, as Kolchanov put it, among regional and municipal state and party organs and Kirov's industrial enterprises, the proceeds never officially documented.

The Dinamo Empire

Kirov's team was one of many football clubs sponsored by a nationwide Dinamo organization whose remit in sports extended well beyond football. In 1923, the State Political Directorate (GPU), responsible for the infant Soviet state's security police, created a "Proletarian Sports Society 'Dinamo'" to promote the physical fitness of its troops.[9] By the end of the decade, the society had branches in two hundred cities, Viatka (renamed Kirov after 1934) included. Each local promoted the physical well-being of its personnel and their family members and, more broadly, youths and adults in the larger community. Throughout the USSR, Dinamo built stadiums for football; facilities for track and field; ice rinks for skating and hockey; courts for basketball, volleyball, and tennis; and a few indoor swimming pools. It also owned, among other facilities, hotels, dormitories, and apartment complexes.

Dinamo supported its sports empire with funds allocated to it by the security police.[10] It also relied on huge profits from its many factories that produced sports equipment and apparel and from the stores that sold them. In the early 1950s, Dinamo transferred the latter to the USSR's Ministry of Trade but retained the factories. By the end of the 1970s, fifty of them employed twenty thousand people and produced almost twenty million items for export as well as for internal consumption. They generated an annual profit of almost 150 million rubles.[11]

Origins of Kirov's Dinamo

In 1923, the GPU's branch in Viatka organized a football team. It played squads in the city and occasionally Dinamo teams from nearby municipalities. After 1932, it had its own Dinamo stadium.[12] By the early 1950s, Kirov's Dinamo competed on a regular basis with other Soviet squads well beyond the city. In 1957, it joined one of the USSR's minor leagues.

Kirov's emergence onto the national football scene occurred in large part thanks to its coach, Aleksandr Andreevich Keller. A 1936 graduate of the USSR's Central Institute of Physical Culture, Keller played for Torpedo in the city of Gor'ky (Nizhnii Novgorod before 1932 and after 1990). From 1940, he coached Stalingrad's Traktor, a team in the USSR's major league. Keller's tenure there was brief. Following the attack on the USSR by Nazi Germany in mid-1941, the Soviet state deported him along with a million of his fellow Soviet citizens of German descent to Kazakhstan. Shortly thereafter, Keller was shipped to the Kirov region's Viatlag, which was under the jurisdiction of the Ministry of Internal Affairs. There he survived in part thanks to his football prowess. In 1946, the camp's commander, Aleksei Dem'ianovich Kukhtikov, called on Keller to manage the sports stadium in the camp's main village, Lesnoe, and serve as a player-coach of its football team. When in 1951 Kirov's regional branch of the Ministry of Internal Affairs resolved to improve the play of its football team in Kirov, it realized that it had just the man for the job. It released Keller from the camp and hired him as Dinamo's coach.[13] Under Keller's guidance, Dinamo, at first with only senior high school pupils, played a limited number of games in a minor circuit of regional teams. In 1956, it played fifteen games, winning ten and losing five. The following year, it advanced to the USSR's minor league where in thirty games, it won eleven. Despite multiple defeats, the club's play attracted enthusiastic crowds. Unable to get into the stadium, fans perched on nearby rooftops, on telephone poles, and in trees. In 1959, Dinamo won fourteen of twenty-eight contests and was the victor at the prestigious Spartakiad of

Kirov's Dinamo Stadium, c. 1950. Note portraits of Stalin and Lenin on the pavilion. *Courtesy of GAKO.*

the Russian Republic. After that successful season, Keller left for Tashkent to coach Pakhtakor, a team that had just advanced to the USSR's major league.[14]

After Keller's departure, Dinamo continued to perform reasonably well until 1971. Thereafter, in the 1970s, except for 1975, Dinamo occupied a spot at the bottom of its zone, winning less than one-third of its games.[15]

The year 1979 began with the usual blossoming of preseason optimism. The region's main newspaper, *Kirovskaia pravda*, hoped that Dinamo might finish in the top ten in its zone. It was a "modest goal," it admitted, "but considering that heretofore the team could not achieve even that, it would not be an easy one."[16] The season was a disaster. "Another loss," *Kirovskaia pravda* repeatedly declared. At midseason, the paper's chief sports correspondent, Viktor Andreevich Chudinovskikh, wrote in an understated fashion: "Again, as in preceding years, Kirov's Dinamo brings no joy to its fans. The question has arisen," he added, "will Dinamo continue to exist."[17] In midseason on July 26, the presidium of the region's Dinamo soviet denounced the team's play and demanded improved performance.[18] It did so in vain.

Amid this disastrous year, buyers descended on Kirov to entice away what little it had in value—its two best players, goalie Sergei Arkad'evich Bubnov

Dinamo, 1957. Keller at the top in the middle column.
Courtesy of GASPI KO.

and midfielder Anatolii Pavlovich Usatov. Bubnov stayed with a promise, soon fulfilled, to provide him with an apartment. Usatov remained as well after, perhaps, a brief departure.[19] Dinamo's play did not improve. Those few fans courageous enough to venture into the stadium departed before the end of another loss.[20] While Kirov's radio refrained from scathing commentary, its television station was not so kind. On October 30, it told the city's viewers that "the present season is the most unsuccessful in the twenty-three years in which the team has participated in a national football league."[21] With only a few games remaining, the coach, Vasilii Shutov, was fired. His replacement from Moscow quit after only a few games.[22] "In Its Same Old Spot," declared *Kirovskaia pravda* at the season's close of the team's occupancy of twenty-first place in a zone of twenty-four teams.[23] In *Komsomol'skoe plemia*, sports reporter Boris Aronovich Kolomensky declared that "fans impatiently waited for the season's close." The team's performance was "a

Kirov's Sports Reporters: Chudinovskikh and Kolomensky. *Courtesy of Viktor Chudinovskikh.*

fiasco, in essence anti-football."[24] A few months later, in February 1980, Kolomensky added that the 1979 season "could be considered with complete justification one of the most unsuccessful in the team's history."[25] As he wrote those lines, more people likely came to Dinamo's stadium for public ice-skating, five hundred to six hundred on weekends, than had recently attended football games.[26]

Disgust with Dinamo's poor performance transcended the Kirov region. In February 1980, the presidium of the Russian Republic's Dinamo soviet pointed out that the team had performed woefully over many years. Attendance had markedly declined. It blamed, in particular, the recently fired Shutov and the deputy chair of Kirov region's Dinamo soviet, Kolchanov.[27]

Poor play and harsh criticism, locally and nationally, brought forth a reckoning in Kirov in late 1979 and early 1980. The region's governing soviet, the branch of the Ministry of Internal Affairs, and the Dinamo soviet confronted an issue long at the forefront of Soviet educational and cultural policy. In their apportionment of funds for the public's physical fitness, amateur sport, and Dinamo, they would have to decide whether in the latter's case "winning was everything."

A Watershed Year

The Soviet government had long imbued its citizens with the notion that life was a form of warfare. It had done so, as Mikhail Prozumenshchikov has observed, with such tropes as "the labor front" or "the battle for the harvest." As we have seen, it was no less true in the realm of football. Leningrad's hosts of the Basque team in 1937, the Soviet national team in the 1952 Olympics, and the USSR's representative in the European Championship in Spain in 1964 discovered that nothing short of total victory was acceptable. After Kirov's Dinamo's disastrous season in 1979, local authorities knew it as well. The team required an infusion of cash to achieve a least a patina of respectability if not consistent victory. In their assessment of the team's needs, the presidium of the regional Dinamo soviet and Kolomensky at *Komsomol'skoe plemia* designated four critical areas. First, Dinamo needed to boost salaries and benefits to acquire and keep better athletes. From 1973 through 1978, inducements offered by other teams had taken away thirty of Dinamo's players. Only the team's doctor, coach, and a few players currently received apartments. Second, it required more and better equipment and its own in-season training facilities in or near Kirov. Third, coaches had to invite more players to preseason training, whatever the added expense, to stimulate competition and find the best players for the upcoming season. In 1979, the team had begun training camp with only eight athletes on hand. Fourth, the region's government had to invest considerably more in the promotion of youth football. The success of a professional team in a provincial city such as Kirov depended on a steady influx of local talent. From 1977 through 1979, Dinamo had added only two athletes from the region to its roster. Moreover, the best players of local "amateur" clubs had demonstrated little interest in playing for the provincial capital's professional team. They preferred the local privileges they now enjoyed over something less they might get in the big city.[28]

In addition, the club's stadium required major repairs. After returning from a road trip in April 1979, Dinamo had to play elsewhere in the city—in the Manpower Reserves (Trudovye reservy) stadium located near the Viatka river. Heavy rains turned the field into a swamp. The ensuing football game, in the words of one observer, was more like water polo.[29] The club had no choice but to host several ensuing games at a facility in a village of thirty-five hundred inhabitants, Mirnyi, located over an hour outside of Kirov city.[30]

Designs for additional funding came at a bad time. The region's Dinamo organization experienced severe financial problems in part, it admitted, because of the current cost of maintaining the football team however poorly it

Mazurenko, 1982. *Courtesy of GASPI KO.*

played.[31] It was in such a financial bind that it borrowed from the state bank office in Kirov to pay for public utilities.[32] Kirov was not unique. In July 1979, Dinamo's central soviet in Moscow issued instructions to all of its affiliates to limit expenditures on their professional football (and hockey) teams to budgets already in place.[33]

In Kirov, the team's patrons plowed ahead regardless of the financial crisis at hand and instructions from Moscow to reign in support for professional sports. The primary impetus for more, not less, funding came from Aleksandr Iakovlevich Mazurenko, the head of Kirov's regional Ministry of Internal Affairs. Mazurenko had come to Kirov in 1978 after eight years as the first deputy and then head of the ministry's regional branch in Voronezh. He was a member of the USSR's Football Federation and, according to a player on Kirov's team in the early 1980s, "loved football up to the point of fanaticism."[34]

Ovchinnikov, 1982. *Courtesy of GAKO.*

Mazurenko's passion for football was not unique for a person in his position. As discussed earlier, Nikolai Starostin managed to survive his imprisonment and exile thanks to heads of labor camps run by the Ministry of Internal Affairs who appointed him to coach their football teams. And so it was in Kirov when the head of the ministry's regional branch plucked Keller from the area's camp to create Dinamo anew. And so it was again with Mazurenko.

At the end of 1979, Kirov's branch of the ministry and the regional soviet's sports committee agreed to spend more on professional football.[35] They began with two new hires: a coach, Valerii Ovchinnikov, and a general manager, Viacheslav Alekseevich Chernozubov. Ovchinnikov arrived from Estonia where the team he coached, Azeri, had been one of the republic's top performers. Chernozubov had previously served as general manager of Moscow's team, Krasnaia Presnia, which played in the second league. To be sure, his team's

Chernozubov, 1982. *Courtesy of GAKO.*

performance was less than spectacular. It took only eighteenth place among twenty-four teams in the second league's first zone in 1979. But Chernozubov promised to bring several of his better players from Moscow.[36]

Ovchinnikov and Chernozubov moved aggressively. In early 1979, they invited more players to the preseason tryout camp than had been the case earlier. The previous year, eleven at the most had attended, the staff filling out the roster just before the season's launch.[37] Now, in 1980, twenty, perhaps as many as twenty-five players came.[38] Only a few were holdovers from the previous season. Ovchinnikov had planned it that way. Thirty-four years later, he boasted that he had arrived in Kirov to clean house. "Right away," he recalled, "I dismissed half the team."[39] As the new season began, the team's main and reserve squad consisted of twenty-three players of whom only seven had been there the previous year. And of that number, five were from Kirov, retained in part, no doubt, because they were local boys. Three of the newcomers arrived, as Chernozubov had promised, from his former team in Moscow.[40] Accommodations for players remarkably improved. Salaries no doubt increased.[41] On December 14, 1979, Mazurenko had asked the Russian Republic's Dinamo soviet for at least 10,000 rubles to house newly recruited players.[42] The following March, the Russian Republic's Dinamo told its sports factory in Kirov to transfer that sum to Kirov's Dinamo.[43]

Kirov's Dinamo football club was part of the larger Dinamo organization that had been founded in 1923 by the Commissariat of Internal Affairs. The Kirov team remained a local amateur team until the 1950s when the regional branch of the Ministry of Internal Affairs recruited Aleksandr Keller, a well-known football player and then coach from the local prison camp, Viatlag. Keller led Kirov's Dinamo to a spot in the USSR's minor league and relatively good play before departing for Tashkent in 1959. Dinamo continued to play reasonably well until the 1970s with the 1979 season being particularly abysmal. In the face of such poor playing, the new head of the Kirov regional branch of the Ministry of Internal Affairs, Mazurenko, spearheaded a drive to secure better funding for the team and better compensation for the players, despite demands from Moscow that teams operate within their budget. To revamp the football club, Dinamo hired a new coach Ovchinnikov and a new club manager Chernozubov who brought in new players with better salaries and expanded the number of people invited to preseason training to try to improve the quality of play. Mazurenko's patronage was key for securing more funds and better players for Kirov's Dinamo.

NOTES

1. See, for example, information on the regional government's budget for 1978 and 1979 in the State Archive of the Kirov Region [henceforth GAKO], f. R-2169, op. 43, d. 2134, ll. 60, 65, 94, 99, d. 2127, ll. 246, 257, and d. 2331, l. 282. Of course, many documents concerning Dinamo in Kirov's two main archives may yet remain classified. I suspect that the Dinamo organization has not turned over all of its materials to those archives or has sent them to Moscow for "safekeeping."

2. State Archive for the Social and Political History of the Kirov Region (GASPI KO), f. R-6766, op. 1, d. 723, ll. 2–3; d. 757, ll. 89, 95–96, 108; d. 763, ll. 35, 37. For more information on the number of people employed at the Dinamo stadium and their salaries in 1980, see GASPI KO, f. R-6766, op. 1, d. 779, l. 57.

3. GASPI KO, f. R-6766, op. 1, d. 757, l. 107.

4. https://www.liveinternet.ru/users/sem_9011/post197942481, accessed August 12, 2020; http://skolko-poluchaet.ru/skolko-poluchayut/skolko-poluchali-v-sssr.html, accessed August 12, 2020.

5. See information in a letter from V. V. Perminov, deputy chair of Dinamo's regional soviet, to the Russian Republic's Dinamo soviet, November 10, 1984, in GASPI KO, f. R-6766, d. 844, l. 52. In an interview on October 2, 2016, in Kirov's Dinamo Stadium, Lev Nikolaevich Usupov, a player for Dinamo from 1972 to 1986, told me that he was not an officer in the armed forces of the Ministry of Internal Affairs. He had a contract with the team.

6. Players received bonuses and awards that were guaranteed for the season whatever the literal meaning of a "bonus" or "award" purportedly for outstanding play in one or several games. The phrase "signing players or coaches to a team without labor books" meant in effect guaranteed but "unofficial" income for players and coaches from any number of sources, including a governmental institution or industrial enterprise where, in fact, they were not employed. At the time, recipients of this relative largesse enjoyed the "extra" benefits, but later, such income, off the books, would not be counted toward configuration of their pension, the amount of which depended in part on past income officially reported.

7. For ticket prices to 10,504 seats for games at Dinamo stadium in 1980 that ranged at a cost from ten kopecks to one ruble, see GASPI KO, f. R-6766, op. 1, d. 779, l. 65. There is incomplete information on ticket sales for Kirov's games in 1982 in GASPI KO, f. R-6766, op. 1, d. 823, l. 31. For the price of tickets in 1981 to 10,500 seats, the cost from 10 kopecks to 1.20 rubles, see a report in January 1982 in GASPI KO, f. R-6766, d. 818, l. 105. Incomplete information about ticket sales may have helped the club to deprive visiting teams of their fair share of gate receipts, as we will see below.

8. Interview with Kolchanov, June 29, 2017, in the Dinamo Sports Pavilion.

9. In 1939, the society's name was changed to the All-Union Lenin Physical and Sports Society. On the early history of the Dinamo organization in Leningrad, see V. G. Bortievsky, "Leningradskoe proletarskoe sportivnoe obshchestvo 'Dinamo' v 1924–1937 gg.," in *Dobrovol'nye obshchestva v Petrograde-Leningrade v 1917–1937 gg.: Sbornik statei* (Leningrad: "Nauka," 1989), 142–151.

10. In 1979, the deputy chair of Kirov's Dinamo society, Kolchanov, wrote to *Kirovskaia pravda* that the society was the "child of two institutions, the Ministry of State Security and Ministry of Internal Affairs." GASPI KO, f. R-6777, op. 9, d. 1840, l. 163. By that time, the security police had been divided into these two separate but interrelated branches. The letter was not published.

11. For Dinamo's factories, see *Sila v dvizhenii: Kniga-al'bom* (Moscow: Fizkul'tura i sport, 1984), 176, 179; *50 let "Dinamo"* (Moscow: Fizkul'tura i sport, 1973), 22, 62, 63; *My iz Dinamo* (Moscow: Fizkul'tura i sport, 1968), 357–358.

12. For the team's early history, see E. Dushkin, *Oni igrali za "Dinamo": Fotoal'bom. Istoriia komandy, predstavliavshei v pervenstvakh RSFSR i SSSR po futbolu Kirov. obl. sovet Vsesoiuz. fizkul'turno-sportivnogo obshchestva "Dinamo"* (Kirov: Kirovskaia oblastnaia tipografiia, 2013), 11–12.

13. On Keller, see Dushkin, *Oni igrali*, 16; Vladimir Luzianin, *Futbol na vsiu zhizn'* (Kirov: Al'fa-Kom, 2009), 33; and an informative essay by Boris Aronovich Kolomensky, "Pod udarami sud'by," published in the Tel Aviv weekly, *Sekret*, no. 1177, November 20, 2016. Keller's professional biography is similar to that of the famous four Starostin brothers, arrested and sent to labor camps, as discussed in chap. 3.

14. In 1960, Pakhtakor finished fourteenth of twenty-teams, tenth in 1961, and fifth in 1962. Keller received the title Meritorious Coach of the USSR. The following year, the team lost several of its best players. Administrators refused to support Keller's measures to discipline several wayward stars. It finished in last place. Management released him in midseason. Keller continued his career in Alma-Ata, Groznyi, Frunze (Bishkek), and again, in 1971, with Pakhtakor. He died in Alma-Ata in 1983.

15. From 1970 to 1979, Dinamo played 388 games, winning 124, tying 96, and losing 168.

16. *Kirovskaia pravda*, March 28, 1979, 4.

17. V. Chudinovskikh, "Kuda idesh' 'Dinamo,'" *Kirovskaia pravda*, July 25, 1979, 4.

18. GASPI KO, f. R-6766, op. 1, d. 742, ll. 30–32.

19. B. Kolomensky, "V ozhidanii luchshikh vremen," *Komsomol'skoe plemia*, July 5, 1979, 4.

20. B. Kolomensky, "Kogda ukhodit bolel'shchik," *Komsomol'skoe plemia*, August 16, 1979, 4; V. Chudinovskikh, "Nedozhidaias' svistka," *Kirovskaia pravda*, September 19, 1979, 4.

21. GASPI KO, f. R-6818, op. 5, d. 1124, l. 141.

22. B. Kolomensky, "Besslavnyi sezon 'Dinamo,'" *Komsomol'skoe plemia*, November 15, 1979, 4.

23. "Na starykh pozitsiiakh," *Kirovskaia pravda*, November 15, 1979, 4.

24. B. Kolomensky, "Besslavnyi sezon 'Dinamo,'" *Komsomol'skoe plemia*, November 15, 1979, 4.

25. B. Kolomensky, "I vnov' futbol i vnov' 'Dinamo,'" *Komsomol'skoe plemia*, February 7, 1980, 4.

26. See a report on March 9, 1980, to the municipal sports committee. On Thursdays, public skating attracted 250–300 people; on Saturdays and Sundays, there were far more. GAKO, f. R-2235, op. 3, d. 567, l. 5.

27. GASPI KO, f. R-6766, op. 1, d. 761, l. 43.

28. For the presidium, see an earlier session of December 22, 1978, GASPI KO, f. R-6766, op. 1, d. 720, ll. 70, 72 and a session of July 26, 1979, GASPI KO,

f. R-6766, op. 1, d. 742, l. 30. B. Kolomensky, "A bolel'shchiki vnov' nadeiutsia," *Komsomol'skoe plemia*, February 22, 1979, 4. See information on the 1978 preseason training camp in GAKO, f. R-1363, op. 4, d. 1405, ll. 13, 15. On the loss of talent in the late 1970s, see information presented at a session of the collegium of the Kirov's regional sports committee, April 19, 1979, in GAKO, f. R-1363, op. 4, d. 1479, l. 32. See also the sports committee's harsh criticism of the state of youth football at its session of January 25, 1978, in GAKO, f. R-1363, op. 4, d. 1405, l. 11. In 1979, the Kirov region had fifty-eight sports schools instructing 17,764 youths, who attended special classes when not in class at a regular school. These sports schools did not, however, emphasize football. On the contrary, they focused on gymnastics, wrestling, and, as a function of Kirov's northern location and climate, skiing and ice-skating. See information on these schools from a session of Kirov's regional sports committee, December 26, 1979, in GAKO, f. R-1363, op. 4, d. 1480, ll. 159–178. Kirov's sports committee sponsored a sports school in the city of Kirov with six sections or specializations, none of which included football. They were wrestling, ice-skating, field events, the ski jump, cross-country skiing, and Nordic combined (a competition in cross-country skiing and the ski jump). See information presented to the party cell of Kirov's sports committee, October 31, 1979, in GASPI KO, f. R-3141, op. 1, d. 62, l. 100. The city also had a sports school that specialized in figure skating (l. 103). Fifty-three of the region's sports schools provided intensive instruction in cross-country skiing. See a report to Kirov's sports committee, January 14, 1980, in GAKO, f. R-1363, op. 4, d. 1547, l. 1. In October 1980, the region had sixty-one sports schools. See information presented to the party organization of Kirov's sports committee, October 28, 1980, in GASPI KO, f. R-3141, op. 1, d. 64, l. 105.

29. B. Arsky, "Futbol, pokhozhii na vodnoe pole," *Komsomol'skoe plemia*, April 26, 1979, 4.

30. B. Kolomensky, "Est' pervaia pobeda," *Komsomol'skoe plemia*, May 1, 1979, 4. Mirnyi is located in the Orichi district.

31. See the soviet's financial report for 1978 in GASPI KO, f. R-6766, op. 1, d. 740, l. 50. The soviet was anxious about paying for public utilities at its main office.

32. See information on the regional Dinamo soviet's budget for 1979 in GASPI KO, f. R-6766, op. 1, d. 758, l. 53.

33. GASPI KO, f. R-6766, op. 1, d. 757, l. 41.

34. On Mazurenko's membership in the Football Federation, see calls for his attendance at its sessions in Moscow in 1980 and 1982 in GAKO, f. R-1363, op. 4, d. 1549, l. 158 and GAKO, f. R-1363, op. 4, d. 1789, l. 141.

35. See information presented later by the Kirov's regional soviet and regional party committee, December 11, 1981, in GAKO, f. R-2169, op. 43, d. 3241, l. 200.

36. Rumors were that Mazurenko may have picked Chernozubov because he was Mazurenko's relative.

37. *Kirovskaia pravda*, July 25, 1979, 4 and *Kirovskaia pravda*, November 12, 1980, 4.

38. On the number in camp, see *Kirovskaia pravda*, November 12, 1980, 4. On the number twenty-five, see Kolomensky's report in *Komsomol'skoe plemia*, October 30, 1980, 4.

39. http://www.sport-express.ru/football/reviews/833276/, last consulted December 30, 2016. Ovchinnikov had a reputation as a tough taskmaster, "a monster," as he quipped in an interview in 2007: interview in *Futbol*, April 13, 2007, https://lokomotiv.info/blogs/130407/2276/.

40. See information in B. Kolomensky, "I vnov' futbol i vnov' 'Dinamo,'" *Komsomol'skoe plemia*, February 7, 1980, 4. The three were Andrei Nikolaevich Moskalev, Zhafiarov, and Sergei Vasil'evich Bazulev. The five local boys on the team: Bubnov, Usatov, Sergei Erdiakov, Lev Isupov, and Starikov.

41. See Chudinovskikh's report on the improvement of living conditions in V. Chudinovskikh, "Do sleduiushchego sezona," *Kirovskaia pravda*, November 12, 1980, 4.

42. GASPI KO, f. R-6766, op. 1, d. 779, l. 130. It seems that Mazurenko wanted Moscow's Dinamo to provide free accommodations, at least temporarily, in the hotel that it owned and operated in Kirov.

43. This information in a letter from Kirov's Dinamo soviet to the local factory in GASPI KO, f. R-6766, op. 1, d. 779, l. 71.

5

SUCCESS!

Dinamo's fans, coaches, and players approached the 1980 season with cautious optimism. Boris Kolomensky modestly hoped "for a more successful performance" than in the past.[1] Days before the first match in early May, coach Valerii Ovchinnikov thought his team might "show fine selfless play with correspondingly good results."[2] On May 9, a Friday, fans packed the stadium despite a temperature of 5 degrees Celsius (41 degrees Fahrenheit) for Dinamo's first home game of the season. At halftime, entrants finished a road race with a lap in the stadium. An hour later, Dinamo sent everyone happily home with a 3–0 victory.[3]

That win on May 9, however, was the team's lone victory in its first six games. Dinamo tied four others and lost one. Then the club's fate changed for the better. It won four of its next seven, tying two others. In mid-June, a confident Ovchinnikov told *Komsomol'skoe plemia* that his team was "in a good fighting mood. Gradually, it is getting a feel for the game."[4]

Fans no longer left matches early but stayed to the end, even in a rainstorm.[5] Kirov's newspapers replaced the previous year's biting sarcasm with high praise for the team's aggressive, attacking style. The team's play, Viktor Chudinovskikh boasted in late May, "doesn't suffer from timidity."[6] At midseason, he observed that after the death watch over the team in previous years, Dinamo's recent performance "inspires hope for the team's rebirth."[7] By midseason, the club had advanced to sixth place in its zone of eighteen teams. At Kirov's television station, chief sports correspondent Gennadii Fediakov gave home games expanded coverage. He was impressed by Dinamo's teamwork on the field.[8] Caught up in the enthusiasm, that July, Dinamo's regional soviet doled out bonuses totaling 620 rubles to the team's staff and

Dinamo, 1980. *Courtesy of Lev Isupov.*

players. It awarded Chernozubov and Ovchinnikov 50 rubles each and 40 rubles each to the assistant coach, Ravil Badrievich Zalialiev, and the team's doctor, Anatolii Nikolaevich Chikishev. It distributed 40 rubles apiece to eleven players.[9]

Better things were to come. That August and September, Dinamo won nine and lost only two (with one tie). Fans expected "not another loss" as in the past but "yet another victory," and a dominant one at that. In August and again in September, Kolomensky cheerfully reported that a match had been played almost in its entirety in front of the opponent's goalposts. At Dinamo's end of the field, its goalie, Sergei Bubnov, "had to endure boredom."[10] The club now fought for one of the league's top three spots. Fediakov spoke approvingly of the "especially tense struggle" in which "the closer to the season's end the more relentlessly tough the games."[11]

In the second half of the season, Dinamo won eleven of seventeen games. With only one game to go, Fediakov seemed pleased that the team was guaranteed at least a fourth-place finish.[12] It won that game at home, 3–0, and ended the season in third with eighteen wins, ten ties, and six losses. At that match's close, fans, players, and staff and officials from the regional party committee and soviet—Aleksandr Mazurenko (head of Kirov's regional Ministry of Internal Affairs) among them—celebrated on the field.[13] The presidium of the regional Dinamo soviet awarded another round of bonuses, totaling 1,000 rubles. It handed out 100 rubles each to Chernozubov and Ovchinnikov, 80 apiece to eight players, and 40 to four.[14]

The Price of Success

Bonuses were a pittance of what Dinamo's personnel and players earned in salaries and other benefits. Winning did not come cheaply.

The team's success fueled continued interest in two of its stars, the goalie, Bubnov, and the midfielder, Anatolii Usatov, on the part of Moscow's Torpedo, a team in the Higher League. In mid-June, Kirov's regional party committee and regional soviet appealed to the USSR's Sports Committee to stop any poaching of the two and to forbid for the foreseeable future recruitment of Dinamo's players.[15] More than likely, it was not a ruling from above but enhanced benefits from below that kept the two players at home. They remained with Dinamo over the next several years.

With improved attendance, ticket sales provided more income than before, but not enough to cover expenses.[16] The football team threatened to bankrupt the local Dinamo soviet. In midseason, Mazurenko asked the Russian Republic's Dinamo soviet for 25,000 rubles. He said that Kirov's Dinamo society owed the regional branch of the state bank 23,000 rubles. The bank refused to advance anything more. Without additional funds, the soviet could not provide its football team with proper equipment and could not pay for public utilities at its headquarters.[17] Moscow instructed its sports factory in Kirov to issue its regional affiliate 20,000, perhaps 23,000 rubles.[18]

The team's successful finish was occasion for more requests for financial help. In early October 1980, the chair of Kirov's regional soviet, Nikolai Ivanovich Pauzin, took up the club's cause by asking Dinamo's central soviet in Moscow to provide the team with a comfortable bus. He wanted the LAZ-697 Tourist, a bus with more than thirty reclining seats commonly used, as its name implied, for transporting tourists from one city to the next. It was needed, he said, to take the team to various training facilities during the preseason and to practice fields during the regular season.[19]

More requests followed. At the end of the month, Mazurenko reminded the Russian Republic's Dinamo soviet of the team's success. He then got straight to the point—he needed a grant from Moscow of 1,100 rubles to cover medical treatment for injured players.[20] On the same day, Mazurenko and Vasilii Egorovich Ochnev, chair of the regional sports committee, asked Nikolai Pavlovich

Chemodanov, deputy chair of Kirov's regional soviet, for assistance. They reprised for Chemodanov, as if he did not know, the team's triumphant season and plans for an even better year to come with a possible promotion to the First League. First, they wanted the regional soviet to help with the construction of a training base in the nearby town of Poroshino, which would include practice fields and housing. Second, they wanted it to create a sports school specializing in football. Third, they asked it to instruct the city's municipal soviet to provide several apartments for the team's players. And fourth, not certain that Dinamo's central soviet would provide the Tourist bus, they called on the regional soviet to purchase it and a microbus and a car as well.[21]

A little over a month later, on December 3, Chemodanov convened a meeting of fifteen regional and municipal officials to discuss how best to support Dinamo's football team.[22] Ochnev and Mazurenko proposed and the session approved the assignment of specific tasks to each of the personnel assembled that day. It told representatives of the tire factory to cede some of the plant's territory at Poroshino to Dinamo for a new training base, ordered heads of the regional construction industry to design and build facilities at the base and additional seating at Dinamo's stadium, instructed officials of the regional and municipal soviet to create a sports school exclusively for football, and demanded that the head of the region's transportation administration procure the Tourist bus. The region's furniture combine and the regional soviet's planning and financial departments were assigned responsibility for finding the raw materials and funds necessary for the construction at the training base and stadium. Finally, the meeting empowered Ochnev and Mazurenko to oversee the implementation by all organizations of the marching orders assigned to them that day.

Chudinovskikh and Kolomensky approved in particular demands for a sports school specializing in football. While sharing everyone's excitement over the 1980 season, they nevertheless were anxious about the future.[23] Dinamo had relied heavily on players invited from other cities. Of the seven athletes from Kirov, only five had played regularly. To be sure, "invited players" were acceptable and necessary for the time being. Yet Dinamo's secure future depended on an influx of local talent. Improved facilities throughout the region and better coaching of amateur squads would likely help. Coaches were to change their approach to the game. Rather than focus on winning by playing adults with their best years behind them, they were to field younger—for the moment, less able—players who, with experience, might have a professional future.

We're No. 1

In 1981, Dinamo hoped to duplicate its success of the preceding year. Many obstacles, however, stood in its way. Two of its stars were poached. Viktor Ivanovich Chipizhny, who had scored twenty-eight goals left for Fakel in the city of Voronezh, a team in the First League.[24] Andrei Andreevich Vostrikov departed for Kryl'ia Sovetov in the city of Kuibyshev (Samara before 1935 and after 1991), a team that had just been relegated from the First League. There he allegedly received benefits judged to be excessive even by lax Soviet standards, as will be discussed below.

Dinamo's management nevertheless remained confident. It retained Chernozubov, Ovchinnikov, and sixteen players, including the goalie, Bubnov, who had just been invited to try out for Moscow's Dinamo in the Higher League. He did not go. Bubnov said he wanted "to defend the sporting honor of his native city."[25] Evgenii Petrovich Kolchanov later recalled that with Bubnov's refusal, he, Kolchanov, was summoned to appear before Dinamo's central soviet to explain the player's behavior. Kolchanov told the Soviet that Bubnov's wife, a native of Kirov, opposed the move. Be that as it may, it was likely that Bubnov received inducements that encouraged him to stay put.[26]

Dinamo signed Aleksandr Georgievich Kozlovskikh, Kirov's favorite son. Born there in 1950, he played for Dinamo in 1968 and 1969. But he was too good to stay home. For the next three years, he joined a team in Perm', which in his final year there joined the First League. Kozlovskikh then played for several of Moscow's teams in the Higher League. Ovchinnikov was keen on signing Kozlovskikh but thought the price too high for a player at the relatively advanced age of thirty-one. Mazurenko thought otherwise. Kozlovskikh later recalled how he returned to his native city "not so much for the club but for individual people, leaders of the highest rank, well-known figures in the country who at the time loved football up to the point of fanaticism. General Mazurenko in Kirov was such a person."[27] As we will see, the investment in Kozlovskikh paid huge dividends.

In January and February, *Kirovskaia pravda* wrote of the team's "rebirth" and its preparation for the upcoming season. On February 20, at 6 p.m., fans were invited to meet the players at the tire factory's House of Culture before the club departed for training camp in Sukhumi, a city on the Black Sea coast.[28] Heretofore uninterested in its professional football team, the Young Communist League reversed course. In late April, its municipal committee agreed to award fifteen rubles each, not an inconsiderable sum, to the top two players after every home game in the upcoming season.[29]

Kozlovskikh, 1981. *Courtesy of GAKO.*

On May 4, the eve of the season's opening, Kirov's television station reported that Dinamo's third-place finish of the year before "inspires new hopes in the hearts of its fans."[30] The club began the season spectacularly with three wins and never looked back. It did not lose until July 12, the twelfth contest. From the end of July to early September, it won eight straight games. "Another victory," *Kirovskaia pravda*'s correspondent Oleg Shcherbakov laconically reported.[31] On August 12, in its seventeenth game, Kozlovskikh scored three goals, a hat trick, giving him an astounding total of twenty-two for the season with many more games to go.[32] At season's end, he had netted thirty-eight goals in thirty-two games.

Not just winning but also a dominating style of play excited fans and reporters alike. An enthusiastic Chudinovskikh wrote after the first game on May 5, a 3–1 win at home, "It's been quite a while since our team began the season with such a convincing victory." Shcherbakov described Dinamo's victory on May 10 as "an attack and still another attack." Kolomensky, who now often traveled with the team, criticized it when, upon acquiring a big lead, it played defensively. He preferred to report that Dinamo played the entire game in front of the opponent's goal.[33]

Fans came out in record numbers. In May, Dinamo's stadium hosted 5,000, then 6,000. On June 21, a warm Sunday of 21 degrees Celsius (70 degrees Fahrenheit), 6,800 came. On September 13 in 13-degree-Celsius weather (55 degrees Fahrenheit), 7,000 watched Dinamo manage only an unusual tie.[34] The increased attendance in Kirov defied a trend of declining numbers elsewhere in the USSR.[35]

On September 8, Fediakov told Kirov's television viewers of the team's latest victory and its "firm grip on first place in the standings." The next day, he seemed bored with its winning ways. "It has already become customary," he told his viewers, that "this season our Dinamo is the victor in almost every game."[36]

It was almost too good to be true. On September 8, an anonymous author, probably Kolomensky, dared to hint at the idea in *Komsomol'skoe plemia* that Dinamo could end the season atop its zone and advance to the playoffs. There it might triumph and enter the prestigious First League. But the author preferred to leave those hopes unsaid, not wishing to jinx the team. Ellipses suggested that readers insert their own optimistic prognostications. "It is not beyond the realm of possibility (we dream, we hope!)," the author wrote, "that Dinamo's players will build on their success and after the playoffs . . . and then perhaps, we will call Dinamo's twenty-fifth season the best in its history. And now, it is possible to think it so that. . . . But you yourself must be the one to say it."[37]

And it was so. Dinamo won its zone with twenty-two wins in thirty-two games. It lost only four times. It outscored its opponents by an incredible margin of sixty-two to twenty-four and led the second-place finisher by an impressive eight points. As the winner of its zone, Dinamo entered the playoffs with eight other teams, champions of their respective zones in the second league. In each of three separate tournaments in late October and early November, three teams played a home-and-home series. The winner of each tournament would join the First League for the 1982 season.[38]

On Friday, October 16, one day after the last regular season game, Kirov's municipal party committee hosted a celebratory session attended by Dinamo's players, coaches, administrators, and a host of assorted government and party leaders. The committee's first secretary, Iurii Ivanovich Derevskoi, congratulated the team for its season and wished it continued success in the upcoming playoffs. Ovchinnikov, team captain Sergei Vasil'evich Bazulev, and star player Kozlovskikh thanked fans and those assembled for their support. Each member of the Dinamo's squad and its staff received a copy of Tolstoy's *War and Peace*.[39]

Dinamo would begin the playoffs on October 28 and continue to play through November 9 with games with Aktiubinets, a team from Aktiubinsk (now Aktobe), a city in Western Kazakhstan, and Krivbass, a team from the city of Krivoi Rog in southeastern Ukraine. It was an expensive proposition. Training for the playoffs and the games extended Dinamo's season by over three weeks. In early October, already assured of his team's participation in postseason play, Kolchanov asked the Russian Republic's Dinamo soviet for 11,600 rubles to cover expenses for training camp in Sukhumi and for the games to follow.[40]

Kirov's Dinamo also needed funds to get its stadium into a condition suitable for such important matches. The stands required repair, lighting had to be improved, and an electrical scoreboard had to be erected. The facility had long been an issue. Built in 1932, its wooden stands deteriorated quickly, requiring overhauls in 1935, 1939, and 1949. In 1952, construction crews removed and replaced the stands in their entirety. Over the next few years, more seats were added. By 1964, the stadium could accommodate 10,800 (including a standing-room-only area).[41]

Kirov's regional soviet had in fact planned capital repairs well before the playoffs. It hoped to pay for it all from its own budget and from donations it coerced from enterprises in the city, chiefly, no doubt, the major defense factories located there.[42] But it was clear from the outset that the soviet could not deliver. Earlier that year, in April, in an orchestrated campaign to entice Moscow to cover the costs, workers at Kirov's tire factory wrote to the editorial board of the national daily, *Sotsialisticheskaia industriia*. As "fans of Dinamo," they complained that the stadium was in a shabby state.[43] On May 6, Dinamo's regional soviet asked the Russian Republic's Dinamo soviet to provide 5,000 rubles for repairs. On August 18, the chair of Kirov's municipal soviet, Anatolii Ivanovich Dziuba, requested 25,000 rubles from the same soviet.[44] In October, with the playoffs looming, lighting in particular became an issue. On October 9, a desperate Mazurenko, commissioned, he said, by Kirov's regional soviet, asked the republic's Dinamo soviet to provide 192 stadium floodlights.[45] On October 20, Chudinovskikh lamented that such a worthy team as Dinamo should not have "to play in such darkness."[46]

Bazulev, 1982. *Courtesy of GAKO.*

Chudinovskikh wrote only eight days before the first playoff game in Kirov. It is unlikely that the stadium met his and Mazurenko's specifications. The games went on nevertheless. On October 28, Dinamo defeated Aktiubinets 3–1 at home before a packed house in 5-degree-Celsius weather (41 degrees Fahrenheit). "It has been a long time," Chudinovskikh wrote two days later, "when we have seen such a great number of spectators."[47] On the road on November 1, Dinamo played Krivbass before twenty thousand rambunctious fans who sounded off on air horns, waved pennants, and unfurled paper streamers.[48] It did not go well for the visitors. Dinamo lost by a two-goal margin, 3–1, its opponent scoring twice in the final five minutes of play. To win the playoff, Dinamo needed to defeat Krivbass by three goals at home on November 5.

Kirov's and league officials compensated for the inadequate lighting by moving the decisive game with Krivbass back from 5:00 p.m. to 2:00 p.m. Despite the early start on a workday and freezing weather of rain mixed with snow,

Dinamo 1981. *Courtesy of Viktor Chudinovskikh.*

another overflow crowd packed the stadium.[49] That day, Dinamo accomplished the impossible, winning 3–0, scoring all three goals in the first half by a relentless attack.[50] Four days later, on November 9 in Aktiubinsk, Kozlovskikh scored both goals in Dinamo's 2–0 victory. Of Dinamo's nine goals in the playoffs, Kozlovskikh had made seven.

Victory made for great news. In its November 11 edition, *Kirovskaia pravda* proclaimed, "Dinamo is in the First League." "What at the beginning of the season could not have been dreamed of has happened. The day of November 9 will be a defining moment in the history of Kirov football."[51] Kirov's radio and television put Ovchinnikov live on the air to celebrate the moment.[52] Kolomensky's article in *Komsomol'skoe plemia* on November 19 began with the headline "A Season for All Seasons."[53]

One pesky matter remained. Kirov's Dinamo had been selected to play in a tournament in Sochi on the eastern shore of the Black Sea. There four clubs would vie for the title of champion of the Russian Republic's second league. They played each other once. Dinamo won the tournament with two victories and one tie.[54] For fans in Kirov, it was no more than an afterthought, if that. *Kirovskaia pravda* and *Komsomol'skoe plemia* gave the games scant coverage.[55]

Proud but Anxious

Despite Dinamo's splendid season and promotion into the First League, Kolomensky remained anxious about the future. The club had succeeded chiefly because of well-compensated athletes recruited from areas beyond the region. He reminded his readers that only seven players on the 1981 squad hailed from Kirov. Prospects for more and thus for Dinamo's long-term future were bleak. The state of the region's youth football program "cried out for serious rescue efforts."[56] Kirov still lacked a sports school specializing in football. Kolomensky pointed out that none other than the head coach of the Russian Republic's national youth team, Azor Kavazashvili, shared his, Kolomensky's, concern. In Moscow, Kavazashvili was not alone. That December, the presidium of the USSR's Football Federation and the collegium of the USSR's Sports Committee chastised a number of teams, Kirov's Dinamo listed among them, for a failure to open their own sports school.[57]

Reports from Kirov's Young Communist League indicated that it was more than a football school that might be needed. As in other regions throughout the USSR, Kirov's Komsomol organized a tourney, the "Leather Ball," with teams arranged into three age categories. Winners would advance to interregional and finally national finals. Kirov's youths failed to respond as hoped. In the early 1980s, Komsomol's district committees reported on the disappointing number of youths who had participated in the competition.[58]

Other problems loomed. Entry into the First League made financing a more challenging task. Dinamo would play not thirty-two regular season games but forty-two. It would take more costly road trips over longer distances (including a game in distant Khabarovsk, almost fifty-four hundred kilometers [thirty-three hundred miles] away). The First League also required that its entries field a reserve squad, a "double" that played games on the road as well as at home.

Well before the season started, the club needed an infusion of cash. In late November 1981, Kirov's Dinamo soviet asked the Russian Republic's Dinamo soviet to help cover preseason training. The cost of room and board for players and staff, of road trips for friendly matches against other teams training in the area, and of equipment and miscellaneous expenses came to a total of 201,200 rubles.[59]

The First League demanded better facilities. Again, in 1981, Kirov's citizens, municipal and regional leaders, and Dinamo's regional soviet emphasized the poor conditions for players and fans alike at the stadium. Little had been done in response. Now with a season in the First League pending, major repairs had begun. On November 11, Kirov's television carried a live report from the arena showing the start of "major reconstruction so that next season it won't be shameful to welcome guests from the First League."[60] The field's drainage system had to be replaced, the lighting improved, and the stands repaired and expanded to accommodate the considerable crowds expected.

Kolchanov hoped the refurbished venue would seat fifteen to twenty thousand people.⁶¹

And yet fresh off a victorious season, it was no time to dwell on the demands of the future. Dinamo had ascended to the heights of the First League. Officials, fans, and reporters wanted to enjoy the miraculous present and lionize those who had made it possible. On October 26, Kirov's municipal committee of the Young Communist League took note of Dinamo players' "great athletic skills and the will to win." For their heroic acts and in recognition of the club's twenty-fifth anniversary, the committee awarded gifts worth 320 rubles to the team.⁶²

Mazurenko merited special praise. In an interview in *Kirovskaia pravda* in October, Bubnov commented that "daily we feel his paternal concern."⁶³ Kolomensky lauded Mazurenko and the efforts of "the city's party and soviet organizations."⁶⁴ On November 19, the national daily, *Sovetskii sport*, published Chudinovskikh's article, "Toughness: Kirov's Dinamo in the First League," a singular honor for both the author and his subject.⁶⁵ "After many years of good-natured contemplation," he wrote, "finally Dinamo's regional soviet had turned its attention squarely to football." It had found the resources to allow Ovchinnikov and Chernozubov to form a roster "to their liking." Buoyed by his enthusiasm for the team's success and the national press in which he could now share it, Chudinovskikh exaggerated by repeating what Ovchinnikov purportedly had said—that for two years the team had experienced "not a single quarrel." Chudinovskikh then knowingly, no doubt, led his audience somewhat astray: "Dinamo's backbone consists of local athletes." He ended by emphasizing that the club had demonstrated throughout the year "an unwavering, pugnacious, and tough character."

On November 20 at 6:00 p.m., hundreds of fans joined the team's coaches, administrators, and local dignitaries, including Mazurenko, Dziuba, and the heads of the city's and region's Young Communist League to celebrate at Kirov's Cosmos Palace of Culture. Fediakov presided. Mazurenko recounted the team's history, emphasizing, no doubt, past misery to highlight present glory. Kavazashvili came from Moscow to address the gathering.⁶⁶ Several days later, Kirov's television transmitted portions of the event with the comment that fans responded to remarks by Kozlovskikh with "stormy applause."⁶⁷ Three weeks later, Kirov's regional soviet and regional party committee recommended both Chernozubov and Ovchinnikov to the USSR's Sports Committee for the title Meritorious Coach of the Russian Republic.⁶⁸ A week later, on December 18, the Russian Republic's Sports Committee gathered documentation to nominate Ovchinnikov as one of the ten best football coaches in the republic.⁶⁹

At the beginning of November, a correspondent for *Futbol-Khokkei*, Aleksei Leont'ev, praised the play of Kirov's Dinamo and the direction provided by its "young mentor," Ovchinnikov.[70]

The key to Dinamo's success was its sponsors raising substantial funds, much of them "off the books," from the national Dinamo organization in Moscow, from Kirov's municipal and regional governments, and from Kirov's major defense plants. With this enhanced financial support, the club recruited a better coach and athletes and played remarkably well in 1980 and 1981. Much to the delight of fans, sports correspondents, and local party and state officials, the team's performance in 1981 earned it promotion to the prestigious First League. Stiffer competition there, however, required ever-greater backing from legitimate as well as illicit sources.

NOTES

1. B. Kolomensky, "I vnov' futbol i vnov' 'Dinamo,'" *Komsomol'skoe plemia*, February 7, 1980, 4.

2. See the interview in V. Chudinovskikh, "'Dinamo' beret start," *Kirovskaia pravda*, April 26, 1980, 4.

3. See the television report of May 10 in the State Archive for the Social and Political History of the Kirov Region (GASPI KO), f. R-6818, op. 5, d. 1243, l. 100.

4. *Komsomol'skoe plemia*, June 14, 1980, 4.

5. *Kirovskaia pravda* reported that a home game in mid-September was played before a full stadium (that could seat more than ten thousand). *Kirovskaia pravda*, September 16, 1980, 4.

6. *Kirovskaia pravda*, May 24, 1980, 4.

7. V. Chudinovskikh, "Vozrozhdenie?," *Kirovskaia pravda*, July 20, 1980, 4.

8. See, in particular, Fediakov's report on July 16, 1980: GASPI KO, f. R-6818, op. 5, d. 1248, ll. 16–18.

9. Bonuses were assigned on July 18, 1980, by the presidium of Kirov's regional Dinamo soviet: GASPI KO, f. R-6766, op. 1, d. 762, l. 47.

10. *Komsomol'skoe plemia*, August 21, 1980, 4. Also, September 4, 1980, 4.

11. See reports of October 1 and 8, 1980, in GASPI KO, f. R-6818, op. 5, d. 1253, ll. 12, 76.

12. See Fediakov's report on October 17, 1980: GASPI KO, f. R-6818, op. 5, d. 1253, l. 26.

13. See the report by B. Kolomensky, "Nastroenie ne osennee," *Komsomol'skoe plemia*, October 21, 1980, 4.

14. GASPI KO, f. R-6766, op. 1, d. 762, l. 82.

15. State Archive of the Kirov Region (GAKO), f. R-2169, op. 43, d. 2719, l. 111.

16. See Mazurenko's acknowledgment of such in his letter at season's end to the Russian Republic's Dinamo soviet, October 31, 1980, in GASPI KO, f. R-6766, op. 1, d. 761, l. 146.

17. GASPI KO, f. R-6766, op. 1, d. 779, l. 32.

18. See information in GASPI KO, f. R-6766, op. 1, d. 779, ll. 34–35.

19. GASPI KO, f. R-6766, op. 1, d. 785, l. 18. Earlier that year, Mazurenko had unsuccessfully submitted such a request to the central soviet. See GASPI KO, f. R-6766, op. 1, d. 760, l. 33.

20. GASPI KO, f. R-6766, op. 1, d. 761, l. 146.

21. GAKO, f. R-2169, op. 43, d. 2719, ll. 240–242. They also requested that the regional government undertake repair of the Dinamo stadium's southwest stands (l. 241).

22. GAKO, f. R-2169, op. 43, d. 2719, ll. 243–244.

23. V. Chudinovskikh, "Do sleduiushchego sezona," *Kirovskaia pravda*, November 12, 1980, 4; B. Kolomensky, "Komu vykhodit' zavtra?," *Komsomol'skoe plemia*, October 30, 1980, 4.

24. In early January 1981, *Kirovskaia pravda* thought that Chipizhny's services might well be retained. It displayed his photograph along with photographs of other top athletes in the region in its edition of January 18, 1981, 4.

25. As quoted by Chernozubov and Ovchinnikov in an interview published in *Kirovskaia pravda*, February 15, 1981, 4.

26. My interview of Kolchanov on June 29, 2017.

27. Vladimir Luzianin, *Futbol'nyi snaiper* (Kirov: Al'fa-Kom, 2010), 87.

28. *Kirovskaia pravda*, January 18, 1981, 4 and February 15, 1981, 4. Quote in the January 18 issue.

29. GASPI KO, f. P-1656, op. 32, d. 3, ll. 176, 208–209. The municipal committee would make the first payment of a total of thirty rubles, for each subsequent game it assigned the responsibility to one of the league's district committees or its cells in the city. It listed fourteen of what would be sixteen total home games for the year.

30. See the report of May 4, 1981: GASPI KO, f. R-6818, op. 5, d. 1414, l. 6.

31. "Ocherednaia pobeda," the title of articles by O. Shcherbakov in *Kirovskaia pravda*, June 20, 1981, 4 and September 18, 1981, 4.

32. See a tally of Kozlovskikh's goals in *Kirovskaia pravda*, August 9, 1981, 4 and O. Shcherbakov, "'Khet-trik' A. Kozlovskikh," *Kirovskaia pravda*, August 14, 1981, 4.

33. V. Chudinovskikh, "Khoroshii start," *Kirovskaia pravda*, May 7, 1981, 4; O. Shcherbakov, "Ataka i eshche raz ataka," *Kirovskaia pravda*, May 12, 1981, 4; B. Kolomensky, "Gol za nebrezhnost,'" *Komsomol'skoe plemia*, June 23, 1981, 4; B. Kolomensky, "S lidera spros osobyi," *Komsomol'skoe plemia*, June 2, 1981, 4.

34. *Komsomol'skoe plemia*, June 23, 1981, 4; September 15, 1981, 4.

35. On declining attendance in the USSR in the late 1970s and throughout perestroika, see Robert Edelman, *Spartak Moscow: A History of the People's Team in the Workers' State* (Ithaca, NY: Cornell University Press, 2009), 178, 291.

36. GASPI KO, f. R-6818, op. 5, d. 1422, ll. 112, 128.

37. *Komsomol'skoe plemia*, September 8, 1981, 4.

38. In 1981, the second league consisted of over 150 teams arranged into nine zones rather than the six of the previous year. On the number of teams and zones, see *Futbol-Khokkei*, no. 3, January 18, 1981, 10–12.

39. See reports by Kirov's television and radio in GASPI KO, f. R-6818, op. 5, d. 1425, l. 33 and d. 1507, l. 193, respectively.

40. See the request of October 2, 1981, in GASPI KO, f. R-6766, op. 1, d. 786, ll. 112–113. Kolchanov wrote his request before he knew the playoff schedule (printed in *Komsomol'skoe plemia* only on October 20). He was also at the time apparently under the impression that the playoffs would occur in one city, Barnaul. The four teams involved played a home-and-home series that made the playoffs an even more expensive proposition than Kolchanov imagined.

41. For a history of the stadium and its constant repair, see V. Zharavin, "Iz istorii stadiona 'Dinamo' v gorode Kirove," in *Pamiatnaia knizhki i kalendar' na 2017 god* (Kirov: Federal'naia sluzhba gosudarstvennoi statistiki po Kirovovskoi oblasti, 2016), 294–303, also available at http://gaspiko.ru/4239.

42. See such plans and commitments in Ochnev's report to the Russian Republic's Sports Committee, March 4, 1981, in GAKO, f. R-1363, op. 4, d. 1671, l. 101. See also information from April 1981 in GASPI KO, f. R-6766, op. 1, d. 784, l. 1. See also a letter from the chair of Kirov's municipal soviet to the Russian Republic's Dinamo soviet, August 18, 1981, in GASPI KO, f. R-6766, op. 1, d. 786, l. 100.

43. A copy of this letter in GASPI KO, f. R-6766, op. 1, d. 784, l. 4.

44. GASPI KO, f. R-6766, op. 1, d. 786, l. 100.

45. GASPI KO, f. R-6766, op. 1, d. 785, l. 63.

46. V. Chudinovskikh, "Ubeditel'naia pobeda. A chto dal'she?," *Kirovskaia pravda*, October 20, 1981, 4. In an interview, Kolchanov indicated that Mazurenko may have acquired for temporary use floodlights from the city's railroad station. My interview of Kolchanov.

47. V. Chudinovskikh, "Tak derzhat' dinamovtsy," *Kirovskaia pravda*, October 30, 1981, 4.

48. V. Chudinovskikh, "Piat' posednikh minut," *Kirovskaia pravda*, November 3, 1981, 4.

49. On game time, conditions, and size of the crowd, see reports by Kirov's television on November 4 and 5, 1981, in GASPI KO, f. R-6818, op. 5, d. 1426, ll. 49, 71–72.

50. See the report on the game: V Chudinovskikh, "Tsel' priblizilas,'" *Kirovskaia pravda*, November 7, 1981, 4. Attendance figures for this game are not available.

51. "'Dinamo'—v pervoi lige!," *Kirovskaia pravda*, November 11, 1981, 4.

52. Kirov's television interviewed Ovchinnikov on November 14, its radio on November 16: GASPI KO, f. R-6818, op. 5, d. 1426, ll. 179, 190 and d. 1508, ll. 205–206.

53. B. Kolomensky, "Vsem sezonam sezon," *Komsomol'skoe plemia*, November 19, 1981, 4.

54. The three other teams: Tekstil'shchik from Ivanovo, Dinamo from Barnaul, and Rotor from Volgograd.

55. Kirov's radio provided somewhat more coverage before and during the competition: see transcripts of its reports in GASPI KO, f. R-6818, op. 5, d. 1508, ll. 138, 248, 311, 390. Dinamo had one other achievement in 1981 that merited at the time little attention. The team's current website as well as several other sources on the team's history emphasize that the club that year won the Dinamo central soviet's tournament. The prize was of little significance. The tournament occurred not in January or February, as usual, but rather in late June in the middle of the football season. Six Dinamo teams competed in a city near Moscow. Kirov's Dinamo won the competition but rested its best players for the ongoing regular season, relying on, as other teams did, its bench and perhaps other athletes from its "reserve." See the report on the tournament on Kirov's television, June 30, 1981, in GASPI KO, f. R-6818, op. 5, d. 1417, l. 197.

56. B. Kolomensky, "Vsem sezonam sezon," *Komsomol'skoe plemia*, November 19, 1981, 4.

57. See the session of the presidium on December 3, 1981, in GARF, f. R-7576, op. 31, d. 7097, l. 182 and the session of the collegium on December 23, 1981, in GARF, f. R-7576, op. 31, d. 6279, l. 35.

58. See, for example, the report from the October district in the city of Kirov to the league's regional committee for the year 1980 in GASPI KO, f. P-1682, op. 28, d. 97, l. 59. For a discussion of an earlier version of the tourney, see N. N. Ozerov, *Vsiu zhizn' za sinei ptitsei* (Moscow: Nauka, 1995), 83–84.

59. GASPI KO, f. R-6766, op. 1, d. 818, ll. 58–59.

60. GASPI KO, f. R-6818, op. 5, d. 1427, l. 15. In his interview on Kirov's radio, November 16, 1981, Ovchinnikov spoke extensively of work already underway at the stadium: GASPI KO, f. R-6818, op. 5, d. 1508, l. 206.

61. On plans for repairs, see interviews by Kirov radio of Ovchinnikov, November 16, 1981, in GASPI KO, f. R-6818, op. 5, d. 1508, l. 206 and of Kolchanov in GASPI KO, f. R-6818, op. 5, d. 1634, l. 85.

62. GASPI KO, f. P-1656, op. 32, d. 6, l. 84.

63. V. Chudinovskikh, "O tekh, kto nas poradoval," *Kirovskaia pravda*, October 11, 9181, 4, an interview with Bubnov.

64. B. Kolomensky, "Vsem sezonam sezon," *Komsomol'skoe plemia*, November 19, 1981, 4.

65. V. Chudinovskikh, "Zakalennyi kharakter: Kirovskoe 'Dinamo'—v pervoi lige," *Sovetskii sport*, no. 267, November 19, 1981, 2.

66. "90 minut s futbolistami," *Komsomol'skoe plemia*, November 24, 1981, 4.

67. GASPI KO, f. R-6818, op. 5, d. 1427, l. 102. The next day, the palace returned to its normal drudgery by hosting a conference, "Ways for Increasing the Effectiveness of Production in the Region's Enterprises in the Context of the Decisions of the Twenty-Sixth Congress of the Communist Party of the Soviet Union": GASPI KO, f. R-6818, op. 5, d. 1427, l. 114.

68. GAKO, f. R-2169, op. 43, d. 3241, l. 200. Chernozubov was awarded the title; Ovchinnikov was not, for reasons that remain unclear. This matter will be discussed later.

69. GAKO, f. R-1363, op. 4, d. 1674, l. 157. The committee asked Kirov's sports committee for Ovchinnikov's resume and a letter of recommendation.

70. Aleksei Leont'ev, "Deviat' izvestnykh," *Futbol-Khokkei*, no. 44, November 1, 1981, 11.

6

FOUL PLAY

After Dinamo's victorious season in 1981, buyers descended on Kirov to pick off its best athletes. The club scrambled to find the resources to keep all but three. Of the group departing, only one, Andrei Nikolaevich Moskalev, had played in more than a couple of games that year.[1] Twenty players returned. Their number included the star, Aleksandr Kozlovskikh, and the talented goalie, Sergei Bubnov. Dinamo even tried to sign Andrei Andreevich Vostrikov, who had played in Kirov in 1980 but had been disqualified the previous July for receiving excessive benefits as a member of Kryl'ia Sovetov (a matter to be discussed immediately below). In February 1982, Iurii Alekseevich Vylegzhanin, deputy chair of Kirov's sports committee, asked—unsuccessfully as it turned out—the USSR's Sports Committee to waive Vostrikov's disqualification and allow him to join Dinamo for the upcoming season. Vostrikov was at that time living in Kirov, Vylegzhanin wrote, and worked diligently at one of the city's major factories.[2] Yet even as it aggressively signed its best players and pursued Vostrikov, Kirov disingenuously denied that it provided athletes with special benefits. It did so knowing full well of efforts nationally, albeit sporadic, to curb such financial and other irregularities.

Rostsel'mash, 1980

The USSR's Sports Committee required that all teams in the second league develop young players for transfer to clubs in the more advanced leagues. It thereby stipulated that coaches limit their roster to no more than six individuals who were older than twenty-five and include at least one person younger than eighteen. In the autumn of 1980, the committee discovered that several teams, most egregiously Rostov-on-Don's Rostsel'mash, violated these rules. It agreed to strip the club of several victories, eventually settling on four.[3] Without such a penalty, Rostsel'mash would have finished the season in first place in its zone, thereby qualifying for the playoffs and earning a chance to advance to the First League. The punishment dropped it to third and out of postseason play, dooming it to spend yet another year in the second league. The USSR's Sports Committee followed with an insistence that now and in the future, sponsors and administrators of second league clubs, Kirov's Dinamo included, learn from Rostsel'mash's demise and compile their roster accordingly. At this juncture, Dinamo need not have worried. Its outstanding performance in 1980 and 1981 had resulted from violations of rules governing benefits provided to players. But it had included on its roster no more than five players over twenty-five and had listed one very young athlete, Leonid Dmitrievich Shatunov, born in 1963. However, there would soon be reason for great anxiety because of the misdeeds of yet another team.

Kuibyshev's Kryl'ia Sovetov, 1979–1981

From 1979 to 1981, Kuibyshev's football club, Kryl'ia Sovetov, provoked the ire, real and feigned, of a host of prominent officials and agencies responsible for the administration of Soviet sports. Trouble was already apparent on June 26, 1979, at a session of the presidium of the USSR's Football Federation. Andrei Starostin, chair of the All-Union Coaches Council, alleged that the city and region of Kuibyshev subsidized their professional football team at the expense of youth and amateur football. Some of those funds, Starostin implied, were the source of illegal benefits given to Kryl'ia Sovetov's players.[4] Far more serious accusations followed.

In October 1980, the USSR's Sports Committee received information that Kryl'ia Sovetov's athletes held fictional jobs and received automobiles among other improper forms of compensation. One player, Arkadii Avetisovich Arutiunian, had allegedly received three cars. Moreover, the club's administrators were accused of extorting money from players for a special fund to bribe referees and opponents. The committee sent a brigade to Kuibyshev where it spent four days investigating the charges. Perhaps because it conducted its work in a sloppy fashion or, more likely, because it understood the commonplace nature of the alleged transgressions, the brigade cleared the club.[5] The story, however, had only just begun.

Kryl'ia Sovetov remained under suspicion. Later that year, Mikhail Kravets, a member of the presidium of the Russian Republic's Football Federation, condemned the club for "the depraved practice" of recruiting players from regions other than its own by implicitly offering improper benefits. This effort and similar attempts by other teams had brought "great harm to our football by the transfer of players from one team to another."[6]

Kravets surely knew more than he said. Although the brigade sent by the USSR's Sports Committee had found Kryl'ia Sovetov blameless, the party's Central Committee thought otherwise. In what was by now an increasingly rare case of the party's direct involvement in the administration of sport, the committee's investigative arm, the Committee for Party Control, sent its own inspectors to Kuibyshev. They submitted their findings and recommendations to the sports committees of both the Russian Republic and the USSR. Their report was devastating. The inspectors found numerous transgressions over the past few years: fictional jobs, improper payment in 1980 of bonuses of 23,000 rubles; an excessive food allowance for coaches and players; the collection of money from players for the creation of a special fund of 6,200 rubles to bribe referees and opponents; and the awarding over the past four years of seventeen cars to players. The committee called for the banning of all players and coaches who had received illegal benefits from professional football. And for the team, it wanted the death penalty—the removal of Kyrl'ia Sovetov from all competition. For good measure, it reprimanded Valentin Lukich Sych, deputy chair of the USSR's Sports Committee, and Viacheslav Koloskov, head of the governing board for football, for improper supervision of the earlier investigation that had found the club free of any and all sins.[7]

On June 8, 1981, the presidium of the USSR's Sports Committee convened to assess Kryl'ia Sovetov's crimes and take punitive action.[8] It summoned to its session the chair of Kuibyshev's regional sports committee, Valentin Mitrofanovich Akulov, and the team's new coach, Boris Nikolaevich Strel'tsov. Both tried their best to elicit sympathy, to deny some of the charges, to insist that corrective action had been taken in other cases, and to persuade the presidium to reject terminating the team. Akulov maintained that he had not been aware of phantom jobs, although he now admitted that numerous illegalities had occurred, such as the abovementioned player, Arutiunian, who had played for the team since 1976, being given three cars. Akulov declared that once his sports committee learned of the club's wrongdoing in early 1980, it fired general manager Mikhail Armaisovich Belagez'ian. In protest, the coach, Viktor Vladimirovich Kirsh, who had played for the team from 1954 to 1960 and had coached it since 1972, resigned, presumably because he now believed his own extra benefits might end. Several of his players followed his example. Kryl'ia Sovetov now consisted of young local boys, Akulov declared, not the outsiders who had demanded improper payments. It would be unfair, he concluded, to insist on killing the team.[9] Strel'tsov hoped to evoke the presidium's sympathy with the claim that his team suffered from a poor playing surface at its training facility and stadium. He echoed Akulov's insistence that the club now consisted primarily of young local boys. Only four players from the previous year were on the roster. The death penalty, he concluded, would be unjust.[10]

Neither Akulov nor Strel'tsov was completely forthcoming. Not four but twelve players on the current roster had played for the club the preceding season. Moreover, when pressed, Strel'tsov admitted that he did not know how many of his current athletes had previously benefited from ghost jobs—perhaps eight, he said.

The presidium's guests pleaded their case in vain; their audience was not kind. Stanislav Vasil'evich Melent'ev, deputy chair of the Russian Republic's Sports Committee, remarked that Akulov's denial of knowledge of improprieties "was not sincere." Akulov had known "all about the illegalities." Nikolai Nikolaevich Riashentsev, chair of the USSR's Football Federation from 1964 to 1967 and the USSR's representative to the Union of European Football Associations (UEFA) at the time, followed that "it was impossible" for Akulov not to have known of the wrongdoing. Sports reporter Boris Fedosov, also a former player and coach, who had headed the USSR's Sports Federation from 1973 to 1980, pointed to Akulov's "weak leadership and insincere remarks."[11]

Not everyone supported the death penalty. Melent'ev opposed it.[12] But Fedosov wanted the sternest punishment possible, to make an example out of the team. "If we limit ourselves to half-hearted measures, then we will never restore order."[13] He got his way. The presidium approved the penalty for "egregious transgressions." Moreover, it banned all eight players from football who held fictional jobs. It stripped Arutiunian and Evgenii Serafimovich Lovchev, a player and coach in 1980, of their titles of Master of Sport of the USSR. It also disqualified former general manager Belagez'ian and Vladimir Vasil'evich Solov'ev, the team's assistant coach from 1975 to 1980, from association with professional football.[14]

Two days later, on June 10, the collegium of the USSR's Sports Committee dispatched its own commission to Kuibyshev. There it met with the leadership of the region's party organization, the soviet, and the sports committee. The accused acknowledged Kryl'ia Sovetov's sins but insisted that corrective action had been taken. The club had a new, presumably law-abiding chief sponsor, an aviation factory (rather than a steel plant). It had ceased to rely on players recruited from outside the region who had demanded and received costly benefits. More funds were now allotted to youth and amateur football in the region.¹⁵

On July 2, the Russian Republic's Sports Committee and two weeks later, on July 15, the USSR's Sports Committee issued official statements accusing Kryl'ia Sovetov of "depraved methods" in the compilation of its roster to include an overreliance on the recruitment of costly outsiders. They enforced the ban of eight players and Belagez'ian from professional football. In addition, they prohibited Kirsh from any association with a professional team and stripped him of his title of Meritorious Coach of the Russian Republic. And yet both committees agreed to commute the death sentence to allow Kryl'ia Sovetov to resume play.¹⁶ Death had lasted all of two contests, the eleventh and twelfth of the season, which were later made up to complete a full schedule of thirty-two games.

At the June 8 session, Sych and Riashentsev acknowledged that sins like Kryl'ia Sovetov's were legion throughout Soviet professional football. They hoped that the punishment of Kryl'ia Sovetov would be a warning to all others to obey football's rules and regulations. Riashentsev wanted a document signed by leaders of local sports clubs verifying compliance with financial regulations.¹⁷ Boris Nikolaevich Topornin, head of the USSR's Football Federation, called on the committee to send its members into the field "to visit teams to explain the essence of what was happening to Kryl'ia Sovetov."¹⁸ On July 15, the USSR's Sports Committee required every club in the USSR's three leagues to convene a special meeting to discuss the misdeeds and punishment of Kryl'ia Sovetov and to submit a summary of its proceedings to the committee's Governing Board for Football.¹⁹

Kirov's regional government and the Dinamo club followed the instructions in short order. They did so, however, not with an honest appraisal of the team's finances but with the launch of a campaign of denial and dissimulation. Upon receiving a copy of the Russian Republic's Sports Committee's July 2 statement, Vasilii Ochnev ordered its submission to the regional sports committee, which he chaired, as well as to the regional council of the Dinamo society and Kirov's club for discussion.²⁰ The following day, the collegium of the regional sports committee met. Kirov's Dinamo was probably no less guilty than Kryl'ia Sovetov of budgetary machinations. But its recent success on the playing field gave it considerable wiggle room. In his opening remarks, Ochnev made no mention of any wrongdoing in Kirov. The collegium affirmed that there would be nothing of the sort in the future. It called on Mikhail Sergeev, deputy chair of the regional Dinamo soviet, to ensure "strict compliance" with regulations governing the team's financial management.²¹

More duplicity followed. That August, general manager Viacheslav Chernozubov; coach Valerii Ovchinnikov; and assistant coach Ravil Zalialiev; representatives from Dinamo's regional soviet, including Evegenii Kolchanov; and eighteen of Dinamo's players met to discuss the charges brought against Kryl'ia Sovetov and the subsequent punishment. The session adopted resolutions that dodged the issue. The club had always sought to recruit not expensive outsiders but local athletes. "For the past three seasons, there have been no financial violations."[22] They all knew better.

Potentially more serious charges followed from Moscow, some of them directed at Kirov's Dinamo. In late November, the presidium of the Russian Republic's Dinamo soviet accused a number of teams of paying players and coaches substantial salaries "off the books" for ghost jobs in factories and government agencies. The presidium singled out Kirov's Ovchinnikov as one such recipient of illegal payments. In addition, it charged that Kirov's Dinamo had paid two players a bonus for games in which they had not participated.[23]

And yet the presidium let Kirov off lightly. It limited its punishment to a mild reprimand of the deputy chair of Kirov's Dinamo society, Sergeev. Praise followed criticism. Caught up in Kirov's enthusiasm over the season just completed, the presidium complimented the team for its promotion to the First League and lauded Aleksandr Mazurenko (head of Kirov's regional Ministry of Internal Affairs) and Anatolii Dziuba (chair of Kirov's municipal soviet) for helping to make it happen. It assigned Kirov's Dinamo 3,600 rubles for distribution to players and coaches for the successful year.[24] One month later, Kirov's sports committee told the Russian Republic's Sports Committee that Ovchinnikov, nominated as one of the ten best coaches in the republic (as discussed previously), deserved the honor whatever his salary "off the books." Ovchinnikov was "married, morally stable, and in his lifestyle modest."[25]

That December, the USSR's Football Federation's presidium hoped to give a personal touch to the center's spasmodic efforts to curb teams' improprieties. It resolved to dispatch its own representatives to individual teams, Kirov's Dinamo among them, to carry out so-called character training.[26] Perhaps the effort brought Dinamo to heel for the moment. In early 1982, it issued a mea culpa, albeit a relatively painless one. On March 26, the presidium of Kirov's Dinamo soviet, attended by Mazurenko and Sergeev, acknowledged inappropriate monetary awards given to players (and, implicitly, staff) in 1980 and 1981. In resolutions that followed, it charged both Sergeev and Chernozubov with "illegal activities related to the payment of bonuses to football players and coaches."[27] It meticulously avoided mentioning and thereby implicating any particular player or coach.

Three weeks later, the collegium of the USSR's Sports Committee took up once more Kryl'ia Sovetov's past disregard for rules and regulations. And once again, it summoned Akulov and Strel'tsov to its session for a thorough grilling. It even considered, before rejecting, a reinstatement of the death penalty. At the session's close, Sych issued a warning to administrators of professional football clubs in the USSR. "I want to warn my comrades once again that if your team conducts itself in an outrageous and illicit manner, no one will defend you and the collegium of the USSR's Sports Committee will remove you from your post."[28]

The warning went largely unheeded in Kirov and elsewhere. But Moscow would soon resort to another indignant outburst at yet another team's commonplace but illegal irregularities. Kirov's Dinamo would once again defend itself by denial and subterfuge.

Vladimir's Torpedo, 1982

In the spring of 1982, Torpedo, the city of Vladimir's entry in the second league, fell under the scrutiny of the party's Central Committee and the sports committees of the USSR and the Russian Republic. The Committee for Party Control had received information on inappropriate payments by Torpedo when compiling its roster for the upcoming season and passed the details to the USSR's Sports Committee. On March 29, the latter sent its agents to the city to pursue the matter, who then sent their findings to its counterpart for the Russian Republic.[29] Two weeks later, on April 19, the republic's Sports Committee denounced Torpedo for "serious financial irregularities."[30] The team's sins were legion. Income from games did not cover the cost of salaries. Players, coaches, and administrators received improper bonuses. They also received hefty payments from various enterprises where, in fact, they were not employed. The committee disqualified Torpedo's general manager, two assistant coaches, and five players from any future association with professional football. It also issued a "stern reprimand" to the chair of the region's sports committee and to the head coach, Valerii Mikhailovich Svintsov (who had played for Kirov's Dinamo from 1960 to 1964 and served as its head coach from 1966 to 1972). It also wanted the death penalty. Within days, the USSR's committee disqualified Vladimir's Torpedo from participation in any league because of "violations of existing regulations regarding the financing of football teams."[31]

The Russian Republic's Sports Committee sent a copy of its denunciation of Torpedo to every professional football team in the country. Someone from Kirov's sports committee underlined in red pencil the key sentences regarding excessive bonuses, fictional jobs, and the club's disqualification.[32] And yet whatever the facts of the matter and Dinamo's admission of financial shenanigans in March, the team's administration now denied any and all wrongdoing. On June 29, the deputy chair of Kirov's sports committee, Nikolai Il'ich Malygin, informed Moscow that an internal review "had found no violations in expenditures for the upkeep of the football team 'Dinamo.'"[33]

And Why Not?

And why should Dinamo's administrators, staff, and players have acted otherwise? Kirov was hardly alone. Their club's misdeeds were ubiquitous in Soviet professional football. At a session of the collegium of the USSR's Sports Committee in July 1982, Koloskov as head of its Governing Board for Football complained that little improvement had followed the previous and much-publicized disqualification of athletes and coaches from association with the sport as well as the death penalty issued to several teams. Clubs continued to recruit at great expense what he called in a fit of pique "notorious drunkards and idlers." Illegal benefits, including excessive bonuses and automobiles, meant that some players in the second league made as much as their brethren in the Higher League. His governing board, Koloskov lamented, "had not yet found sufficiently effective means of struggle with dealers on the make" who helped make it so.[34]

Koloskov surely knew that there was little he could do to correct the behavior of most clubs, especially the victorious ones. Winners, whatever their wrongdoing, had privileges. One of them, Kirov's Dinamo, had performed spectacularly well in 1980 and 1981 in large part because it violated the rules, and, as we will see, it played reasonably well at the outset of its first season in the First League. Losing, on the other hand, had consequences far beyond an unenviable place in a league's standings. To be sure, Rostsel'mash, a winner in 1980, had been severely punished. But it had violated the second league's inflexible rule limiting the use of older veterans. Unlike under-the-table and off-the-books benefits, Rostsel'mash's transgression lacked plausible deniability; its sin was easily verified by the names and birthdates of players on file in the league's office.

Moscow singled out Kryl'ia Sovetov, a loser, for its poor performance on the field *despite* its financial shenanigans. It won the First League in 1978 and thereby earned promotion to the Higher League in 1979. There it finished in last place, eighteenth of eighteen teams. Relegated back to the First League in 1980, it ended the season in twenty-second place among twenty-four teams and suffered another relegation, this time to the second league. There, in 1981,

Kryl'ia Sovetov, a team that only two years before had performed in the Higher League, won only eleven of thirty-two games for a seventh-place finish among seventeen teams.[35] In a classic display of schadenfreude in late 1981, the Russian Republic's Sports Committee noted the team's "rapid descent from the Higher League to the second league in a space of two years."[36] A failure, Kryl'ia Sovetov was fit for scapegoating for Soviet football's many financial irregularities.[37]

Like Kryl'ia Sovetov, Vladimir's Torpedo was probably no more guilty of "crimes" than were other teams. Torpedo's fault had been its poor performance on the field despite its financial irregularities. In 1980, Torpedo had finished ninth among nineteen teams in its zone in the second league, in the following year, seventeenth of seventeen.[38] In its case, death lasted through the 1982 and 1983 seasons. Returning to play in 1984 in the second league, Torpedo finished seventeenth and last in its zone, winning only two of thirty-two matches.

In Kirov, the lesson was clear. Its Dinamo would have to keep on winning or else.

Hypocrisy

Kirov's disingenuity was more than matched by its hypocrisy. While poaching athletes from other teams, Dinamo's and Kirov's leaders, Ochnev and Chernozubov prominent among them, belligerently condemned similar attempts by other teams and cities to purchase, as it were, Kirov's own. In December 1980, Mazurenko, Sergeev, and Ochnev denounced the city of Odessa when it pursued Kirov's wrestlers. Weeks earlier, Kirov's German Pavlovich Baboshin, Meritorious Coach of the Russian Republic, and three of his top wrestlers, Vasilii Fomin, Vladimir Galkin, and Gennadii Skriabin, all Masters of Sport and members of the USSR's national team, announced their departure for better accommodations in the Ukrainian port city. After scorching comments on December 24 by Mazurenko, Sergeev, and Ochnev, Kirov's sports committee duly condemned Baboshin for "a lack of gratitude, a dearth of patriotic feelings for Kirov, and contempt for the ethos of a Soviet athlete."[39] It recommended that the USSR's Sports Committee strip him and his three wrestlers of their titles. It also wanted the removal of the trio from the USSR's national team.

In Moscow, Viktor Andreevich Ivonin, born in Kirov in 1927 and now deputy chair of the USSR's Sports Committee, took up his native city's cause.[40] His committee demanded the return of the coach and the three wrestlers to Kirov. By late February 1981, Galkin and Fomin (and presumably Baboshin) were back in the city. Nevertheless, the committee reprimanded both athletes and demanded that the Ukrainian Republic's Sports Committee compel the errant

Skriabin's return. For good measure, it stripped Skriabin of his Master of Sport of the USSR title. At the same time, the Russian Republic's Sports Committee deprived Baboshin of his title of Meritorious Coach of the Russian Republic. These measures and—no doubt—enhanced benefits kept the coach and his charges safely in Kirov.[41] Baboshin soon regained his status as a local hero. The following August, in celebration of the Day of Physical Culture and Sport, Ochnev spoke glowingly on Kirov's radio of Baboshin as one of Kirov's best coaches.[42]

Ochnev likewise vigorously opposed any raid on the region's professional hockey team, Olimpiia, that played in the city of Kirovo-Chepetsk, a fifty-kilometer drive from the provincial capital. In May 1981, in a letter to the USSR's Sports Committee, he complained that each year Olimpiia lost four to six players to other teams who tempted the athletes with inappropriate benefits. Just that month, two players had deserted the squad for the club Khimik, located near Moscow. Ochnev wanted their return and a ban on all such departures over the next two to three years.[43] Less than a month later, on June 18, the head of the Governing Board for Hockey of the USSR's Sports Committee ordered the return of the two players in question.[44] A year later, on May 3, Ochnev informed Moscow's committee that the two had ignored the order and had continued to play for Khimik and that a third player had just departed for the same team.[45]

Many years later, Olimpiia's coach at the time, Dmitrii Viktorovich Dumarevsky, was still bitter over the abrupt loss of so many of his athletes. When asked in 2015 if he understood that his team had failed over the years to advance from the second league to the First League, Dumarevsky responded "as if [his interlocutor wrote] much had built up in his soul." "Of course," Dumarevsky immediately replied, "how could I not understand! Where could the team go if each year five or six players left my team for a club in the First or Higher League. They took the very best."[46] A year later, Olimpiia's administrator since the 1960s, Ararat Artashesovich Popov, ruefully recalled the flow of home-grown talent to other teams. "Who in our country," he mused, "can match Olimpiia in the training and cultivation of young talent for clubs of a higher division?"[47]

In still another case, Kirov proposed a shameless nullification of a sport's most basic protocols in early 1981. It did so to protect Rodina, its entry in the Higher League for bandy, a game of hockey played with a ball on a rink the size of a football field. In the season just completed, the team had finished dead last among fourteen teams and was therefore doomed to relegation to the First League. On March 23, the heads of Kirov's regional party committee and regional soviet appealed to the USSR's Sports Committee to void the demotion.

Bandy, they insisted, enjoyed great popularity throughout the city and region of Kirov. Up to twelve thousand fans attended Rodina's home games. In the past year, the club's inaugural season in the Higher League, its young inexperienced players had performed as well as could be expected. The plaintiffs thought they had a splendid solution—the league's expansion to sixteen teams to include Rodina.[48] Two weeks later, the USSR's Sports Committee rejected the request and confirmed Rodina's relegation.[49] Kirov would have to make do with the new bright star in the town's firmament, Dinamo.

Dinamo's need for enhanced funding came precisely at a time when Moscow's organs for the administration of sport renewed spasmodic efforts to limit payments of improper benefits to players and coaches. But when these agencies did so, they usually pounced on a losing team, such as Kuibyshev's Kryl'ia Sovetov and Vladimir's Torpedo as their victims. Through evasion and dissimulation, Kirov's Dinamo wriggled free of any punishment for its illegal behavior, thanks to its winning ways. Also worth noting here is the hypocrisy of Kirov's municipal and regional governments. Even as these bodies helped Dinamo raid other football clubs of their best athletes, they vehemently tried to protect their own teams. They protested the poaching of players from the region's hockey team and of Kirov's nationally renowned wrestlers and their coach. They attempted to keep Kirov's bandy team in the Higher League by bending the rules as well. Rules clearly applied to others if they protected Kirov's interests, but they could be bent or ignored if they did not.

NOTES

1. In addition to Moskalev, they were Aleksandr Komarov and Vladimir Lazarev. All three went to teams in the second league.

2. State Archive of the Kirov Region (GAKO), f. R-1363, op. 4, d. 1780, l. 6. Vostrikov had played for Dinamo from 1974 to 1980. It did not happen. Vostrikov did not play professionally again until 1985 when he joined Kirov's Dinamo.

3. See this information in a report sent in late October 1980 by Pavlov, chair of the USSR's Sports Committee, to the Central Committee: RGANI, op. 5, op. 77, d. 149, ll. 124–125. See also M. Iu Prozumenshchikov, *Bol'shoi sport i bol'shaia politika* (Moscow: ROSSPEN, 2004), 385.

4. State Archive of the Russian Federation (GARF), f. R-7576, op. 31, d. 5417, ll. 118–119. Starostin also criticized Minsk's Dinamo.

5. For information on the charges and the investigation that followed, see the opening remarks by Viacheslav Koloskov, head of the Governing Board for Football of the USSR's Sports Committee, at a session of the presidium of the USSR's Football Federation, June 8, 1981: GARF, f. R-7576, op. 31, d. 7096, l. 218.

The committee had received, Koloskov said, an anonymous letter setting forth the allegations.

6. See V. Liubimov, "Mera otvetstvennosti," *Futbol-Khokkei*, no. 51, December 21, 1980, 12.

7. This information is from Koloskov's remarks at a session of the presidium of the USSR's Football Federation, June 8, 1981: GARF, f. R-7576, op. 31, d. 7096, l. 218 ob. The Central Committee had received a letter analogous to the one submitted earlier to the USSR's Sports Committee.

8. For the complete record of this session, see GARF, f. R-7576, op. 31, d. 7096, ll. 218–222.

9. GARF, f. R-7576, op. 31, d. 7096, ll. 219–219 ob.

10. GARF, f. R-7576, op. 31, d. 7096, l. 219 ob.

11. GARF, f. R-7576, op. 31, d. 7096, l. 219 (Melent'ev); l. 220 (Riashentsev); l. 221 (Fedosov). Fedosov was by this point a prominent journalist.

12. GARF, f. R-7576, op. 31, d. 7096, l. 219 ob.

13. GARF, f. R-7576, op. 31, d. 7096, l. 220.

14. GARF, f. R-7576, op. 31, d. 7096, l. 222. The eight disqualified: Anatolii Fetisov, Andrei Vostrikov, Aleksandr Nikanorov, Aleksandr Kupriianov, Iurii Akhmerov, Sergei Zolotovsky Vladimir Ersiukov, and Arkadii Arutiunian. Lovchev was also banned from coaching a professional team: see comments at a session (April 4, 1983) of the presidium of the USSR's Football Federation: GARF, f. R-7576, op. 31, d. 9301, ll. 41–42. In 1981, Zolotovsky's disqualification was lifted. The other seven and Lovchev had to wait until early 1983. In 1981, Lovchev appealed his punishment to the Central Committee: GARF, f. R-7576, op. 31, d. 9301, ll. 41–42. Four of them never played again. In 1985, Kirsh returned to coaching, and in 1992, he arrived in Kuibyshev (now Samara) to coach its team in the second league. Akulov remained head of Kuibyshev's sports committee well into the 1980s. Belagez'ian returned to serve as president of Samara's Kryl'ia Sovetov from 1991 to 1995.

15. This information from a session of the presidium of the USSR's Football Federation, July 3, 1981: GARF, f. R-7576, op. 31, d. 7097, l. 3.

16. For the statement of the Russian Republic's Sports Committee, see information in GARF, f. R-7576, op. 31, d. 7097, ll. 3–4 and GAKO, f. R-1363, op. 4, d. 1672, ll. 137–138. For the statement from the USSR's Sports Committee: GAKO, f. R-6766, op. 1, d. 785, ll. 50–51. On July 3, the presidium of the USSR's Football Federation approved the request of the Russian Republic's Sports Committee to annul the death penalty: GARF, f. R-7576, op. 31, d. 7097, l. 4.

17. GARF, f. R-7576, op. 31, d. 7096, ll. 220, 220 ob.

18. GARF, f. R-7576, op. 31, d. 7096, l. 221 ob.

19. GAKO, f. R-6766, op. 1, d. 785, l. 51.

20. See Ochnev's handwritten note, dated July 15, at the top of the copy: GAKO, f. R-1363, op. 4, d. 1762, l. 137.

21. GAKO, f. R-1363, op. 4, d. 1678, l. 16.

22. State Archive for the Social and Political History of the Kirov Region (GASPI KO), f. R-6766, op. 1, d. 785, l. 57. The resolution even implied that the team had added a number of young players to its roster and would continue to do so in the future.

23. GASPI KO, f. R-6766, op. 1, d. 806, ll. 10–11. The two were Viacheslav Belov, who had played in nineteen games in 1981, and Leonid Shatunov, a local boy who had played in twenty-three.

24. GASPI KO, f. R-6766, op. 1, d. 806, l. 11. Dinamo's central soviet had previously reprimanded Sergeev.

25. GAKO, f. R-1363, op. 4, d. 1674, l. 159.

26. GARF, f. R-7676, op. 1, d. 9301, l. 20. "Character training" used a presumed devotion to Marxist-Leninist principles to compel proper behavior on and off the field by a team's athletes and staff.

27. GASP KO, f. R-6766, op. 1, d. 808, l. 28. Sergeev specified the second half of 1981. And yet despite the charge, on April 21, 1983, the collegium of Kirov's sports committee, upon the request of the regional Dinamo soviet, awarded Sergeev (as well as Kolchanov, Mazurenko, and M. F. Efremov) certificates of honor: GAKO, f. R-1363, op. 4, d. 1889, l. 93.

28. GARF, f. R-7576, op. 31, d. 6429, l. 171.

29. See the letter from the Sports Committee's deputy chair, Sych, to the head of the Vladimir region's party committee, March 29, 1982, in GARF, f. R-7576, op. 31, d. 7573, l. 83.

30. GAKO, f. R-1363, op. 4, d. 1783, ll. 56–58. The committee issued its decree jointly with the Bureau of the All-Union Soviet of Voluntary Sports Societies of Professional Unions. On June 11, 1982, the Russian Republic's Sports Committee found similar "gross violations" committed by a basketball team in the city of Gor'ky. Players and at least one coach were paid handsomely for fictional jobs: GAKO, f. R-1363, op. 4, d. 1783, l. 138.

31. See information on the decision of the USSR's Sports Committee in *Futbol-Khokkei*, no. 19, May 9, 1982, 16. Information on the Russian Republic's decree is also in this issue of *Futbol-Khokkei*. Svintsov returned to Vladimir's Torpedo as head coach in 1985 and continued in that position until 1987.

32. GAKO, f. R-1363, op. 4, d. 1783, ll. 56–57.

33. See the report to the Russian Republic's Sports Committee: GAKO, f. R-1363, op. 4, d. 1783, l. 132.

34. GARF, f. R-7576, op. 31, d. 7527, l. 128.

35. Ironically, it competed well against the zone's winner, Kirov's Dinamo, with a 2–2 tie on May 28 in Kirov and a 2–0 victory at home on September 24.

36. See information from the Russian Republic's Sports Committee submitted to the USSR's Football Federation as mentioned in the deliberations of the federation's presidium, December 3, 1981: GARF, f. R-7576, op. 31, d. 7097, l. 182.

37. In 1983, Kryl'ia Sovetov won its zone in the second league and the playoffs that followed. It thereby earned promotion to the First League. The team had a young roster, fourteen of the twenty-three players were twenty-three or younger. However, of the twelve who played in more than twenty contests, only three belonged to that age cohort. The average age of the other nine was twenty-seven. These veterans probably reaped considerable benefits beyond their official salary. But winning now absolved the team of any and all sins. It skirted but did not violate regulations regarding the number of players over twenty-five allowed on a team, and it had at least one player who was eighteen or younger.

38. Information on Torpedo from its website: http://fc-tv.ru/history.htm.

39. See discussions of the collegium of Kirov's sports committee, December 18 and 24, 1980, in GAKO, f. R-1363, op. 4, d. 1553, ll. 182–184, 214–215, quote on l. 214.

40. Ivonin's letter to the Central Committee, February 25, 1981, in GARF, f. R-7576, op. 31, d. 6414, l 3.

41. In my interview with Kolchanov, he recalled that Mazurenko had phoned the Ministry of Internal Affairs in Moscow and arranged to cancel any and all promises to provide Baboshin with an apartment and other perquisites in Odessa. In April 1984, Kirov's sports committee asked the Russian Republic's Sports Committee for financial assistance to provide better housing for a number of people, including Baboshin: GAKO, f. R-1363, op. 5, d. 3, l. 55. In early 1982, Fomin became the champion of the USSR in his weight category: GASPI KO, f. R-6818, op. 5, d. 1548, l. 92. All three continued to represent Kirov in national and international tournaments. Speaking about Fomin and Galkin as well as other wrestlers, Kirov's television station declared on February 12, 1982: "Of course, we are pleased, that such a large group of able warriors are in Kirov": GASPI KO, f. R-6818, op. 1548, l. 191. See references to the presence in 1984 of Fomin, Galkin, and Skriabin in Kirov: GAKO, f. R-1363, op. 5, d. 1, l. 59 and d. 3, l. 4. In mid-1984, Kirov's authorities again focused attention on the area's loss of athletes, who had been purchased, as it were, by other regions. Several skiers had recently left for better benefits: V. Shishkin, "'Akai,' na prodazhu," *Kirovskaia pravda*, June 20, 1984, 4. (Akai is a Japanese brand.) Athletes must resist the "disease of acquisitiveness." Players were to be athletes in the "spiritual as well as physical sense [because] for hundreds of thousands of people they are the ideal, the idol, if you like."

42. GASPI KO, f. R-6818, op. 5, d. 1638, l. 52.

43. GASPI KO, f. R-1363, op. 4, d. 1670, l. 49. On July 11, 1984, Kirov's sports committee asked the USSR and the Russian Republic's Sports Committee to forbid for two to three years transfers from Olimpiia to other clubs: GAKO, f. R-1363, op. 5, d. 14, l. 3.

44. GASPI KO, f. R-1363, op. 4, d. 1670, l. 60.

45. GAKO, f. R-1363, op. 4, d. 1780, l. 44.

46. Maksim Makarychev, *Gorod masterov: Letopis' Kirovo-chepetskogo khokkeia* (Kirov: Kirovskaia oblastnaia tipografiia, 2016), 109. Dumarevsky added that he encouraged his players to depart for a better team and enhanced compensation. But he wanted them to let him know in advance of their departure. Many did not. Dumarevsky recalled his chance to leave for a position in Khar'kov at the end of the 1981–1982 season: "I didn't give it a thought, I grabbed my bags and left" (109). In 1973, Dumarevsky coached Kirov's Dinamo. That year, he began his coaching career with Olimpiia.

47. Makarychev, *Gorod masterov*, 148. The two most famous of Olimpiia's prodigies had left years before. After two years at Olimpiia, Aleksandr Mikhailovich Mal'tsev departed in 1967 for Moscow's Dinamo, where he played through the 1983–1984 season. He appeared in three Olympics with the USSR's national team. Vladimir Semenovich Malkin, a goalie, left Olimpiia in 1972 for twenty years of play for two of Moscow's teams, including Dinamo. He played in two Olympics for the USSR's national team.

48. GARF, f. R-7576, op. 31, d. 6489, ll. 45–47. In the 1980–1981 season, in twenty-six contests, Rodina had won only six, tied six, and lost fourteen.

49. GARF, f. R-7576, op. 31, d. 6489, l. 44. The next year, Rodina won its zone in the First League and the ensuing playoff to earn promotion to the Higher League.

7

THE FIRST LEAGUE

Now that Dinamo had won promotion to the First League, anyone in Kirov who was the least bit interested in football looked forward to the upcoming season. In the meantime, the club repeatedly demonstrated that it might not be ready for the big time.

In early January 1982, the Russian Republic's Dinamo soviet invited a number of coaches, Valerii Ovchinnikov included, to a clinic to be held in Kiev from the twenty-first to the twenty-fourth. Ovchinnikov failed to attend and could not, according to the soviet, provide a reasonable explanation.[1] The Central Dinamo soviet invited eight of its teams from across the USSR, including Kirov's squad, to participate in a tournament in Moscow's indoor Olympic stadium from January 26 to 30. Teams were told to arrive on the twenty-fifth. Kirov's Dinamo showed up from its preseason training camp in Tsakhkadzor, Armenia, on the twenty-sixth. The delay scrambled the host's arrangements for the team's accommodations.[2]

Once in Moscow, Dinamo played reasonably well, taking third place out of eight participants.[3] But outside the stadium, it earned not victories but multiple reprimands. On the night of January 27, at the camp near Moscow where all the teams stayed, Kirov's team doctor, Anatolii Chikishev, appeared in public in an inebriated state. Once detained, he caused such a commotion that authorities locked him up in his hotel room for the night.[4] The next day, the entire team missed "an important political event." Of all the squads in the tournament, it was the only one that failed to appear for a special ceremony on Red Square to place wreaths at Lenin's Mausoleum and the nearby Tomb of the Unknown Soldier.[5] In response to this series of misdeeds, the Russian Republic's Dinamo soviet rebuked Ovchinnikov, coach Chikishev, and general manager Viacheslav Chernozubov.[6]

Less than a month later, at another tournament, Kirov's Dinamo was on its best behavior. From February 20 through March 4, it appeared in the preseason USSR Cup, an event held in several cities in Armenia. Kirov's entry lost its first three contests but followed with two victories. Among the seven teams involved, Kirov finished in fourth place behind three clubs from the Higher League and avoided any scandals.[7]

High Expectations

Despite an admission in March 1982 of undue remuneration of players, Kirov's Dinamo's expensive roster for that year's season remained largely unchanged. The team's fans waited anxiously for the competition to begin with their team now in the First League. Viktor Chudinovskikh and Boris Kolomensky shared their enthusiasm. Both correspondents attended the tourney in Moscow, and Kolomensky attended the USSR Cup in Armenia. His spirits buoyed by Dinamo's third-place finish in the nation's capital, Chudinovskikh described Dinamo as a "combative group with the strength not to get lost in the First League."[8] In April, the city's Komsomol committee pledged bonuses of ten rubles each to Dinamo's two best players in each of the club's upcoming home games.[9] Although the committee had handed out fifteen rubles the previous year rather than ten, the schedule in the First League involved far more games.

On April 8, the day before the regular season's opening, Natal'ia Zenina, a local radio correspondent, interviewed Dinamo's administrator, Evgenii Kolchanov. Neither of them could conceal their enthusiasm and great hopes for the year. Zenina began, "The people of Kirov await with considerable impatience the current football season. There's so much talk." Kolchanov responded that Dinamo's initial game in the prestigious First League "is a holiday for Kirov's fans."[10] Kolchanov then made the best of a difficult situation. Repairs of the home stadium that had begun immediately after the close of the 1981 season had not yet been completed, failing spectacularly to meet expectations. As it turned out, Dinamo played all of its games in the first half of the season at the tire factory's field, Shinnik. And once refurbished, Dinamo's arena could accommodate no more spectators than it had previously, far short of the fifteen thousand to twenty thousand Kolchanov had hoped for. Kolchanov told his listeners that because of limited seating first at Shinnik and then at Dinamo—where, temporarily, because of ongoing construction fewer seats would be available than last year—they should assure themselves of a place by buying season tickets now available at the offices of Dinamo's regional soviet.[11]

Ovchinnikov was upbeat but cautious about his team's prospects. In an interview the previous month, he claimed with little exaggeration that "we have kept in full last year's squad" and had added several excellent new players. But the coach understood the difficulties posed by the tougher competition in the First League. "Our mission," he said, was to avoid relegation, "to hold on to our position in the First League. A debutante in it cannot set its sights on a higher goal."[12]

On the first day of the regular season, at a home game on April 9, *Kirovskaia pravda* carried a headline marking the occasion: "Hello, Football." Greetings followed from Kirov's favorite son, Soviet cosmonaut Viktor Petrovich Savinykh, who had spent ten weeks in space the previous year. He wished the team a successful start and hoped that "it would remain in the First League."[13] At 2:00 p.m. in 7-degree-Celsius weather (45 degrees Fahrenheit) and rain mixed with snow, thousands packed the stands at Shinnik Stadium, and thousands more stood on surrounding hills and the balconies and rooftops of nearby buildings. A presentation of flowers, a gift from the city's Rodina sports club, preceded a solemn flag-raising ceremony, later shown that day by Kirov's television station.

Dinamo dominated its guest, Kiev's Army Sports Club, but in the end had to settle for a 0–0 tie.[14] Huge turnouts continued for subsequent matches. Ten thousand or more attended games in April and May, a number well beyond Shinnik Stadium's capacity. Many of Dinamo's fans traveled over eight hundred miles to watch their team play Spartak on May 6 in the city of Smolensk. Unfortunately for them, Dinamo lost 1–0, only its second defeat of the young season.[15] On May 11, their enthusiasm unabated, more than ten thousand fans filled Shinnik and nearby hills and perches to watch Kirov's Dinamo defeat a team from Volgograd, 2–1.[16] On July 12, in 26-degree-Celsius weather (79 degrees Fahrenheit), a game played in the newly opened Dinamo stadium drew an overflow crowd of 11,200 spectators. Their team prevailed over a squad from the city of Zaporozh'e 1–0.[17]

In April, the season's first month, Dinamo won two games, tied three, and lost one to occupy eighth place in the league of twenty-two teams. League inspectors in attendance reported that win, lose, or draw, Dinamo played an interesting attacking game.[18] An April 18 report in the national weekly, *Futbol-Khokkei*, expressed pleasure with the team's performance.[19] Five days later, Kirov's radio interviewed an upbeat Kolomensky. Like the fans, he regretted the losses, but he reminded his listeners, "Don't forget that our team is a debutante in the First League. Games at and around the [opponent's] goalposts, as it happened [the year before] with Kirov's team in the second league, can't be expected." Every match is difficult, he continued, "the team needs our goodwill and support. The players are in a fighting mood. Therefore, we can expect beautiful, attacking, contemporary football." He wished the team success in its quest "to represent our region in a dignified way during this important and highly challenging season."[20]

Cause for Concern

By mid-May, Dinamo had four wins, five ties, and two losses, good enough for seventh place. It was an impressive record for a newcomer in a highly competitive league. Nevertheless, fans and the team's reporters had begun to worry. In a game on May 11, goalie Sergei Bubnov was injured, a "great loss," *Kirovskaia pravda* reported.[21] He joined several other injured players who, once they returned, were unable to play as well as before.[22]

At this point in the season, an expert commentator in Moscow warned about a possible deterioration of Dinamo's play as a result of the coach's tactics. In March, Ovchinnikov had expressed his concern about how his players from the previous year might respond to the tougher play of the First League. There, the competition presented a physical challenge and, as Ovchinnikov put it, a "psychological barrier."[23] Perhaps he overcompensated by demanding too much too early from his athletes. Valerii Karpov, chair of the coaches' council of the All-Russian Football Federation, certainly thought so. On May 16, he expressed his anxiety in *Futbol-Khokkei*. Under Ovchinnikov's demanding leadership, Dinamo's athletes exerted maximum effort in each game. "To continue this style of play for a whole season," Karpov added, "is practically impossible, it requires too much energy. It will be interesting to see how the team performs later in the season, when the level of skill becomes of paramount importance." Karpov also thought that Dinamo relied excessively on Aleksandr Kozlovskikh, a player now thirty-two years of age, who would tire over the course of the season.[24] Karpov's warning proved more prescient than he could have imagined.

At the end of May, Dinamo's season began to unravel. On May 28, an inspector commented that in a loss on the road in Lanchkhuti, a city in the republic of Georgia, Dinamo's squad seemed especially tired in the second half.[25] From that day forward until the midseason break in mid-June, the team won only one game, tied one, and lost four. It now occupied sixteenth place. It did not help matters that the league had disqualified one of Kirov's best players, defender Sergei Bazulev, for four games for repeatedly rough and reckless play.[26] At home on the eleventh, Dinamo displayed minimal effort in a 3–0 loss to a team from Vilnius.[27] That defeat especially troubled Kirov's sports correspondents. The home team must win, Chudinovskikh wrote; "this is the unwritten rule of football."[28] On that day in *Komsomol'skoe plemia*, an anonymous author—probably Kolomensky—wrote that Dinamo suffered a "major defeat" brought on in part by the "impotent play of its forwards."[29]

The team faced other challenges. As discussed earlier, Kirov's Dinamo successfully parried implicit and explicit criticism of improper remuneration of its players and coaches in 1981 and 1982. But now Dinamo faced greater threats closer to home. As previously mentioned, the team had opened its 1982 season not in its own stadium, then under repair, but at the tire factory's Shinnik where they continued to play the first half of the season. During the two-week break at midseason, the club needed a field where it could practice and improve its skills following its dismal performance in May and June. The training facility at Poroshino was not yet suitable, and for reasons unclear, neither was Shinnik. Dinamo requested permission to use the field at the city's Rodina stadium, which belonged to the Lepse defense factory and its Rodina sports club. In a departure from the club's gracious presentation of flowers at Dinamo's opening home game on April 9, it turned down the request, telling Kolchanov that Rodina needed the time to prepare the field for the celebration of "City Day" on July 25. When Kolchanov pursued the matter, he uncovered a more likely reason. Dinamo owed the factory money for its previous use of the facility.[30] The sports society Progress, under the jurisdiction of another defense plant, Maiak, also refused Dinamo the use of its field. At this crucial juncture of the season, Kirov's professional football club had no choice but to train on another, far inferior field.

The uncooperative attitude of the two factories and their sports clubs enraged Chudinovskikh and Kolomensky and, no doubt, many fans. They hoped that midseason workouts might somehow save Dinamo's season. In an article published on July 1, "Turned Away at the Goalposts," Chudinovskikh accused Rodina's leaders of "parochial interests." While he acknowledged that Dinamo owed Rodina a considerable sum, Chudinovskikh nevertheless hoped (in vain, as it turned out) that municipal and regional officials might pressure Rodina to cooperate.[31] On the same day, Kolomensky published "In Search of a Shelter," an angry denunciation of Rodina and Progress. He accused both of "narrow institutional interests." Whom did Dinamo represent, he asked rhetorically, "only Dinamo or the entire city and the entire region?"[32] Meanwhile, repair work at Dinamo's stands and field proceeded so slowly that Kolomensky thought the team would have to schedule its first two home games after the break, matches of July 12 and 15, in the city of Izhevsk, located over 400 kilometers (263 miles) driving distance from Kirov.[33] As it turned out, the games were played in Dinamo's home stadium. But it remained so unfit, especially for a team in the First League, that in late July, the Governing Board for Football of the USSR's Sports Committee sent a threatening letter to Kirov's sports committee. It would ban all games there in the 1983 season if the stands, field, and locker rooms were not greatly improved.[34]

On July 12, Dinamo finally managed to win its first game at its own stadium. This was achieved in 24-degree-Celsius weather (75 degrees Fahrenheit) before a standing-room-only crowd of 11,200 fans.[35] The team's subsequent performance vanquished any hopes that arose that day. There followed two road losses and, worse, a tie and a loss at home.[36] "Our team," Kolomensky observed somewhat charitably on July 17, "stays in the saddle only with difficulty."[37] On July 27, Chudinovskikh observed that the opposition had suffocated Kozlovskikh. The player's inability to score as well as Ovchinnikov's defensive tactics had accounted for a dreadful road record. In seven away games, Dinamo had scored a total of only one goal. It had lost seven times and tied three, all of the latter by a score of 0–0.[38] On August 2, following a recent loss at home to Moscow's Lokomotiv, Gennadii Fediakov told his television audience that Dinamo had failed to score on four or five excellent opportunities. "And then," he lamented, "the deadly law of football came into play—if you don't score, they'll score on you." With six minutes remaining in the game, Lokomotiv netted a goal for a 1–0 victory.[39]

The first secretary of Kirov's municipal party committee, Iurii Derevskoi, tried his best to remain positive. On July 24, on the occasion of "City Day," he discussed the state of amateur and professional sports on Kirov's radio. "Recently, Dinamo's athletes have brought us joy."[40] Few of his listeners, if any, agreed. Well past disappointment, angry fans wrote to *Komsomol'skoe plemia* "to suggest radical measures," presumably a wholesale dismissal of coaches and players.[41] Dinamo's poor play caught the attention of the national press, *Futbol-Khokkei*. On August 1, Evgenii Kucherevsky, the coach of Kolos, Dinamo's rival in the First League, from the Ukrainian city Nikopol', reported on developments in the league. At the time, his team stood atop its standings, while Dinamo occupied sixteenth place. Kirov's entry "had such a promising start at the season's outset," Kucherevsky wrote, "but it was then unable to live up to expectations." The author censured the play of the club's star, Kozlovskikh. Opponents closely marked him wherever he was on the field, but in response, he "had not refashioned his game. Perhaps he does not want to?"[42] Kozlovskikh's performance had, in fact, deteriorated as the season wore on. To be sure, he was playing hurt, but it seemed that age and the level of play in the First League contributed to his woes. When Chudinovskikh asked Chernozubov in late August about the star's disappointing performance, he candidly responded, "We very much counted on him, but unfortunately he has lost the skills necessary for the contemporary game."[43] Chernozubov refrained from any public criticism of Ovchinnikov. The coach, in the meantime, held out hope. He and the staff, he said in late August, "still believe in our boys."[44] Despite three wins (and four losses) that month, on the thirty-first, Dinamo occupied seventeenth place.

In late August, the presidium of the USSR's Football Federation summoned Ovchinnikov to Moscow to its session on the twenty-seventh held jointly with the All-Union Coaches Council. Several of those in attendance repeated Karpov's May criticism of Ovchinnikov's methods. A representative from the Russian Republic's Dinamo Council, former player and coach Ivan Ivanovich Mozer, noted by way of implicit disapproval the coach's demanding approach and his adherence to "his own principles." Kachalin, the famed coach of numerous USSR national teams, called on Ovchinnikov to proceed with more caution in holding two-a-day workouts so that his team might successfully finish the season. While Ovchinnikov remarked that he relied primarily on local players from Kirov, Aleksei Aleksandrovich Paramonov, famous for his play with Moscow's Spartak from 1947 to 1959, correctly pointed out that fifteen of the twenty-two athletes on Dinamo's squad had been recruited from teams in other cities. Moreover, Paramonov continued, Ovchinnikov failed to properly train and prepare the club's double, the players in reserve. The prospects for an immediate improvement in play were not, therefore, particularly bright.[45]

Two weeks after the session, Kirov's Dinamo suffered another extended disqualification of one of its best players, the defender Iurii Vladimirovich Starikov. On three previous occasions that year, referees had penalized him for reckless and dangerous play. On September 13, a commission of referees in Moscow summoned Starikov, several teammates, and an assistant coach to discuss the player's behavior. Starikov's teammates rushed to his defense by emphasizing that in general, he played well and by the rules. Undaunted, the commission resolved to ask the Governing Board for Football to ban Starikov for two contests. A chastened Starikov apologized, saying that he "was letting his team down at a critical moment."[46]

Three games later, when Starikov rejoined his teammates on the field, it made little difference to Dinamo's plunging fortunes. From the beginning of September through mid-October, the team played nine games, winning three and losing six. Falling to twentieth place, it seemed doomed to be one of the three bottom dwellers slated for relegation to the second league. Ovchinnikov remained hopeful. In his article in *Futbol-Khokkei*'s October 12 edition, he pointed out that Dinamo's relative early success in the year was due to his players being in excellent physical shape and the fact that the opposition underestimated his team. He still hoped that the conditioning of his athletes, a result of his demanding ways, and a necessary change in game tactics (implicitly more offense), would keep his team afloat and free of relegation.[47]

To be sure, more than Ovchinnikov's coaching had contributed to a rash of injuries and team fatigue. A brutal schedule played its part. After the close of the 1981 regular season, Dinamo played four intensely fought games in the playoffs from October 28 to November 9. Then, at the end of November, the club played three matches in the Russian Republic's championship. In January 1982, it broke camp to compete in five matches in the Dinamo tournament in Moscow. A month later, it played five more contests in the USSR Cup in Armenia. Then, from April to mid-October, it had thirty-eight regular season games plus a friendly match in Kirov against the Ethiopian national team. Thus, from late October 1981 to mid-October 1982, Dinamo played a total of fifty-six games, more than enough to break the body and spirit of the ablest of athletes.

To Be or Not to Be

By mid-October, only four matches remained in the season, two of them at home. Dinamo needed wins in two, perhaps three, to save the season and avoid relegation. "To Be or Not to Be," Chudinovskikh aptly titled his article in *Kirovskaia pravda* on October 17.[48]

Ovchinnikov did not get a chance to see his hopes through for any last-minute heroics. Within days, if not hours, after Dinamo's road loss on October 14, Chernozubov, with Aleksandr Mazurenko's full support, fired his coach. The club announced that Ovchinnikov had "taken a leave for family reasons."[49] No one believed it. Kolomensky reported a month later that Chernozubov had concluded that Dinamo had come to a "difficult moment, when the team was psychologically fractured and had lost faith in itself."[50] Kolomensky added that Ovchinnikov's excessive insistence on conditioning had worn his team out physically and mentally. "The young coach was not yet ready to head a team in the First League."[51] Years later, in a 2006 interview, Ovchinnikov recalled his dismissal as "painful." "I was young and cocky," he admitted.[52] Ovchinnikov did not elaborate further on his firing.[53] More simply but correctly put, despite Kirov's massive investment in the club, Ovchinnikov had not won in 1982. He had to go.

In Moscow, Karpov, a critic in May of Ovchinnikov's training methods and tactics, now came to his defense in *Futbol-Khokkei*. Karpov denounced the unjustified—he thought—firing of many coaches with, implicitly, Ovchinnikov uppermost in his mind. "It is not surprising," Karpov wrote, "that our prominent and most able football coaches taste the bitterness of unfair expectations and involuntary early dismissal from their post with the formula 'by their own request.'" Karpov called on the USSR's Sports Committee to compel clubs to honor their contracts with their coaches.[54]

Yet Ovchinnikov's departure seemed to inspire Dinamo's players. Under the direction of assistant coach Ravil Zalialiev, the team won its next two games, both at home, with scores of 3–0 and 2–0. A win on the road in the next contest would ensure the team's stay in next season's First League. On November 1, it did just that with a 1–0 victory over Kiev's Army Sports Club. A local Ukrainian correspondent reported "much rejoicing" in Dinamo's locker room.[55] Fediakov told his television audience that it no longer needed to "worry about the fate of our Dinamo."[56]

Dinamo earned these wins; they were not giveaways or thrown contests. On October 22 at home, it defeated Odessa's Army Sports Club, a team also struggling at the time to avoid relegation. Odessa's loss contributed to its own finish in twentieth place and demotion to the second league.[57] Kiev's team also fought to avoid relegation. With its loss to Dinamo, it ended the year in twenty-first place and banishment to the second league. Dinamo played so well in Kiev that, according to an inspector in attendance, it won the approval of many of the five thousand spectators.[58] In something of an anticlimax, Dinamo played its last game of the season, November 5, in Voroshilovgrad, to a 1–1 tie. The club ended the season in fifteenth place among twenty-four teams with fifteen wins, eight ties, nineteen losses, and thirty-eight points. It was a close call, but Kirov survived to see another day in the First League. "Many thousands of Dinamo's fans in the city and region of Kirov," Kolomensky reported, "breathed a sigh of relief."[59]

Dinamo was no doubt fatigued at the end of the season, but it still had more matches to go. Moscow sent the team to Laos, Kampuchea, and Vietnam for eight friendlies from November 28 to December 14 with local and national teams.[60] Several games drew thirty thousand spectators. A match in Kampuchea attracted seventy thousand fans. Ho Chi Minh City hosted a game in 40-degree-Celsius weather (104 degrees Fahrenheit). Dinamo won six of the eight. It lost to a Laos army team coached by a former Soviet goalie and tied with the Ho Chi Minh City team.[61]

Perhaps Dinamo's players understood the trip as something of a reward for their late-season success.[62] If so, the collegium of the regional sports committee

Dinamo in Vietnam, 1982. *Courtesy of Lev Isupov.*

thought the team's management should be rewarded as well. On November 18, it bestowed its chair, Mazurenko, with a badge of honor "For the Development of Physical Culture and Sport." At the same time, it awarded Zalialiev the title "Distinguished Representative of Physical Culture and Sport." The collegium made no mention of Ovchinnikov.[63]

The celebratory awards temporarily masked serious problems. The team had barely avoided relegation. Its key players, now a year older, would tire more quickly in 1983. In their postseason assessments, both Chudinovskikh and Kolomensky confided that the young players on the team, when asked to play for injured veterans, had performed poorly.[64] Much had been made the previous year of the performance of Kirov's youngster, Leonid Shatunov, who in 1981 had played in twenty-three games. In 1982, however, he matched up poorly against skilled First League competitors and appeared in only three games. Chudinovskikh and Kolomensky continued to complain of the poor state of youth football in the Kirov region. It was an unlikely source of recruits in the foreseeable future.

As in the past, Dinamo needed still more financial assistance locally and from Moscow. First Mazurenko then Dinamo's deputy chair, Mikhail Sergeev, asked Kirov's governing organs and the Russian Republic's Dinamo soviet for help in completing construction of the training base in Poroshino.[65] In Kirov,

Shatunov, 1982. *Courtesy of GAKO.*

the stadium needed major work. It still had, as Chudinovskikh put it in November, "an antediluvian scoreboard" and stands that "are an anachronism in our rapidly changing century."[66]

And just when Dinamo needed financial support at year's end to fill its roster for the upcoming season, Mazurenko told the Russian Republic's soviet that Kirov's Dinamo society was bankrupt. He used the same language employed in earlier appeals: on November 16, he wrote that his Dinamo society found itself in "an extremely difficult financial situation." The State Bank's regional branch refused to extend any more credits and threatened to cut off public utilities. Mazurenko asked for 50,000 rubles to cover his organization's debts.[67]

With Mazurenko again hat in hand, Dinamo, now something less than a winner, had to admit to financial irregularities, including excessive expenditures in the season just completed. On December 16, 1982, the Russian Republic's Sports

Committee launched yet another campaign to rein in costs incurred by professional football teams. It instructed regional committees to review the finances of their teams and report their findings by January 15, 1983.[68] On January 7, chair of the regional sports committee Vasilii Ochnev responded. He found what he surely already knew to be the case. Dinamo had shortchanged visiting teams of their legally required share of gate receipts. Moreover, the club had exceeded by 22 percent (32,400 rubles) the amount allowed for expenditures on training camps. And it had received, by purchase implicitly, more than the allowable amount of sports equipment.[69] He said nothing about excessive benefits. His disclosures nevertheless meant that in the coming season, a chastened Dinamo would have to cut costs even as it struggled to remain in the First League. The city's Young Communist League remained willing to help. In April 1983, it again pledged ten rubles each to Dinamo's two best players in the upcoming season's home games.[70]

Dinamo's promotion to the First League was exciting for the team's supporters. Initially, the club's performance justified fans' fondest hopes even as doubts arose about the long-term effect of its coach's tactics. The season then unraveled; the team seemed doomed to relegation. After firing the head coach before the end of the season, a miracle finish saved the day. Dinamo would live to see another year in the First League but was forced to ask once again for more money to support the foundering club. The Dinamo organization was also forced to admit to financial irregularities, which left them even more vulnerable to criticism or censure, as they were no longer winners. Further losses would make the team even more vulnerable.

NOTES

1. This and additional information below on Dinamo's poor behavior is in documentation provided on February 4, 1982, by V. I. Nikolaev, a deputy chair of the Russian Republic's Dinamo soviet, in the State Archive for the Social and Political History of the Kirov Region (GASPI KO), f. R-6766, op. 1, d. 807, l. 14.

2. GASPI KO, f. R-6766, op. 1, d. 807, l. 14.

3. Dinamo played its first game on the very day, January 26, it arrived in Moscow. Weary from travel, it lost the match 6–1. Chudinovskikh, who attended the game, allowed that Kirov's athletes were not accustomed to playing on an artificial surface. V. Chudinovskikh, "Strogii ekzamentor," *Kirovskaia pravda*, January 28, 1982, 4. See reports on the tournament by Kirov's television in GASPI KO, f. R-6818, op. 5, d. 1547, l. 169 and d. 1548, l. 14.

4. GASPI KO, f. R-6766, op. 1, d. 807, ll. 14–15. It was not the first time Chikishev appeared drunk in public. In February 1978, an inebriated Chikishev cursed loudly in the Sport café in Kirov: GASPI KO, f. R-6766, op. 1, d. 721, l. 8.

5. GASPI KO, f. R-6766, op. 1, d. 807, l. 14.

6. See information in a letter of February 4, 1982, from the Russian Republic's Dinamo soviet to Mazurenko: GASPI KO, f. R-6766, op. 1, d. 807, l. 15.

7. See reports on the games in *Kirovskaia pravda*, February 25 and 27, March 3 and 6, 1982, and by Kirov's television in GASPI KO, f. R-6818, op. 5, d. 1549, ll. 86, 122 and d. 1550, ll. 25, 38, 89.

8. V. Chudinovskikh, "Stali prizerami," *Kirovskaia pravda*, February 2, 1982, 4.

9. GASPI KO, f. P-1656, op. 33, d. 11, ll. 9, 33. As before, after making the initial payment, the municipal committee assigned the responsibility to Komsomol district committees and cells in the city.

10. GASPI KO, f. R-6818, op. 5, d. 1634, l. 84.

11. GASPI KO, f. R-6818, op. 5, d. 1634, l. 85.

12. An interview conducted at the aforementioned preseason USSR Cup in Armenia, in *Futbol-Khokkei*, no. 10, March 7, 1982, 13.

13. "Zdravstvui, futbol," *Kirovskaia pravda*, April 9, 1982, 4.

14. See an inspector's report on the game and efforts by the Dinamo club to make the field as playable as possible: State Archive of the Russian Federation (GARF), f. R-7676, op. 31, d. 8209, ll. 495–496. This and other inspectors of games in the First League submitted their reports to the Governing Board for Football of the USSR's Sports Committee. Bad weather continued through April to make for a poor playing field at Shinnik: see inspectors' reports from late April in GARF, f. R-7576, op. 31, d. 8209, ll. 443–444.

15. See the inspector's report in GARF, f. R-7576, op. 31, d. 8209, ll. 431–432.

16. See the inspector's report in GARF, f. R-7576, op. 31, d. 8209, ll. 418–419.

17. *Komsomol'skoe plemia*, July 15, 1982, 4. A report to the First League's office gave the field's condition a 4 out of a possible 5: GARF, f. R-7576, op. 31, d. 8205, l. 37.

18. See inspectors' reports on May 14 and 19 in GARF, f. R-7576, op. 31, d. 8209, ll. 393–394, 404–405.

19. *Futbol-Khokkei*, no. 16, April 18, 1982, 10.

20. GASPI KO, f. R-6818, op. 5, d. 1634, ll. 248–249.

21. *Kirovskaia pravda*, May 13, 1982, 4.

22. In addition to Bubnov, Vladimir Statkevich and Oleg Petrovich Kulakov were injured. Later in the year, Kozlovskikh suffered an injury, although he continued to play. A report of September 22, 1982, noted that chiefly because of injuries, Oleg Kulakov, Sergei Bazulev, Anatolii Usatov, and Vladimir Ivanovich Parkhomenko played for the double. See *Kirovskaia pravda*, September 22, 1982, 4.

23. Interview in March 1982, in *Futbol-Khokkei*, no. 10, March 7, 1982, 13.

24. Valerii Karpov, "Zagadki i razgadki," *Futbol-Khokkei*, no. 20, May 16, 1982, 6–7. Karpov indicated his own bias—he wanted Dinamo and other teams to put less emphasis on winning. Rather than relying on more skilled but older players,

they should focus on the development of young players who might soon be of value to teams in the Higher League.

25. GARF, f. R-7576, op. 31, d. 8209, ll. 378–379.

26. GARF, f. R-7576, op. 31, d. 8205, l. 60. That year, Bazulev played in thirty-three of Dinamo's forty-two regular season games.

27. See an inspector's report in GARF, f. R-7576, op. 31, d. 8209, ll. 333–334.

28. V. Chudinovskikh, "Ne nashli vernyi put,'" *Kirovskaia pravda*, June 13, 1982, 4. As of June 20, Dinamo had five wins, six ties, and six losses. An article in the national press was more upbeat about the club: A. Leont'ev, "Priroda neudach," *Futbol-Khokkei*, no. 24, June 13, 1982, 3. As a debutante, the author noted, the team played well. However, the paper's correspondent wrote this piece when Dinamo had played only fourteen games and occupied eighth place in the league.

29. "Au, forvardy," *Komsomol'skoe plemia*, June 15, 1982, 4.

30. See information in V. Chudinovskikh, "Ot vorot povorot," *Kirovskaia pravda*, July 1, 1982, 4. Kolchanov negotiated with I. A. Mil'chakov, an official of the Rodina sports club. There had been a plan to use the Rodina stadium earlier for regular season games. In late 1980 and early 1981, Dinamo had used the Rodina sports club's facilities for training: see the interview of Ovchinnikov in B. Kolomensky, "Poka molchat tribuny," *Komsomol'ksia plemia*, January 24, 1981, 4.

31. V. Chudinovskikh, "Ot vorot povorot," *Kirovskaia pravda*, July 1, 1982, 4.

32. B. Kolomensky, "V poiskakh priiuta, ili gde treniruiutsia debiutantam pervoi ligi," *Komsomol'skoe plemia*, July 1, 1982, 4.

33. Kolomensky, "V poiskakh priiuta, ili gde treniruiutsia debiutantam pervoi ligi," 4.

34. GAKO, f. R-1363, op. 4, d. 1780, l. 86. On August 22, 1982, the national newspaper, *Futbol-Khokkei*, published an article critical of five playing surfaces at stadiums of the First League, including Dinamo's, that "did not meet elementary requirements." Garrinal'd Nemirovsky, "Bez sushchestvennykh izmenenii," *Futbol-Khokkei*, no. 34, August 22, 1982, 5. The author was also critical of the transportation and hotel accommodations provided to visiting teams. It is curious that inspectors throughout the second half of the year had usually given Dinamo's field a rating of 4 out of 5: GARF, f. R-7576, op. 31, d. 8206, ll. 28, 70, 80, 112, 122, 178, 189, 218.

35. *Komsomol'skoe plemia*, July 15, 1982, 4.

36. On July 26, Dinamo played the young Ethiopian national team. Dinamo won 3–1. *Kirovskaia pravda*, July 28, 1982, 4. The game drew 6,049 fans and 8,300 rubles. It is one of the few occasions that we know the precise attendance and gate: see information from the Finance-Planning Department of Kirov's regional Dinamo soviet, January 9, 1983, in GASPI KO, f. R-6766, op. 1, d. 823, l. 31.

37. B. Kolomensky, "Kak utverzhdat'sia v sedle?," *Komsomol'skoe plemia*, July 17, 1982, 4.

38. V. Chudinovskikh, "Ataka—put' k uspekhu," *Kirovskaia pravda*, July 27, 1982, 4.

39. GASPI KO, f. R-6818, op. 5, d. 1560, l. 12. The game was played on July 30.

40. GASPI KO, f. R-6818, op. 5, d. 1637, l. 273.

41. B. Kolomensky, "Igrat' tak, chtoby kazhdyi match zapomnilsia," *Komsomol'skoe plemia*, July 29, 1982, 4.

42. Evgenii Kucherevsky, "Vybor puti," *Futbol-Khokkei*, no. 31, August 1, 1982, 5.

43. V. Chudinovskikh, "My verim v Vas, rebiata!," *Kirovskaia pravda*, August 24, 1982, 4.

44. Chudinovskikh, "My verim v Vas, rebiata!," 4.

45. GARF, f. R-7576, op. 31, d. 8201, ll. 116–118. The session adopted a resolution that pro forma labeled Ovchinnikov's work "satisfactory" but more significantly called on Ovchinnikov to carefully consider the advice issued to him that day. Ovchinnikov may well have missed Dinamo's game on the twenty-eighth in Volgograd.

46. GARF, f. R-7576, op. 31, d. 8202, ll. 67–68. Starikov played in thirty-eight of Dinamo's forty-two games that year.

47. Valerii Ovchinnikov, "Znakomimsia i uchimsia," *Futbol-Khokkei*, no. 37, October 12, 1982, 6–7. Ovchinnikov also thought that some of his younger players, on whom he relied in midseason, had not played well.

48. V. Chudinovskikh, "Byt' ili ne byt'? Etot vopros ostro vstal pered dinamovtsami," *Kirovskaia pravda*, October 17, 1982, 4.

49. Kolchanov so told Chudinovskikh: V. Chudinovskikh, "Byt' ili ne byt'?" In 2008, Chudinovskikh asked Kolchanov what the reason was for Ovchinnikov's dismissal. Kolchanov responded that the coach resented that Chernozubov—not he, Ovchinnikov—was awarded the title "Meritorious Coach of the Russian Republic" at the close of the 1981 season. Out of personal pique, Ovchinnikov decided that he could not work with Chernozubov. One of them had to go, and Mazurenko supported Chernozubov. Thus "Ovchinnikov picked up his suitcase." See Chudinovskikh, *Ispoved'*, 39. In my June 12, 1983, conversation with Lev Isupov, who played for Dinamo from 1972 through 1986, he mentioned Ovchinnikov's pique as a reason for his dismissal or resignation. It is curious, to say the least, that Ovchinnikov would wait so long to precipitate his dismissal and at such a critical moment in the team's season. Moreover, although it is true that Ovchinnikov, despite a nomination, did not receive the honor, he was nominated for an award as one of the ten best coaches in the Russian Republic. Ovchinnikov went on to a successful career as a coach for teams in Tiumen', Ordzhonikidze (Vladikavkaz), Tallinn, Nizhnii Novgorod, and Cheliabinsk, among others. In an October 2, 2016, interview at Kirov's Dinamo Stadium, Usupov told me that Ovchinnikov had been a good coach. He indicated that the relationship between Ovchinnikov and Chernozubov was a tense one. Neither Kirov's television nor

its radio reported Ovchinnikov's dismissal. The center's dissatisfaction with Ovchinnikov, as previously discussed, certainly contributed to his dismissal.

50. B. Kolomensky, "Sezon debiuta i ispytanii," *Komsomol'skoe plemia*, November 18, 1982, 4.

51. Kolomensky, "Sezon debiuta i ispytanii," 4. In a 1992 interview, Ovchinnikov mentioned that he had gained in football circles the nickname of Martin Bormann. See the report on the interview in Simon Kuper, *Soccer against the Enemy*, 2nd ed. (New York: Nation Books, 2006), 42. It was said that he had been so named because of a remarkable physical resemblance. It is tempting to add that Ovchinnikov might have earned the moniker because of his demanding ways. In the interview, Ovchinnikov insisted that the nickname resulted from his administration of a club's books in much the same way that Bormann had managed the finances of the Nazi Party's insurance fund. I have found no reference to "Martin Bormann" during the period Ovchinnikov coached Kirov's Dinamo. In my correspondence with them, neither Kolomensky nor Chudinovskikh recalled its use at that time.

52. Interview of Ovchinnikov in *Sport-Ekspress*, October 27, 2006, https://www.sport-express.ru/newspaper/2006-10-27/9_1/.

53. Nor did Ovchinnikov elaborate on his dismissal in his brief autobiography when addressing his relationship with Mazurenko. He simply referred to "negative experiences." See http://www.loko.nnov.ru/borman/biography.htm.

54. Valerii Karpov, "Trener i ego komanda," *Futbol-Khokkei*, no. 44, October 31, 1982, 12–13. Quote on 13.

55. P. Leiko, a correspondent of the newspaper *Molodezh' Ukraina*, "Tak mnogo znachila igra," *Komsomol'skoe plemia*, November 4, 1982, 4. Bubnov played especially well.

56. GASPI KO, f. R-6818, op. 5, d. 1566, l. 35.

57. An inspector wrote that it was a hard-fought contest in which both teams played well with frequent counterattacks: GARF, f. R-7576, op. 31, d. 8209, ll. 48–49.

58. GARF, f. R-7576, op. 31, d. 8209, ll. 18–19.

59. B. Kolomensky, "Sezon debiuta i ispytanii," *Komsomol'skoe plemia*, November 18, 1982, 4.

60. On the decision in early November to send Dinamo to Southeast Asia, see Mazurenko's letter to Dinamo's central soviet, November 10, 1982, in GASPI KO, f. R-6766, op. 1, d. 807, l. 105. This letter indicates that Dinamo would spend eighteen days abroad, beginning on November 25.

61. See a report in *Kirovskaia pravda*, December 16, 1982, 4, and an account by Dinamo's general manager, Chernozubov: V. Chernozubov, "Pod zharkim nebom Azii," *Komsomol'skoe plemia*, December 28, 1982, 8. For the dates and results of the eight games, see Z. Dushkin, *Oni igrali "Dinamo": Fotoal'bom: Istoriia*

komandy, predstavliaavshei v pervenstvakh RSFSR i SSSR po futbolu Kirov. obl. sovet Vsesoiuz. fizkul'turno-sportivnogo obshchestva "Dinamo" (Kirov: Kirovskaia oblastnaia tipografiia, 2013), 89.

62. On the way, team members received sports equipment worth 1,577 rubles (shoes, jerseys, warm-up suits, sports bags) to distribute to players and administrators abroad. They probably kept some of the items for themselves and picked up many other valuable items on the way. On distribution of equipment, see GASPI KO, f. R-6766, op. 1, d. 825, l. 29.

63. GAKO, f. R-1363, op. 4, d. 1788, l. 112. Nor did the collegium mention Ovchinnikov at its next session, December 16, 1982: GAKO, f. R-1363, op. 4, d. 1788, ll. 146–151. Earlier, on November 22, the presidium of Dinamo's regional soviet approved a request from Ovchinnikov, the nature of which is unspecified: GASPI KO, f. R-6766, op. 1, d. 808, l. 94.

64. V. Chudinovskikh, "Novichka. Nelegkii put,'" *Kirovskaia pravda*, November 11, 1982, 4; B. Kolomensky, "Sezon detiuta i ispytanii," *Komsomol'skoe plemia*, November 18, 1982, 4.

65. See Mazurenko's request in April in GASPI KO, f. R-6766, op. 1, d. 807, l. 58 and Sergeev's request in December in GASPI KO, f. R-6766, op. 1, d. 807, l. 112. In 1983, work was still ongoing at the base: GASPI KO, f. R-6766, op. 1, d. 824, ll. 70, 89. By December 1983, the base could accommodate Dinamo: GASPI KO, f. R-6766, op. 1, d. 824, l. 122.

66. Chudinovskikh, "Novichka. Nelegkii put,'" 4.

67. GASPI KO, f. R-6766, op. 1, d. 818, l. 28.

68. GAKO, f. R-1636, op. 4, d. 1877, l. 80.

69. GAKO, f. R-1363, op. 4, d. 1877, l. 79. Dinamo had assigned for training camps a total of 280 days rather than the allowed 250. Chernozubov may have taken the fall for these financial irregularities.

70. GASPI KO, f. P-1656, op. 34, d. 3, ll. 182, 205.

8

DEAD LAST

In 1983, Dinamo's play lacked all the drama of the previous year. From midseason to finish, it occupied the First League's basement. The year before, Valerii Ovchinnikov had been dismissed for reasons never adequately explained. Soon after Dinamo's Southeast Asia trip, general manager Viacheslav Chernozubov left without explanation.[1]

Self-Hypnosis

Ravil Zalialiev replaced Chernozubov, and Boris Evgen'evich Iakovlev became the new head coach. Neither inspired much confidence. Zalialiev had been Dinamo's assistant coach from 1979 through the 1982 season. His new post required far more responsibilities. Iakovlev came with a relatively unimpressive resume to coach a team in the First League. To be sure, he had been a head coach since 1957 and had guided a team in the Higher League, the Army Sports Club of Rostov-on-Don, in 1972 and 1973. That squad, however, finished twelfth in his first year there and sixteenth and last in his second season. In the two years before his appointment to Kirov's Dinamo, Iakovlev coached a second league team, Riazan's Spartak, to a ninth- and then eleventh-place finish in a zone of sixteen teams.[2]

Kirov's Dinamo had barely avoided relegation in 1982. It needed talented reinforcements to ensure an improved performance in 1983. And yet it lost key players from its squad when it could not match better offers by other clubs. Three players left for teams in the Higher League. Vladimir Parkhomenko left for Donetsk's Shakhter. Sergei Bazulev departed for Moscow's Spartak. Vladimir Anatel'evich Er'ko went to Moscow's Dinamo. Three other prominent players from the 1982 squad left for teams in the second league.[3]

Parkhomenko, 1982. *Courtesy of GAKO.*

Iakovlev nevertheless seemed confident. He would stock his new team, he said, with skilled youngsters from the region. On January 12, he told Viktor Chudinovskikh, "I believe that the team must consist basically of local players." Iakovlev rose from his chair and walked to a wall to point to photographs of Kirov's own. "There they are, one, a second, a third, a seventh."[4] The next month, Iakovlev told Boris Kolomensky of the need for a "fundamental reliance on local players."[5]

Iakovlev surely knew better. Local prospects could contribute little to a team competing in the First League. He hoped that one local athlete might help. Iakovlev immediately pursued the region's star, Aleksandr Kozlovskikh, to convince him to remain with the team for one more year. After a subpar and injury-riddled season in 1982, Kozlovskikh decided to enter Moscow's Advanced Coaches School.[6] Iakovlev successfully convinced him to stay home to play and also serve as one of the team's assistant coaches.⁷ Kozlovskikh proceeded to have a good year, playing in forty games (four more than in the previous season) and scoring ten goals. His teammates did not fare as well.

Iakovlev set out to recruit talented players from other teams. He and Zalialiev pursued a number of them too aggressively, or so it seemed. In early January, the USSR's Football Federation told Kirov's Dinamo that First League regulations permitted Dinamo to sign only three of the four players it now sought from other squads.⁸ Yet, as in so many other instances involving transfers and benefits, the federation was not as good as its word. Dinamo proceeded to sign and play that year all four athletes in question.⁹ "We now have," Zalialiev told Kirov's radio listeners on April 8, the eve of the new season, "experienced players."¹⁰

Iakovlev's hopes notwithstanding, there was cause for concern about the skills of the four new recruits even if they had not come cheaply. Three left a team in the second league. Only Sergei Anatol'evich Kamzulin had played for a club, Kostroma's Spartak, in the First League, and it had just finished in twenty-second place, seven places below Dinamo. Two recruits from the second league, Evgeni Borisovich Khrabrostin and Vladimir Semenovich Peregontsev, had likely seen their best days. The former was thirty-one, and Peregontsev had just turned thirty-four. Two additional signees from other teams, Viktor Danilovich Buivolov and Viktor Borisovich Kas'ian, came to Kirov from clubs in the second league.

Yet Dinamo's performance in several preseason tournaments gave doubters reason to pause and fans cause for optimism. In the tournament of Dinamo teams held in Moscow in late January, after two initial losses (one to Moscow's Dinamo with a score of 1–0), Kirov's entry tied teams from Samarkand and Barnaul. It then lost to Vologda. In the subsequent USSR's Cup, Dinamo played in two games, winning its first on February 19 in Ashkhabad and losing its second in Sochi on February 24. The loss, however, came on penalty kicks after a 0–0 tie in regulation and after an overtime period.¹¹ Taking hope from these games as well as from the previous year's season-ending surge, on March 25, Kirov's regional Dinamo soviet complimented its team on its apparent ability to fulfill its given task "to hold on to its place in the First League."¹²

Dinamo began the regular season as if it might well justify the soviet's praise. It achieved a 0–0 tie in its first two games, both away games. A road tie was rightly considered a moral victory and, better yet, a point in the standings. Dinamo returned to play its first home game on April 17 at Shinnik, because its own stadium was once again undergoing repairs. The venue in no way dampened the city's or region's enthusiasm. "Long before the match's beginning at 6:30 p.m., fans had filled up the stadium's stands" on this cloudy and cold

Sunday of 3 degrees Celsius (37 degrees Fahrenheit).[13] They were not disappointed. Dinamo won a "convincing victory," as Kirov's television reported, 3–0. Kozlovskikh scored one of the goals.[14] Even more supporters, fifty-eight hundred, gathered three days later for the next game, also at Shinnik. It went badly; the home team lost 2–1. It was the first of a string of defeats and mounting bitter disappointment.

The Monotony of Defeat

After a loss and a tie on the road, Dinamo lost at home, on May 4, before a Wednesday crowd of fifty-eight hundred in 3-degree-Celsius weather (37 degrees Fahrenheit). "Our players looked lifeless," Chudinovskikh observed. "They lost naturally enough," Kolomensky wrote. "We have a right to demand more," he added, "of players and coaches for last year demonstrated how such insipid play is fraught with consequences."[15] Two more ties at home on May 7 and 21 provoked the headline "Again a Struggle for Survival" and the comment "Once more Kirov's players have disappointed their followers."[16] Dinamo had scored only seven goals in eleven games, "a result, of course," Kirov's television reported, "beneath contempt."[17] Kolomensky responded to a win on May 24 with the banner "At Long Last a Victory."[18]

Perhaps Kolomensky meant his article's title to be somewhat sarcastic. At that point, Dinamo had won only two of twelve matches, tying six and losing four. The national press's coverage of Kirov's Dinamo was not so coy. At the end of May, Valerii Karpov chastised the team for boring defensive play designed to gain a tie and thus a single point in the standings. Dinamo was "like a hen adding as if by one grain at a time a point to its money-box."[19]

Dinamo's play did not improve. "Again a Loss" and "Another Tie," the region's newspapers announced in June.[20] After a home loss on June 15, Dinamo had only two wins to go, with seven ties and seven losses. *Komsomol'skoe plemia* headlined "Heading for the Second League?"[21] A home win on July 5 prompted Chudinovskikh to ask, "Perhaps everything is fine with the team?" He hastily answered, "Not so."[22] On June 16, Kirov's television announced that the team was at the bottom of the standings and "there's no room for it to retreat any farther."[23] Dwindling attendance exemplified fans' loss of hope. On June 18, a Saturday in pleasant weather of 20 degrees Celsius (68 degrees Fahrenheit) only two thousand came to watch yet another tie at home.

At midseason, after twenty-one games, Dinamo occupied twentieth place in the league with a record of three wins, ten ties, and eight losses. Chudinovskikh's assessment was brutal. Players lacked the necessary skills and, worse, physical conditioning. The staff, Iakovlev in particular, had failed to demand more from their athletes.[24] The coach had erred badly when he permitted some of the team's veterans, outsiders with homes in Moscow, to stay in the capital on their way back from road trips. They were allowed to do so as well during a break in the home schedule. Dinamo thereby became a house divided, split into "Moscow" and "Kirov" camps, the latter resentful of the privileged treatment of the Muscovites.[25] Iakovlev realized his mistake too late. "The seeds of individualism and fragmentation had already taken root."[26]

The two outsider recruits, Khrabrostin and Peregontsev, played especially poorly and antagonized fans, coaches, and fellow teammates. Before a home game on May 24, Khrabrostin loudly and effusively cursed his fellow players.[27] After appearing in only fourteen games, he was released. Shortly thereafter, the team benched Peregontsev, who had appeared in only fourteen games as well. With Khrabrostin and Peregontsev in mind, Kolomensky blamed Iakovlev for a "blind reliance on fading stars."[28] Their poor play prompted Chudinovskikh to insist in desperation on the need to somehow find local boys to play. A professional football team "is strong when its roots are in the soil, the sporting honor of which it defends."[29] He pleaded in vain, as he surely knew.

Chudinovskikh proceeded to acknowledge, as he had many times before, the poor state of youth and amateur football in the region. Even the roster of Dinamo's second string contained relatively few skilled local athletes. Coaches of the region's amateur teams continued to focus on winning games by relying on veterans rather than by developing young prospects. Scandalous behavior by young players made matters worse. At a tournament of the region's best youth teams in September, a player from one squad joined a gang that broke into a hotel to attack a competitor.[30] Later in the year, the much-ballyhooed youngster from Kirov, Leonid Shatunov, just twenty years of age, ran afoul of the region's sports committee. It provisionally disqualified him from playing for one year for poor performance and other inappropriate but unspecified behavior.[31]

Kirov's regional government also harshly judged the team's players and staff. With the season only a little more than half over, Kirov's sports committee and the regional football federation formed a commission to review the team's performance. In its report issued in late August, it faulted Zalialiev and Kolchanov for "malfeasance and shortcomings."[32] On September 2, the presidium of Kirov's regional Dinamo soviet blamed Zalialiev, Kolchanov, Iakovlev, and the team's doctor, Anatolii Chikishev. Zalialiev proved incapable of coping with his duties. Kolchanov exercised "weak supervision" over the team and its staff. Iakovlev recruited and signed "outsider graybeards." Chikishev failed to provide regular medical examinations. Perhaps hoping that declarative judgments might turn the season around, the presidium issued a "stern warning" to Iakovlev and reprimanded Kolchanov.[33]

Local officials and fans alike thought the harsh verdicts were fully justified. Dinamo's performance deteriorated in the second half of the season. On August 2, it lost 6–1 on the road in Voroshilovgrad. After another loss at home on August 8, Chudinovskikh turned to the realm of boxing to characterize the team's sorry state. Dinamo, he said, "has suffered a knockdown."[34] In its report on the same game, Kirov's television told its viewers that "again Dinamo's players have brought grief to their followers."[35] On August 21, Valentin Vasil'evich Fedorov, a Master of Sport of the USSR since 1943 and Meritorious Coach of the Russian Republic since 1965, denounced Dinamo's performance in *Futbol-Khokkei*. The club relied on outsiders who cared little about representing the city and region of Kirov. Peregontsev, Evgenii Borisovich Khrabostin, and Kamzulin, in particular, had performed poorly. But everyone was responsible for the team's dismal play, coaches and athletes alike. "It seems," Fedorov concluded, "that players and coaches have given up and only a miracle can save the team from relegation to the second league."[36] A week later in the weekly, Aleksei Leont'ev, a former player and now member of the presidium of the RSFSR's Football Federation, took the occasion of Dinamo's loss in Voroshilovgrad to point out that the opponent's forward had scored five goals under the "personal tutelage" of Dinamo's defender, Kamzulin.[37] On August 27, Dinamo's occupancy of last place in the league's standings prompted the headline in *Komsomol'skoe plemia*: "Done For."[38]

Fans inundated the press with denunciations of the team's play.[39] Attendance dwindled to two thousand and then to eight hundred at one game late in the season. In admittedly bad conditions, 6 degrees Celsius (43 degrees Fahrenheit) and rain mixed with snow, many of that latter group left early.[40] Mounting losses and a "shabby stadium with stands still under repair" further soured fans' mood.[41] Earlier in the season, in mid-May, "overheated" fans repeatedly and loudly cursed during games. One spectator complained that law enforcement largely ignored such behavior.[42] The police did eventually increase their presence and added more volunteer security personnel.[43]

After a road loss on September 6, Chudinovskikh repeated his previous year's declaration "To Be or Not to Be."[44] Six days later, Kirov's television reported that Dinamo's chances to remain in the First League "are only theoretical."[45] On September 17, after still another loss, Chudinovskikh "flunked the team for its play." Dinamo could "feel the breath," he observed, "of the second league on its neck."[46] After so many losses, a rare win on September 18 against one of the worst clubs in the league was "no cause for joy," as *Kirovskaia pravda* put it.[47] Kirov's television announced ruefully that "this is only the fifth victory of our team this season."[48]

Dinamo lost its last nine games, four of them at home. *Kirovskaia pravda* and the city's television and radio monotonously covered the defeats: "Again a loss," they declared, "Dinamo continues to lose," "Dinamo suffers another loss," "Yet again a defeat."[49] Like the team, by season's end, *Kirovskaia pravda*'s sports desk was a spent force. For the final game of the season, a 1–0 loss at home, the paper reported only the score. Dinamo finished dead last in twenty-second place, with five wins, eleven ties, and twenty-six losses, a full five points (and three wins) behind the team ahead of it. Its opponents had outscored it by a margin of sixty-three to twenty-nine. On the road, Dinamo won no contests, achieved five ties, and lost sixteen times, outscored by thirty-seven to eight.

Your Just Desserts

Harsh postmortem analyses, one tripping over the other, followed the team and its sponsor, now losers. On November 9, only four days after the final game, Kirov's sports committee criticized Kolchanov, Iakovlev, and Zalialiev. In a thinly veiled reference to the side trips of players to Moscow, the collegium denounced Iakovlev for "insufficient toughness" in allowing "violations of proper regimen." "The team was not a single cohesive whole." It called for Iakovlev's dismissal, rebuked Zalialiev, and "sternly reprimanded" Kolchanov.[50]

On November 16, the presidium of Kirov's regional Dinamo soviet chaired by Mazurenko approved the sports committee's harsh recommendations and reprimands. It then criticized a number of players, including, ominously, local boys, heretofore almost untouchable. The soviet singled out Iurii Vladimirovich Starikov, who joined Dinamo in 1976 at the age of nineteen; Lev Isupov, who joined in 1972 when he was sixteen; Sergei Erdiakov, who joined in 1973 at eighteen; and the stellar goalie, Sergei Bubnov, who joined the team in 1975 when nineteen.[51] As previously mentioned, Kirov's sports committee had already disciplined another of Kirov's own, Shatunov. It had also, later in the season, placed Erdiakov and Isupov on two years' probation for unspecified violations of "sports regimen."[52]

Meanwhile, on November 10, *Kirovskaia pravda* printed Chudinovskikh's postmortem.[53] Although Iakovlev had mistakenly relied on "experienced players." Chudinovskikh admitted that the Kirov region could not provide capable replacements. Iakovlev had been insufficiently tough on many of the players. In contrast to the previous year's staff, the club's current coaches, Iakovlev and

Starikov. *Courtesy of GAKO.*

Zalialiev, "were gentle, and democratic, who saw in their players not robots but people." "But football players," Chudinovskikh continued, "are grownup adults who do not appreciate kindness. More than that, they considered it a weakness." On that same day, November 10, Kolomensky published his conclusions in *Komsomol'skoe plemia*. Iakovlev had relied on "fading stars," notably Khrabrostin and Peregontsev, neither of whom wanted "to work for the glory of a Dinamo that was completely alien to them."[54] Kolomensky went further, however, than people on the field in assigning blame. He chastised the regional Dinamo soviet and Kirov's sports committee for hiring Iakovlev in the first place.

Speaking for the regional sports committee, its chair, Vasilii Ochnev, seemed to agree in an article in *Kirovskaia pravda* almost a month later.[55] But he would go only so far. After acknowledging his committee's "own guilt" for the team's relegation to the second league, Ochnev deflected much of the blame by saying that his agency had been too kind. It had not "always been sufficiently strict and

Isupov. *Courtesy of GAKO.*

principled," implicitly with Iakovlev and Zalialiev and their policies. The sports committee would proceed to focus its attention not on signing "outsider 'stars'" but on working with "local boys."

The unkindest cut of all came at the end of the year. On December 27, the Russian Republic's Dinamo soviet took Iakovlev to task more harshly than any of his detractors in Kirov had done. When compiling the team's roster, he "had invited a group of hopeless players who had been dismissed from other teams for poor play." Insufficient toughness on his part meant that "players failed to take training and the games seriously."[56]

The national soviet proceeded to acknowledge a more fundamental underlying reason for its disgust with the performance of Kirov's Dinamo and other teams as well. Their fans had abandoned them in droves with a resulting "financial deficit." The agency knew all too well that gate receipts even in the best of years hardly covered costs. Its subsequent demand, therefore, was all the more ominous. Kirov's professional club and others like it should adopt "the strictest measures in limiting expenses."[57] In so many words, if a club spent lavishly, the team had to win or else.

Kirov could hardly have been surprised. Several months before, Mazurenko again turned to Dinamo's central soviet with an urgent plea for financial help. He needed more than 300,000 rubles to complete repairs on a number of the region's sports facilities, but chiefly Dinamo's stadium. Kirov's regional soviet and regional party committee had promised to help, as had a number of local enterprises. Perhaps they might provide some assistance, but Mazurenko wanted Moscow to immediately provide 113,000 rubles to cover outstanding debts. To justify his request, he turned egregiously disingenuous. Funds were needed to cover the repair of the stadium of a First League team where "a large number of spectators have attended games."[58] Mazurenko knew well by this point that Dinamo would return to the second league and that attendance had collapsed. Moscow knew it as well.

Declining attendance at football games not only in Kirov but at all levels throughout the USSR made economizing by cutting back on illegal benefits most urgent, especially for losing teams. From 1987 to 1990, attendance for games in the Higher League fell by half. In the First League, average attendance fell from well over 11,000 in 1979 and 1980 to 9,600 in 1981 and 7,600 in 1982.[59] In Kirov, even in its team's better year of 1982, only 4,600 fans attended on average.[60]

It was all too much for Moscow and Kirov. At the season's end, Chudinovskikh candidly acknowledged that the city of Kirov "has not yet arrived at the point where it could be in the First League."[61] This time, the city's Komsomol committee lost interest and made no pledge to provide bonuses to the team's best players in the season to follow.

Improved play in the First League and avoidance of relegation required even greater financial support. It was not forthcoming. A poor choice of new and costly recruits added to the team's woes. Dinamo finished at the bottom of the league and suffered relegation. "The else" in "win or else" now came into play. The loss provoked the disgust of its fans and sports correspondents. It also prompted the condemnation of the team, now a loser, by regional governing bodies and serious charges of fiscal mismanagement by the sport's governing organs in Moscow.

NOTES

1. Perhaps Chernozubov was still blamed for the team's tardy arrival at the Dinamo tourney in January 1982 and failure to show up at Red Square to lay a wreath at Lenin's Mausoleum. Local authorities may also have held him

responsible, fairly or otherwise, for failures that led to talk in *Futbol-Khokkei* that Kirov provided visiting teams with a "most cold reception"—poor transportation upon arrival and poor accommodations. See Garrinal'd Nemirovsky, "Bez sushchestvennykh izmenenii," *Futbol-Khokkei*, no. 34, August 22, 1982, 5. I cannot find information on Chernozubov's career in 1983. In 1984, he became the general manager of Ordzhonikidze's Spartak. He would later have a distinguished career as a sports administrator in Moscow.

2. In 1979 and 1980, Iakovlev coached a First League team, Voronezh's Fakel, to fifth- and tenth-place finishes in a twenty-four-team league.

3. They were Sergei Kozlov, who played in twenty-three games in 1982; Aleksandr Nikolaevich Golokolosov, who played in twenty-nine games; and Vladimir Vasil'evich Statkevich, who had been in twenty-six games. On Bazulev's subsequent career, see V. B. Pomelov, *"Kogda pobedy byli bol'shimi . . .": Ocherki o viatskikh futbolistakh* (Kirov: Gertsenka, 2018), 42–45.

4. V. Chudinovskikh, "Tri voprosa," *Kirovskaia pravda*, March 25, 1983, 4. No doubt Iakovlev pointed to some players who had heretofore been designated for Dinamo's double, the second team, not the main squad. As it turned out, the double in 1983 consisted of relatively few of Kirov's own.

5. B. Kolomensky, "Snova zhivem ozhidaniem," *Komsomol'skoe plemia*, February 2, 1983, 4.

6. Even before the beginning of the 1982 season, Ochnev wrote the Russian Republic's Sports Committee, nominating Kozlovskikh for admission: State Archive of the Kirov Region (GAKO), f. R-1363, op. 4, d. 1782, l. 97. Following the 1982 season, Kozlovskikh remained determined to study there. See Kolomensky's interview in B. Kolomensky, "Aleksandr Kozlovskikh: 'Zaviduiu mal'chishkam,'" *Komsomol'skoe plemia*, November 6, 1982, 4.

7. On Iakovlev's determination to convince Kozlovskikh to stay, see V. Chudinovskikh, "B. Iakovlev. 'Nastroenie delovoe,'" *Kirovskaia pravda*, January 12, 1983, 4.

8. See information on the decision in V. Asaulov, "V interesakh komand i zritelei," *Futbol-Khokkei*, no. 4, January 23, 1983, 7. They were Evgenii Borisovich Khrabrostin, Vladmir Semenovich Peregontsev, Sergei Anatol'evich Kamzulin, and Dmitrii Borisovich Kuritsyn.

9. They were Evgenii Borisovich Khrabrostin, Vladmir Semenovich Peregontsev, Sergei Antol'evich Kamzulin, and Dmitrii Borisovich Kuritsyn.

10. State Archive for the Social and Political History of the Kirov Region (GASPI KO), f. R-6818, op. 5, d. 1788, l. 92.

11. *Kirovskaia pravda*, January 27, 1983, 4, February 2, 1983, 4, and February 26, 1983, 4.

12. GASPI KO, f. R-6766, op. 1, d. 825, l. 15.

13. B. Kolomensky, *Komsomol'skoe plemia*, April 19, 1983, 4.

14. *Kirovskaia pravda*, April 19, 1983, 4. For the television report: GASPI KO, f. R-6818, op. 5, d. 1693, l. 87.

15. V. Chudinovskikh, "Vtoroe porazhenie na svoem pole. Ne mnogo li?," *Kirovskaia pravda*, May 6, 1983, 4. B. Kolomensky, "Pod diktovku gostei," *Komsomol'skoe plemia*, May 7, 1983, 4.

16. B. Kolomensky, "Opiat' bor'ba za vyzhivanie," *Komsomol'skoe plemia*, May 12, 1983, 4. V. Chudinovskikh, "Ne komu bylo zabivat,'" *Kirovskaia pravda*, May 24, 1983, 4.

17. GASPI KO, f. R-6818, op. 5, d. 1697, l. 121.

18. B. Kolomensky, "Nakonets-to pobeda," *Komsomol'skoe plemia*, May 26, 1983, 4.

19. Valerii Karpov, "Chetvert' puti," *Futbol-Khokkei*, no. 22, May 29, 1983, 4.

20. "Snova proigrysh," *Kirovskaia pravda*, June 4, 1983, 4; B. Kolomensky, "Ocherednaia nich'ia," *Komsomol'skoe plemia*, June 14, 1983, 4.

21. "Kurs na vtoruiu ligu?," *Komsomol'skoe plemia*, June 18, 1983, 4. No author.

22. V. Chudinovskikh, "Ataku nachal vratar,'" *Kirovskaia pravda*, July 7, 1983, 4.

23. GASPI KO, f. R-6818, op. 5, d. 1701, l. 34.

24. V. Chudinovskikh, "Defitsit masterstva," *Kirovskaia pravda*, July 13, 1983, 4.

25. In this midseason assessment, Chudinovskikh made only a vague reference to this "violation of the sports training regimen," as he called it. His meaning became clear in his postseason assessment and in an article by Kolomensky. See V. Chudinovskikh, "Sluchainost' ili zakonomernost'? O prichinakh neudachnogo vystupleniia futbolistov kirovskogo 'Dinamo' v nyneshnem sezone," *Kirovskaia pravda*, November 10, 1983, 4 and B. Kolomensky, "Vremia eshche est,'" *Komsomol'skoe plemia*, August 18, 1983, 4.

26. Chudinovskikh, "Sluchainost' ili zakonomernost'?"

27. B. Kolomensky, "Nakonets-to pobeda," *Komsomol'skoe plemia*, May 26, 1983, 4.

28. B. Kolomensky, "Vremia eshche est,'" *Komsomol'skoe plemia*, August 18, 1983, 4. Hoping to catch lightning in a bottle, other teams signed at considerable cost veterans who were well past their prime and only going through the motions: see remarks by Koloskov, head of the Governing Board of the USSR's Sports Committee at a session of the committee's collegium, July 28, 1982, l. 128.

29. V. Chudinovskikh, "Defitsit masterstva," *Kirovskaia pravda*, July 13, 1983, 4.

30. B. Kolomensky, "Kogda raskaliaiutsia strasti," *Komsomol'skoe plemia*, September 22, 1983, 4. See also Kolomensky's comments on coaches in B. Kolomensky, "Kompromiss s sovest'iu," *Komsomol'skoe plemia*, October 4, 1983, 4.

31. See the letter from Ochnev to the Russian Republic's Sports Committee, October 12, 1983, in GAKO, f. R-1363, op. 4, d. 1880, l. 45. In 1983, Shatunov played in nineteen games and scored two goals.

32. See a report on the commission's findings by Ochnev in V. Ochnev, "V opasnoi zone," *Kirovskaia pravda*, August 31, 1983, 4.

33. GASPI KO, f. R-6766, op. 1, d. 825, ll. 52–56, quotations on l. 55 and l. 56.

34. V. Chudinovskikh, "Dinamovtsy igrat' nado!," *Kirovskaia pravda*, August 10, 1983, 4.

35. GASPI KO, f. R-6818, op. 5, d. 1708, l. 53.

36. V. Fedorov, "Vse—v ataku i koe-kto—v zashchitu," *Futbol-Khokkei*, no. 34, August 21, 1983, 4–5, quotation on 5.

37. Aleksei Leont'ev, "Risk na prochnom fundamente," *Futbol-Khokkei*, no. 35, August 28, 1983, 6–7.

38. "Zamknuli tablitsu," *Komsomol'skoe plemia*, August 27, 4.

39. "V opasnoi zone," *Komsomol'skoe plemia*, July 21, 1983, 4; B. Arskii, "Chto vyuchil kommentator?," *Komsomol'skoe plemia*, September 8, 1983, 4.

40. See a report on attendance in L. Opalev, "Porozhenie za porazheniem," *Komsomol'skoe plemia*, October 18, 1983, 4.

41. On the stadium, see Chudinovskikh, "Sluchainost' ili zakonomernost'?"

42. *Kirovskaia pravda*, May 20, 1983, 4.

43. See a report by an official of Kirov's regional sports committee, "Get Hooligans Out of the Stadium": V. Krinitsyn, "Khuliganov—so stadiona," *Kirovskaia pravda*, July 7, 1983, 4.

44. V. Chudinovskikh, "Povremenim s prognozami," *Kirovskaia pravda*, September 7, 1983, 4.

45. GASPI KO, f. R-6818, op. 5, d. 1710, l. 11.

46. V. Chudinovskikh, "Dvoika za igru," *Kirovskaia pravda*, September 17, 1983, 4.

47. O. Shcherbakov, "Trudnaia pobeda," *Kirovskaia pravda*, September 20, 1983, 4.

48. GASPI KO, f. R-6818, op. 5, d. 1710, l. 156.

49. V. Andreev, "Snova proigrysh," *Kirovskaia pravda*, October 16, 1983, 4. *Kirovskaia pravda*, October 25, 1983, 4; *Kirovskaia pravda*, October 29, 1983, 4; *Kirovskoe pravda*, November 3, 1983, 3. See Kirov's television reports of early November in GASPI KO, f. R-6818, op. 5, d. 1715, ll. 52, 150.

50. GAKO, f. R-1363, op. 4, d. 1890, ll. 90–91. On November 11, Ochnev sent the recommendation for Iakovlev's firing to the sports committees of the USSR and the Russian Republic. For the former, GAKO, f. R-1363, op. 4, d. 1876, l. 218, and the latter, GAKO, f. R-1363, op. 4, d. 1880, l. 69.

51. GASPI KO, f. R-6766, op. 1, d. 825, ll. 62–65.

52. See information presented at a session of the presidium of Kirov's Dinamo soviet, January 27, 1984, in GASPI KO, f. R-6766, op. 1, d. 846, l. 14. It is not clear why Isupov and Erdiakov had been singled out. That season, Isupov had been yellow-carded at least three times for relatively minor infractions: GARF, f. R-7576, op. 31, d. 9310, ll. 137, 163, 217. Referees had carded Erdiakov twice for rough play: GARF, f. R-7576, op. 31, d. 9310, l. 165 and d. 9311, l. 13.

53. Chudinovskikh, "Sluchainost' ili zakonomernost'?" Earlier in the year, Chudinovskikh repeated without comment Iakovlev's claim that Dinamo's

players were in good physical shape: V. Chudinovskikh, "Tri voprosa," *Kirovskaia pravda*, March 25, 1983, 4.

54. B. Kolomensky, "Zaplanirovannoe porazhenie?," *Komsomol'skoe plemia*, November 10, 1983, 4.

55. "Kurs—na mestnykh igrokov. Gorovit predsedatel' oblsportkomiteta V. E. Ochnev," *Kirovskaia pravda*, December 4, 1983, 4.

56. GASPI KO, f. R-6766, op. 1, d. 822, l. 138.

57. GASPI KO, f. R-6766, op. 1, d. 822, l. 139.

58. GASPI KO, f. R-6766, op. 1, d. 823, ll. 96–97. Mazurenko sent this request on October 18. A month earlier, on September 14, he sent a less detailed but similar letter to Dinamo's central soviet: GASPI KO, f. R-6766, op. 1, d. 823, ll. 89–89 ob.

59. See figures, slightly conflicting, on attendance in *Futbol-Khokkei*, no. 15, April 11, 1982, 7 and in *Futbol-Khokkei*, no. 15, April 10, 1983, 6. Goldblatt reports that attendance in other countries collapsed. In just ten years, attendance at all English professional league games fell precipitously from 25 million in 1975 to less than 17 million in 1986. In West Germany, after peaking at 26 million in the late 1970s, crowds declined to 18 million in 1990: David Goldblatt, *The Ball Is Round: A Global History of Soccer* (New York: Riverhead Books, 2008), 546–547. Sweden and Denmark experienced a "catastrophic decrease in attendance in the 1970s." Torbjörn Andersson and Aage Radmann, "Football Fans in Scandinavia: 1900–97," in *Fanatics! Power, Identity and Fandom in Football*, ed. Adam Brown (New York: Routledge, 1998), 149. With attendance in mind, historian James Walvin wrote in 1975, "The halcyon days of professional football most notably in the late 1940s are not likely to return": James Walvin, *The People's Game: A Social History of British Football* (London: Allen Lane, 1975), 186.

60. See information from the Finance-Planning Department of Kirov's Dinamo soviet, January 9, 1983, in GASPI KO, f. R-6766, op. 1, d. 823, l. 31. One match brought in 9,700 rubles. Figures for 1983 are not available. In 1983, Kirov region's professional hockey team, Olimpiia, which played in Kirovo-Chepetsk, had been victimized by transfers, as previously discussed, and received dramatically less income because of low attendance. Despite the team's resulting poor play on the ice and financial woes, on July 4, 1983, the chair of Kirov's regional soviet and head of its regional party committee asked Moscow (the Central Committee of Professional Unions) to allow Olimpiia to continue to compete in the second league. See GAKO, f. R-2169, op. 43, d. 3476, l. 138. In the 1982–1983 season, Olimpiia finished in tenth place in a zone of thirteen teams in the second league. The club survived to finish tenth of fourteen in its zone in the next season.

61. Chudinovskikh, "Sluchainost' ili zakonomernost'?"

9

FALLEN FROM GRACE

Dinamo's fling with the upper reaches of the USSR's football empire had ended. The club fell from the grace of the First League's twenty-two teams to the second league's 162.[1] Aleksandr Mazurenko remained the head of the regional Ministry of Interior and a key figure in Dinamo's affairs. But now his influence, if not commitment—financial and otherwise—lagged far behind what it had been. Dinamo's regional soviet cut back on its support of the team.[2] One story has it that Mazurenko received a call from Moscow's Ministry of Internal Affairs. He was told to pay less attention to football and more to criminal behavior.[3]

Despite the criticism of their performance in 1983, Dinamo retained Kirov's native sons Leonid Shatunov, Sergei Bubnov, Sergei Erdiakov, and Lev Isupov. It also resigned Konstantin Vasil'evich Olenev, a young goalie, and several other players from the 1983 squad. It did not keep Sergei Kamzulin. Aleksandr Kozlovskikh left to enter the Advanced Coaches School in Moscow. In their stead, Dinamo brought in players who had just launched their professional careers, who had returned to play after a year or more off, or who had played the year before on a second league team.[4]

The new head coach seemed fitting for this scaled-down version of Dinamo. Aleksandr Aleksandrovich Sokovnin, a local boy, played for Kirov's Dinamo from 1965 through 1974. He then coached amateur teams in Kirov. His designation as Dinamo's coach was his first for a professional team. Local affiliation and, presumably, fewer costs also contributed to the appointment of Aleksandr Kuz'mich Vozhegov as Sokovnin's assistant. Vozhegov had played for Dinamo in the 1970s and was its assistant coach in 1983. The new general manager, Ivan Pavlovich Anisimov, had few qualifications and probably came at relatively little cost.⁵ Further savings occurred when the club did not renew its contract with the team physician, Anatolii Chikishev. It proceeded through 1984 without a team doctor.⁶

Whatever the apparent difficulties facing the team, Sokovnin thought that it might do well. On two occasions before the season's start, he asserted that Dinamo could finish the year no lower than sixth place in its zone. It could do so, he said, because of a reliance on local talent. It would take time for the youngsters to develop, he admitted, but their play would improve and Dinamo's season would end successfully.⁷ He did have a number of Kirov's own at his disposal, although not all of them had yet demonstrated skill at the professional game. Sokovnin counted on the rapid improvement of what he did have on hand with the help of the recently completed training base in Poroshino. It now had two football fields, a cafeteria, a hotel that could accommodate fifty people, a training room, and a banya (and guard dogs).⁸ But the facility could not turn mediocre players into talented ones overnight.

Dinamo performed reasonably well at first. It played in the Dinamo tourney in Moscow in late January, losing one game and tying another.⁹ On February 18, it lost the USSR Cup to Pamir, a team from Tajikistan's capital, Dushanbe. For Dinamo, it seemed a moral victory: Pamir played in the First League, and Dinamo tied the game in regulation 1–1. Kirov's television agreed. On April 25, it reported that "it is a new season and new hopes."¹⁰ One day later, Dinamo lost, 2–1, in a match in the Russian Republic's Cup for second league squads to a team also just relegated from the First League, Torpedo, from the city of Togliatti. The game was played in the city of Kirov at Rodina's stadium, perhaps one good sign, at least, that for the time being, Dinamo and Rodina had set aside their squabbles of the past.

On May 2, Dinamo opened the regular season at home with a victory. The team's followers, more realistic than Sokovnin, responded with little enthusiasm. They remained distressed over the team's dismal showing of the year before and its current mere existence, win or lose, in the second league. After the match, an unenthused Viktor Chudinovskikh wrote of Dinamo, "Alas, not in the First League as in the past two seasons."¹¹ Neither for this game nor for any other did his newspaper or *Komsomol'skoe plemia* report attendance as it had in the previous year. A meager turnout, no doubt, accounted for the silence. As in years past, *Futbol-Khokkei* largely ignored the second league. Kirov's television limited its coverage to a report on the distressing results, finding neither the time nor the energy for any commentary.

And yet Dinamo stumbled on with a win here and there. After a home victory on July 5, it had four each of wins, ties, and losses. Still unmoved after this latest victory, Chudinovskikh headlined his report with "Points Earned, but No Game."[12] Another home victory on September 5 failed to shake Chudinovskikh out of his doldrums. Dinamo's players, he commented, exhibited no joy either during the game or at its end. Chudinovskikh shared their distress. Despite the win, "it is generally not going well."[13] Dinamo occupied fourteenth place in its zone of seventeen teams.

The season was going so badly that a victory literally turned into defeat. Chudinovskikh had responded unenthusiastically to his team's win on opening day, May 2. He had more reason to be despondent than he thought. The match turned a subsequent win into a loss. In that first game, referees issued two warnings (two yellow cards) to Erdiakov. The second penalty required his removal from the game and disqualification from the following contest. Erdiakov, however, played in the next game. When in August Moscow became aware of such a serious infraction of league (and football) rules, it changed the results of Dinamo's win, a lopsided 7–0 victory on July 22 over Volga from Gor'ky, into a defeat.[14] A month later, the league's office had more reason for disapproving of Dinamo. The club failed to provide a bus to transport the visiting team, Izhevsk's Zenit, to the railroad station for its departure from Kirov.[15]

On September 22, Dinamo won at home by a commanding score of 6–0. Unlike the earlier lopsided win, this victory remained in the win column. It made little difference. In the next six and final games of the season, Dinamo won one and lost five. It ended the year in twelfth place among the zone's seventeen teams.[16] Chudinovskikh understated his and the fans' dismay. "We still do not have good local players," he said again as he had so many times before. He then allowed himself and the team's followers a whiff of good cheer so lacking throughout the year. "People are forbearing and continue to believe in better times. They have always been and are still with you, 'Dinamo!'"[17]

The following year, Dinamo managed to take third place in its zone, but as Chudinovskikh and the faithful understood too well for their comfort, their club remained in the second league. There until the end of the decade, it could manage no better than an eighth-place finish in its zone.

Stripped of much of its financial backing and the support of fans, the team stumbled badly in its zone in the second league in 1984. Never again would Dinamo achieve anything resembling the glorious years of 1980 and 1981. Local talent alone was insufficient to allow even competitive play in the second league let alone a return to the First League. And, as a loser, Dinamo could not marshal the financial or personnel resources it needed to be competitive again. It was, however, lucky to escape with mere censure rather than being made an example of like Kuibyshev's Kryl'ia Sovetov or Vladimir's Torpedo had been

Left to right: Aleksandr Kozlovskikh, the author, Lev Isupov. Dinamo Stadium, Kirov, September 22, 2022.

earlier. But Dinamo would never recover from its funding cuts and the resulting decrease in talent and play.

NOTES

1. In 1984, the second league consisted of 162 teams: *Futbol-Khokkei*, no. 15, April 15, 1984, 5.
2. See Viktor Chudinovskikh's comment on the soviet's interest in Chudinovskikh, "Gde iskat' kliuchi k vorotam," *Kirovskaia pravda*, July 31, 1984, 4. Mazurenko continued in that post until 1987 when he returned to Voronezh.
3. Interview with Evgenii Kolchanov on June 29, 2017.
4. Eduard Il'dusovich Akbarov and Iurii Vladimirovich Tiul'kin came from second league teams. Pavel Viktorovich Iurtsev came from Moscow's Torpedo, a team in the Higher League, but he had played only for its double.
5. It took some time to appoint Anisimov. As of March 15, 1984, the collegium of Kirov's sports committee had not yet chosen a general manager. In an interview on June 29, 2017, Evgenii Kolchanov indicated that the delay was a technical matter. Anisimov had to clear his release from the army and complete the necessary paperwork before he was officially designated the team's general manager. I am unable to find information on Anisimov before this appointment. He

continued in his post in Kirov through the 1989 season. In my interview on June 29, 2017, Kolchanov indicated that perhaps earlier, while serving in the army, Anisimov had been posted to Kirov and had played there.

6. Chudinovskikh reported the lack of a team doctor in Chudinovskikh, "Gde iskat' kliuchi k vorotam," 4.

7. See interviews of Sokovnin in *Kirovskaia pravda*, February 1, 1984, 4 and A. Sokolov, "Aprel' primeniaet futbolku," *Kirovskaia pravda*, April 26, 1984, 4.

8. See information on the base in reports dated January 9, 1984, and October 26, 1984, in the State Archive for the Social and Political History of the Kirov Region (GASPI KO), f. R-6766, op. 1, d. 822, l. 137 and d. 844, 49. See also information from sports correspondent Oleg Shcherbakov after he visited the base in *Kirovskaia pravda*, February 1, 1984, 4.

9. See only mention of Dinamo's participation without any results in *Komsomol'skoe plemia*, January 19, 1984, 4 and *Kirovskaia pravda*, February 1, 1984, 4.

10. GASPI KO, f. R-6818, op. 5, d. 1838, l. 120.

11. V. Chudinovskikh, "Nachali s pobedy," *Kirovskaia pravda*, May 4, 1984, 4.

12. V. Chudinovskikh, "Ochki est'—igry net," *Kirovskaia pravda*, July 7, 1984, 4.

13. V. Chudinovskikh, "Dva nepokhozhikh taima," *Kirovskaia pravda*, September 7, 1984, 3.

14. On the scandal, see information provided by the deputy chair of Dinamo's regional soviet, August 22, 1984, in GASPI KO, f. R-6766, op. 1, d. 845, l. 47. See the official modification of the result at http://footballfacts.ru/matches/552247-dinamo-kirov-volga-gorkij-, last consulted January 31, 2017.

15. On September 21, the deputy chair of the Dinamo's regional soviet reprimanded Dinamo's administrator, Vladimir Petrovich Kiselev, for a failure to provide transportation on September 20. GASPI KO, f. R-6766, op. 1, d. 845, l. 55. Dinamo had played Zenit to a 0–0 tie on September 19.

16. The year ended with eleven wins, six ties, and fifteen losses. The opposition outscored Dinamo by a 50–29 margin.

17. V. Chudinovskikh, "Sezon nesbyvshikhsia nadezhd," *Kirovskaia pravda*, November 1, 1984, 4.

CONCLUSION

Sporting Dialectics

Soviet sport is a study of contrasts. In 1925, the Central Committee condemned competitive sport. In 1926, the Fifteenth Party Conference promoted it. In 1930, the Soviet state created a Council of Physical Culture that denied legitimacy to sport as traditionally understood. In 1936, it added *sport* to the council's title. Twelve years later, the party's Central Committee demanded world domination by Soviet athletes in all major sports. In the citadel of socialism, as early as the 1920s, a freewheeling market ruled the recruitment and benefits paid to athletes. An elaborate bureaucracy for the administration of sports, one enamored with its own power of diktat, could not in fact control what it sought to regulate. Prisoners coached the teams of their jailers. In Kirov, inmate Aleksandr Keller jumped overnight from Kirov's concentration camp to the training camp of its professional football team. Some venues, most notably the newspaper *Pravda*, frequently resorted to hyperbole when criticizing and praising Soviet football. *Krasnyi sport* and its successor, *Sovetskii sport*, as well as the latter's weekly supplement, *Futbol-Khokkei*, often rendered sober assessments and avoided self-aggrandizing posturing. From 1979 to 1985, Kirov's Dinamo lurched in the standings from the bottom to the top and back to the bottom again.

A Must Win

Prominent state and party organs insisted that Soviet football clubs, especially the USSR's national team, dominate international competition. Ironically, and in sharp contradiction to the competitive spirit, that demand resulted in games with far inferior, often amateur squads or a frequent avoidance altogether of play in the international arena. Multiple losses to the touring Basques in 1937 demonstrated, as Soviet commentators painfully put it, the fiction of Soviet football's invincibility. Dinamo's tour of Great Britain in 1945, however, prompted hyperbolic remarks about the "excellence of Soviet football." Seven years later, the failure to win in the USSR's first Olympics brought about the disbandment of the Red Army Club team, which had made up the core of the national squad. Eight years later, a first-place position in the inaugural European Football Championship led once again to an understandable but exaggerated commentary about the "brilliance of Soviet football." Over the next quarter of a century, the national team performed admirably well with multiple finishes in the top four in European and world tournaments. Yet many state officials and sports administrators responded with disappointment, even anger at the team's failure to win it all. Nothing short of victory would do for a USSR that insisted on its ideological and political superiority.

Kirov's Dinamo was victimizer and victim in this system of "win or else." As much as they occasionally said otherwise, Viktor Chudinovskikh, Boris Kolomensky, and municipal and regional officials approved an aggressive and expensive recruitment of athletes from other teams. The long-term future of Kirov's Dinamo might lie in an intensive investment in youth football, but for the moment, it could win only by paying dearly for outsiders. Meanwhile, the regional soviet's sports committee hypocritically condemned other organizations when they raided players from the region's professional hockey team and its renowned wrestling coach and his star athletes. The duplicity was all the more galling for Dinamo's magistrates and fans when its heavily recruited and compensated stars in 1982 and 1983 played so poorly.

To be sure, the Dinamo organization in Moscow and the sports committees of the Russian Republic and the USSR issued regulations to contain exorbitant spending on professional football. But they enforced them spasmodically. When they pounced on a team for violations of rules, it was an exercise in showmanship and scapegoating with little or no effect on other clubs. And it was the conspicuously unsuccessful teams that Moscow punished. "We are because we win," journalist Eduardo Galeano observed about football teams. "If we lose, we no longer exist."[1] As Soviet teams understood all too well, losing had its disadvantages well beyond the won-loss column.

Yet winning also had its disadvantages. Teams that spent lavishly "off the books" had to keep winning or else. Kirov's Dinamo knew it well to its benefit and detriment. In July 1981, the sports committees of the Russian Republic and the Soviet Union condemned Kuibyshev's Kryl'ia Sovetov for the excessive financial benefits it provided to its athletes (and coaches). When all other clubs were asked to consider the relevance of the charges to their own ventures, Dinamo's administrators, coaches, and players disingenuously dismissed any such possibility. It was an easy thing to do with Dinamo in the middle of its most successful season ever. Later that year, in November, the Russian Republic's Dinamo soviet accused its Kirov branch of inappropriate payments to the team's coach and several players. Poised to strike a blow for rules and regulations, the accusing soviet then relented. Kirov's Dinamo was too good to "fail"; it had just won its zone and promotion to the First League. The soviet issued only a mild reprimand to a relatively minor administrator in Dinamo's regional soviet. In March of the following year, Kirov's Dinamo soviet precluded any serious punitive action by blaming the same administrator and the team's general manager, not any coach or player, for "illegal activities regarding the payment of bonuses."

That April, the Russian Republic's Sports Committee disbanded Torpedo, the team from the city of Vladimir, which had just finished last in its zone, for "grave financial violations." Now required, as all teams were, to examine their own budgets, Kirov's Dinamo, still basking in its successful entry into the First League, found no violations. But later that year, in December, after barely escaping relegation, Kirov's Dinamo, now something far less than a winner, admitted to excessive expenditures. A year later, after Dinamo's woeful season and relegation to the second league, the Russian Republic's Dinamo soviet insisted that the team reduce expenses.

The soviet had good reason to do so. Dinamo had lived well beyond its means. In its best and most expensive years, it had repeatedly begged the regional government and Dinamo's national organization for funds to pay even for utilities. And it passed the hat to other agencies and enterprises in the city and region, which were asked, if not compelled, to uphold municipal and regional pride. For the moment, Dinamo succeeded beyond all expectations. Administrators from Kirov and Moscow basked in Dinamo's success. They joined the on-field celebration following the 1980 campaign and the ceremonious gathering at the Palace of Culture after the 1981 season. The cost of success, however, was not sustainable, especially for a team that would begin to lose. Patrons in Moscow and Kirov would not continue to provide such lavish support for a loser. Even promises of local governing organs and industrial enterprises to help repair and upgrade Dinamo's stands, field, and lighting were often honored in the breach. At a critical juncture in the 1982 season, the Lepse factory and the sports society Progress refused Dinamo use of their facilities.

A Little Habitat of Freedom

And yet whether a team won or lost, football nationally and in Kirov provided for administrators, players, fans, and reporters a "little habitat of freedom of expression" in the highly authoritarian Soviet Union. After losses to the Basques in 1937, journalists, one of them a foreigner, used the Soviet press to criticize the nation's administrators, coaches, and players. High-ranking officials in the state and party bureaucracy boldly objected, albeit often in vain, to the inappropriate sponsorship and financing of teams by powerful figures in the country's armed forces and security apparatus. Players enjoyed something akin to free agency by demanding greater compensation and moving to and fro in its pursuit. Fans freely expressed their sentiments by their attendance or lack thereof and, when in the stadium, by their boisterous approval or disapproval of a team's play. Reminiscing about Soviet football during the tense decade of the 1930s, Spartak's Nikolai Starostin recalled that at the time "for most people, football was the only and sometimes the very last, chance and hope of retaining in their souls a tiny island of sincere feelings and human relations."[2] After the USSR's loss to Portugal for the bronze in the 1966 World Cup, Nikolai and his brother, Andrei, insisted that Soviet football instill in its athletes root and branch, from its youth programs to the training camp for the national squad, "the creative freedom" to play with initiative and innovation. Journalists Gennadii Radchuk, Lev Filatov, and Vladimir Ponedel'nik excoriated the USSR's administrators, coaches, and players for a lack of imagination in contrast to their victorious foreign counterparts. Iurii Il'ich Van'iat blamed the USSR's governing organs for football for some of the national team's woes. For their readers starved for information about football abroad, *Sovetskii sport* and *Trud* provided strikingly extensive and objective reports on the European Championship and World Cup even when the Soviet national team was not involved.[3]

Composer Dmitrii Shostakovich, a self-described football fanatic, associated the sport with unbounded joy and an escape from the constraints of Soviet life. He tried not to miss a football game because "I love all kinds of spontaneous cheerful gatherings, and my profoundly lowbrow devotion to soccer knows no bounds."[4] From 1937 to 1941, when he taught at the Leningrad Conservatory, he was nowhere to be found on game day.[5] When away from Leningrad or, later, Moscow, Shostakovich bombarded his friends with requests for the latest scores and for tickets to games to follow his impending return home.[6] In late November 1945, after Dinamo's first three games in Great Britain (two victories and a tie), Shostakovich wrote in *Izvestiia* of "his right to be proud" of the club's achievements. English football has always been considered the best in the world, he continued, but now with Dinamo's success "Soviet football has grown into an international force." "Hurrah for Dinamo, which has upheld the honor of Soviet sport."[7] At about the same time, cellist Boris Vasil'evich Dobrokhotov described the composer's Moscow apartment. "I was amazed that in his office nothing spoke of his profession. Nowhere were there musical scores, but on its tables everywhere magazines about football were strewn about."[8] Shostakovich purportedly confided to friends that the stadium had become, as he put it, "the single place where one can loudly tell the truth about what one sees."[9] As Laurel Fay has aptly concluded in her biography of Shostakovich, football for him "offered an escape both from music and from the cares of daily life."[10]

In his book about the Barcelona football club, Jimmy Burns noted that the team, "the people's passion [and] the world's most politicised club," represented a distinct Catalan language and culture in Spain.[11] One fan told the author that "the club is a way of saying that we do not want the rest of Spain to repress us—the stadium was the only place where we could express ourselves freely."[12] In the last decade of the existence of the East German police state, fans and journalists vociferously objected to the state's support of the secret police's team, the Berliner Football Club Dinamo.[13] In a seminal article on Moscow's Spartak team, historian Robert Edelman uncovered a similar phenomenon. "Sport was one of the relatively free places in Soviet life."[14] By its support of Spartak, the "people's team," as opposed to Moscow's Dinamo, the club sponsored by the state's police, fans found what Edelman calls "a small way of saying no." They did not seek regime change, but by their attachment to their team, they found "a way to demonstrate a measure of agency denied them in other parts of their lives." "Supporting Spartak may have been a small way of saying 'no,'" Edelman concludes, "but if the gesture were small, it nonetheless spoke volumes."[15] When in 1950, Spartak's star, Sergei Sal'nikov, was transferred to Moscow's Dinamo, irate fans bombarded newspapers, the Central Committee, and Soviet leaders with their complaints.[16] In an analysis of fans' letters, telegrams, and postcards about a single match between Moscow's Torpedo and Kiev's Dinamo, in November 1966, Manfred Zeller found a similar use of the game to express feelings that transcended sport. Wide-ranging support of Kiev's entry, he found, demonstrated not necessarily anti-Soviet sentiment but nevertheless antipathy toward the center.[17]

Fans and local officials sent letters to the central press and the party's Central Committee objecting to the draft of their players by the nation's armed services to bolster Red Army and Dinamo squads. Televised matches in the 1970s and thereafter, reasonably free of an ideological and political framework, as Edelman has pointed out, helped Soviet citizens "create meaningful identities and recapture some small piece of themselves." Matches could, of course, divide viewers by their choice of competing teams, but they could also undermine "those processes of atomization that were so long thought to buttress the authority of Soviet power."[18]

In Kirov, players, fans, and reporters expressed their own interests in a remarkably aggressive way. Dinamo's players came and went in search of the most advantageous benefits. The city's native son, Aleksandr Georgievich Kozlovskikh departed in 1970 for greener pastures, then returned in 1981 for the same reason. In 1983, the team's administrators discovered to their chagrin that they had badly overpaid new recruits and aging stars Evgeni Khrabrostin and Vladimir Peregontsev, the former released in midyear and the latter benched. Dinamo's fans turned out in droves when their team performed well. On one occasion, more than eleven thousand overwhelmed their stadium. In October, during the disappointing season of 1983, in admittedly poor weather, only eight hundred came. Many of them departed at halftime. The mood of the city's sports correspondents likewise rose and fell with Dinamo's fortunes on the field. Following the 1983 season, Kolomensky surely spoke for most of his readers when he openly criticized not only the club's players but also the regional Dinamo soviet and regional sports committee. He and his audience well understood that such criticism was also directed, if explicitly unsaid, at the club's chief sponsor, the powerful regional branch of the Ministry of Internal Affairs and its head, Aleksandr Mazurenko.

Misdeeds on a Grander Scale

This story often highlights the seamier side of Soviet football. It is not grounds, however, for a smug condemnation of Soviet sport. Financial shenanigans so evident in Dinamo's history (and that of other teams) occurred in many other realms of Soviet life. Administrators of collective farms and industrial enterprises falsified production to meet and exceed quotas. Governing party and state officials turned a blind eye to the practice to protect and advance their own careers. Industrial enterprises hired "special agents" (*tolkachi*) to procure illegally necessary goods and services well outside the parameters of Moscow's central plan.[19] Denunciation of those engaged in any such illegal activities—scapegoats, as it were—usually occurred in the most egregious of cases or when an enterprise could not meet its quota despite its illegal capers. In the immediate postperestroika years, a largely unregulated "free market" destroyed many of the institutions, enterprises, and people who were supposed to benefit from the change. Some football teams became the plaything of what historian

K. Manuel Veth has called the "futbolcracy." Oligarchs used the sport for domestic political gains and as a part of a shady business empire that involved, among other illicit activities, money laundering and even murder.[20] The Russian government's unhealthy obsession with winning led to state-sponsored doping of many of its athletes at recent Winter and Summer Olympics.

The mix of politics, money, and sports has been an unhealthy phenomenon beyond the former Soviet Union. Corruption, match fixing, bribery of referees, and a corrosive obsession with victory have dominated much of the history of Italian football.[21] British football has likewise been riddled with scandals. Until the elimination there of the maximum wage for the sport's athletes in 1961, few individuals dared to challenge its violation precisely because of its ubiquity.[22] The US government has used the Olympics for political purposes, providing financial support to its Olympian athletes before the practice was sanctioned. Almost one-third of the representatives of the United States in the 1956 games in Melbourne served in the American armed forces, which lavishly supported their training.[23] Privately owned professional teams in the United States draw on public funds for their livelihood. Teams play in stadiums built and maintained by local governments that receive little in return. Clubs rely on athletes trained in large part by state universities at taxpayers' expense. Public funds have supported a youth football permeated with such ills as fake birth certificates, waivers for children flunking in schools, recruitment through favors, and an obsession with victory.[24] A permissive transfer portal in college sports allows, in effect, athletes to move at will to the institution that enables them to best profit from the sale of their "name, image, and likeness."

Kirov's Mazurenko has many protégés in contemporary football—owners and administrators whose relationship to the sport is, as one commentator has labeled it, one of "love vanity, and insanity."[25] Rich and politically ambitious figures—"power freaks"—have dominated the history of Italian football, among them more recently Silvio Berlusconi, media magnate, owner of a Milan football club (AC Milan), and prime minister of Italy in four governments.[26] Many of the shenanigans highlighted in this story, including "financial doping," as a critic has called it, currently prevail in big-time European football.[27] Corruption in the International Federation of Association Football (FIFA) has had a long history. Galeano described FIFA's president from 1974 to 1998, João Havelange, as an "old-style monarch."[28] "His body glued to the throne," Galeano wrote, "Havelange reigns in his palace in Zurich surrounded by a court of voracious technocrats."[29] Corruption became more rampant with Havelange's successor, Sepp Blatter, who served as FIFA's president from 1998 to 2015.

"A master at cooking the books," Galeano commented, "Blatter the untouchable turned Havelange into a Sister of Charity."[30]

By 2014, FIFA knew a reckoning was in the offing. That year, it spent thirty million dollars to produce the film *United Passions*. Its portrayals of Havelange and Blatter presented them as idealists and warriors for the game's integrity and global reach. "The worst film ever screened," it flopped at the box office.[31] It may nevertheless be worth watching for one especially memorable line. When acknowledging evidence of corruption at FIFA, Blatter confides, "I know I wasn't joining a chess club."

Football's World Cup "is awash," as author Pete Davies has characterized it, "with strange and feverish money."[32] Accordingly, Brazil, Russia, and Qatar have spent ghastly sums to host the World Cup in 2014, 2018, and 2022, respectively.[33] In Qatar, desert temperatures can reach the high forties (Celsius) in the summer. Much to the consternation of football devotees, the games therefore occur not in midyear but rather in November and December. This "looming travesty" prompted philosopher and avid football fan Simon Critchley to angrily declare, "Personally, I'd like to see Qatar declared a rogue state and the World Cup taken away."[34] It should be noted, however, that Qatar has promised air-conditioned stadiums and that heretofore, the World Cup has been played in high temperatures (and in the oxygen-depleted high altitude of Mexico City).

More to the point of this current work, in their mad dash for victory, owners of several teams have been accused of circumventing Financial Fair Play (FFP) regulations adopted by the Union of European Football Associations (UEFA) in 2010. Those rules stipulated that, with few exceptions, clubs could spend no more than what they earned. In 2015, UEFA banned Moscow's Dinamo from European club competition in 2015–2016 (from participation in the Europa League) for violation of FFP. A more recent and egregious example of a violation of the FFP has been Manchester City in England's Premier League, a club owned by the brother of the ruler of the petrostate United Arab Emirates. In 2018 and 2019, UEFA charged that the club had consistently concealed the owner's massive infusions of cash through phony contracts with allegedly independent sponsors as well as from firms paying for players' image rights. In 2020, UEFA fined the club thirty million euros and barred it for two seasons from playing in the Champions League, a yearly tournament of the best football teams worth millions for a participating team.[35] The club appealed the ruling to the independent Court of Arbitration. That July, the court ruled that many of the charges fell outside UEFA's own statute of limitations. It lifted the ban on play in the Champions League and reduced the fine to ten million euros.³⁶ The very validity of FFP has, as a result, come under question.³⁷ A grab for money by twelve of the top football teams in Europe in April 2021 to create a superleague of their own was aborted only when officials, other club owners, players, and fans vigorously objected. In 2022, UEFA replaced FFP with a so-called Financial Sustainability and Club Licensing Regulations that set limits on expenditures and above all on the amount and duration of deficit spending. It remains to be seen if these restrictions will have much of an effect.

The "win or else" mentality in the USSR and abroad has promoted illicit behavior and hypocrisy. Within a highly authoritarian Soviet Union, there appeared "a little habitat of freedom of expression." Whether their national team or local club won or lost, administrators, players, fans, and reporters expressed their heartfelt pleasure or displeasure with their team's performance. They even suggested modest reforms of football (and government?) to improve the overall play of their favorite. The presence of financial tricks and scapegoating so evident in Soviet football was present in other spheres of Soviet life and may be understood as a key feature of both the Soviet system and organized sports in general. Many countries outside the USSR also engaged in financial shenanigans or other unethical practices to win at all costs.

NOTES

1. Eduardo Galeano, *Soccer in Sun and Shadow*, trans. Mark Fried (New York: Nation Books, 2013), 230.

2. Nikolai Petrovich Starostin, *Futbol skvoz' gody* (Moscow: Molodaia gvardiia, 1989), 83. Eric Dunning speaks of sports as providing "enclaves of autonomy." "An important aspect of sports in modern societies," he has written, "consists in their development as an enclave where people are permitted to experience a relatively high—but crucially variable—degree of autonomy as far as their behaviour, identities, identifications and relationships are concerned." Eric Dunning, *Sport Matters: Sociological Studies of Sport, Violence and Civilization* (New York: Routledge, 1999), 3–4.

3. For example, see coverage of the 1966 World Cup in *Sovetskii sport*, July 23, 1966, 4–5 and July 24, 1966, 4–5, and coverage of the 1982 World Cup in issues of July 3, 1982, 1, July 4, 1982, 3–4, July 6, 1982, 1, 3, and July 7, 1982, 1, 3.

4. Dmitrii Dmitrievich Shostakovich, *Testimony: The Memoirs of Dmitri Shostakovich* as related to and edited by Solomon Volkov, trans. Antonina W. Bouis (New York: Harper & Row, 1979), 237. "I'd be very happy if they managed to find some famous humanist who could be trusted, with whom you could chat about flowers, brotherhood, equality and liberty, the European soccer championships, and other lofty topics. But no such humanist has been born," 204. On his passion

for football, see also 113, 204, 237. I am aware of the controversy over the authenticity and reliability of *Testimony*. See in particular the review of *Testimony* by Laurel E. Fay, "Shostakovich Versus Volkov: Whose Testimony?," *Russian Review* 39, no. 4 (October 1980): 484–493 and a summary of the opinions expressed in the controversy in David Caute, *The Dancer Defects: The Struggle for Cultural Supremacy during the Cold War* (Oxford: Oxford University Press, 2003), 434–440. Upon noting the various points of view, Caute observed, "Clearly the grave of the greatest of Soviet composers retains a full orchestra," 440. See also essays in Malcolm Hamrick Brown, ed., *A Shostakovich Casebook* (Bloomington: Indiana University Press, 2004).

For a repudiation of the criticism of *Testimony*, see Allan Benedict Ho, *Shostakovich Reconsidered* (New York: Toccata, 1998), especially 16–23, 33–45. Questions have arisen chiefly over Volkov's compilation of the memoirs and the veracity of Shostakovich's criticism of the Soviet artistic intelligentsia and party's leadership. His passion for football is not in doubt. In her biography of the composer, Fay acknowledges his "love for the beauty of the game, its artistry": Laurel E. Fay, *Shostakovich: A Life* (Oxford: Oxford University Press, 2000), 110–111, 134, 148, quote on 111. Other biographers note that "Shostakovich was a longstanding and passionate soccer fan": Dmitri Sollertinsky and Ludmilla Sollertinsky, *Pages from the Life of Dmitri Shostakovich*, trans. Graham Hobbs and Charles Midgley (New York: Harcourt Brace Jovanovich, 1980), 93. On the composer's passion for the game and participation in pick-up contests, see Elizabeth Wilson, *Shostakovich: A Life Remembered*, 2nd ed. (Princeton, NJ: Princeton University Press, 2006), 226–227.

5. Sollertinsky and Sollertinsky, *Pages from the Life*, 93.

6. See Shostakovich's persistent requests from 1940 to 1957 of Levon Tadevosovich Avton'ian in *Dmitrii Shostakovich v pis'makh i dokumentakh*, ed. I. A. Bobykina (Moscow: RIF "Antikva," 2000), 249, 266, 286, 291–293, 299, 302, 305. See also similar requests of other people, 396, 437.

7. D. Shostakovich, "Komande 'Dinamo'—fizkul't ura!," *Izvestiia*, November 22, 1945, 3.

8. *Dmitrii Shostakovich v pis'makh i dokumentakh*, 518.

9. Ivan Tiantov, "O futbole v zhizni i tvorchestve velikogo kompozitora," https://www.sports.ru/tribuna/blogs/field_notes/1063679.html, accessed October 4, 2020. Jim Riordan cites a similar remark by Shostakovich: "Football is the only place in our country where you can say what you think of what you see." See Jim Riordan, "More Serious than Life and Death: Russian and Soviet Football," in *The Organisation and Governance of Top Football across Europe: An Institutional Perspective*, ed. Hallgeir Gammelsaeter and Benoit Senaux (New York: Routledge), 224. Shostakovich was such an enthusiast that in 1935, he completed a course to become a referee, although he never found time to pursue the profession.

10. Fay, *Shostakovich*, 111.

11. Jimmy Burns, *Barça: A People's Passion* (New York: Bloomsbury, 1998), 330. The club was a "potent symbol of political and cultural identity" because of its "identification with Catalan culture, society, and politics," x, xv. On the club and its expression of a changing meaning of Catalan identity, see Joan Barcelo, Peter Clinton, and Charles Samper Seró, "National Identity, Social Institutions and Political Values. The Case of FC Barcelona and Catalonia from an Intergenerational Comparison," *Soccer & Society* 16, no. 4 (July 2015): 469–481. For the view that interprets the club's recent association with the Catalan nationalist movement as an expression of democratic rights and consensus, see Carlos Pulleiro Méndez, "The Political Stance of Sport: FC Barcelona and the Sovereignty of Catalonia, 2012–2017," *Soccer & Society* 23, no. 2 (2022):144–158.

12. Burns, *Barça*, 27.

13. Alan McDougall, "Eulogy to Theft: Berliner FC Dynamo, East German Football, and the End of Communism," in *The Whole World Was Watching: Sport in the Cold War*, ed. Robert Edelman and Christopher Young (Stanford, CA: Stanford University Press, 2020), 121.

14. Robert Edelman, "A Small Way of Saying 'No': Moscow Working Men, Spartak Soccer, and the Communist Party, 1900–1945," *American Historical Review* 107, no. 5 (December 2002): 1444.

15. Edelman, "A Small Way of Saying 'No'": 1442, 1467, 1473. Galeano noted that in Spain, during Franco's regime, Catalonians and Basques used football to express their own brand of forbidden ethnic pride. "During the long dictatorship of Franco, two stadiums, Camp Nou in Barcelona and San Mames in Bilbao, were sanctuaries for outlawed nationalist sentiment. There, Catalonians and Basques could shout and sing in their own languages and wave their outlawed flags. The first time the Basque standard was raised without provoking a beating from the police was in a soccer stadium." Galeano, *Soccer in Sun and Shadow*, 127.

16. Robert Edelman, "Romantic Underdogs: *Spartak* in the Golden Age of Soviet Soccer, 1945–1952," in *Euphoria and Exhaustion: Modern Sport in Soviet Culture and Society*, ed. Nikolaus Katzer et al. (New York: Campus, 2010), 238–240.

17. Manfred Zeller, "'Our Own Internationale,' 1966: Dynamo Kiev Fans between Local Identity and Transnational Imagination," *Kritika* 12, no. 1 (Winter 2011): 53–82.

18. Robert Edelman, "Sport on Soviet Television," in *Sport and the Transformation of Modern Europe: States, Media and Markets, 1950–2010*, ed. Alan Tomlinson, Christopher Young, and Richard Holt (New York: Routledge, 2011), 112.

19. For an extended discussion of this practice, see Oleg V. Khevniuk, "'Tolkachi,' Parallel'nye stimuly v stalinskoi ekonomicheskoi sisteme 1930-e–1950-e gody," *Cahiers du Monde Russe* 59, nos. 2–3 (2018): 233–254.

20. K. Manuel Veth, "The Berlusconization of Post-Soviet Football in Russia and the Ukraine: Money Scores Goals, Goals Win Titles, and Titles Win Popularity," *Journal of Sports History* 41, no. 1 (Spring 2004): 55–72. See also K. Manuel Veth, "Sovintersport and the Cashing in on Soviet Football," *Soccer & Society* 18, no. 1 (January 2017): 132–143. In 1990, Robert Edelman expressed fears of potential abuse: Robert Edelman, "The Professionalization of Soviet Sport: The Case of the Soccer Union," *Journal of Sports History* 17, no. 1 (Spring 1990): 44–55.

21. John Foot, *Winning at All Costs: A Scandalous History of Italian Soccer* (New York: Nation Books, 2006).

22. Simon Inglis, *Soccer in the Dock: A History of British Football Scandals, 1900–1965* (London: Willow Books, 1985), 118. For a discussion of the toxic mix of military dictatorship, football, warfare, and diplomacy, see Jon Spurling, *Death or Glory: The Dark History of the World Cup* (Kingston upon Thames: Vision Sports, 2010).

23. Toby C. Rider, *Cold War Games: Propaganda, Olympics, and U.S. Foreign Policy* (Urbana: University of Illinois Press, 2016), 92. On an earlier marriage of sports and the US armed forces, see Wanda Ellen Wakefield, *Playing to Win: Sports and the American Military, 1898–1945* (Albany: State University of New York Press, 1997).

24. See a discussion of Pop Warner football in Miami, Florida, for children between the ages of six and fifteen in Robert Andrew Powell, *We Own This Game: A Season in the Adult World of Youth Football* (New York: Atlantic Monthly, 2003).

25. Kieran Maguire, *The Price of Football: Understanding Football Club Finance* (Newcastle: Agenda, 2020), 169. Football as vanity ownership as well as a business opportunity helps explain foreign ownership of teams in England's top two leagues. At the start of the 2016–2017 season, 57 percent of clubs in the Premier League and Football League Championship were owned or controlled by foreign investors. Daniel Geey, *Done Deal: An Insider's Guide to Football Contracts, Multi-Million Pound Transfers and Premier League Big Business* (London: Bloomsbury, 2019), 74.

26. Foot, *Winning at All Costs*, 355–390, quote on 362.

27. See the article by Rory Smith in the online edition of the *New York Times*, November 9, 2018, https://www.nytimes.com/2018/11/09/sports/manchester-city-united-football-leaks.html.

28. Galeano, *Soccer in Sun and Shadow*, 167. Investigative reporter Andrew Jennings wrote of a "mobbed-up" Havelange, one of whose "great achievements was to conceal his criminal activities behind the aristocratic mask of a tough but benevolent gentleman": Andrew Jennings, *The Dirty Game: Uncovering the Scandal at FIFA* (London: Arrow Books, 2015), 3, 35.

29. Galeano, *Soccer in Sun and Shadow*, 166.

30. Galeano, *Soccer in Sun and Shadow*, 254. Andrew Jennings described Blatter as an "organised crime boss": Jennings, *Dirty Game*, 194. For one of many books on "corruption on a dizzying, entrenched scale" at FIFA, see David Conn, *The Fall of the House of FIFA: The Multimillion-Dollar Corruption at the Heart of Global Soccer* (New York: Nation Books, 2017), quote on 7. Conn and other critics acknowledge that both Havelange and Blatter contributed significantly to the global popularity of football.

31. Jennings, *Dirty Game*, 8.

32. Pete Davies, *All Played Out: The Full Story of Italia '90* (London: Yellow Jersey, 1990), 110. See also chap. 3, "Money," in Alan McDougall, *Contested Fields: A Global History of Modern Football* (Toronto: University of Toronto Press, 2020), 41–62.

33. On the projected expense of the 2018 World Cup in Russia, see Martin Müller and Sven Daniel Wolfe, "World Cup Russia 2018: Already the Most Expensive Ever?," *Russian Analytical Digest*, no. 150, June 25, 2014, 2–6.

34. Simon Critchley, *What We Think about When We Think about Soccer* (New York: Penguin Books, 2017), 74.

35. On Financial Fair Play, see the chapter on the subject in Maguire, *The Price of Football*, 93–105. Ironically, the FFP was designed in part to protect the wealthy elite, a status already attained by Manchester City, by precluding competition from other clubs blessed with a sudden infusion of large amounts of cash. Goldblatt reported that play in 2006 in the Champions League guaranteed a team with a major television market 110 million pounds just for showing up. David Goldblatt, *The Ball Is Round: A Global History of Soccer* (New York: Riverhead Books, 2008), 695. For contrasting opinions on the FFP, see Markus Sass, "Glory Hunters, Sugar Daddies, and Long-Term Competitive Balance under UEFA Financial Fair Play," *Journal of Sports Economics* 17, no. 2 (2016): 148–158; Egon Franck, "Financial Fair Play in European Club Football: What Is It All About?," *International Journal of Sport Finance* 9, no. 3 (2014): 193–217; Stefan Szymanski, "Fair Is Foul: A Critical Analysis of UEFA Financial Fair Play," *International Journal of Sport Finance* 9, no. 3 (2014): 218–229.

36. The court ruled that some of the charges were not proven and that other "alleged breaches were time-barred" because of a five-year window for imposition of any punishment as put forth in UEFA's own regulations. A portion of the fine remained because of the club's failure to fully cooperate with UEFA investigators.

37. See the article by Rory Smith, "Manchester City Won. Now Brace for the Losses," *New York Times*, July 13, 2020, https://www.nytimes.com/2020/07/13/sports/soccer/man-city-ffp.html.

EPILOGUE

Until the mid-1990s, Dinamo usually finished the season in the middle or near the bottom of its zone. Perestroika and the collapse of the Soviet Union made the situation worse. In the final years of the USSR and in the Russian Federation, football clubs scrambled to convince a large factory, individual oligarchs, and governmental organs to support them. Kirov's Dinamo could not do so successfully. A sharp reduction of the center's defense spending had disastrous consequences for Kirov, a city and region heavily invested in the Soviet military-industrial complex. Its deteriorating stadium earned the team no extra revenue from advertising boards or a rechristening after a private firm at a handsome price. The team could hardly generate investment by an outside oligarch, a benevolent carpetbagger, as it were. Its bare existence was not unlike the perilous state of minor-league teams around the globe.[1] Due to a lack of funds, Kirov's professional football team ceased to exist from 1994 through 1998. After Dinamo's reappearance in 1999, its performance was mediocre at best, and from 2010, it was abysmal with finishes at or near the bottom of its zone.

In July 2017, the administration of Dinamo's football club disbanded the team, pointing out that for the past four years, the team had relied exclusively on funds from the municipal government. In an article titled "Wave Goodbye," published in the region's newspaper, *Viatskii krai*, correspondent Artur Masal'tsev hardly regretted the loss. He wrote that for years, Dinamo had been "the worst team in the [entire] second division."[2] This rude dismissal of the team's disappearance aside, Kirov's citizens lost something of importance. In a different setting, that of contemporary England, journalist David Goldblatt spoke eloquently about a "football culture" in the periphery and what is forfeited when a team vanishes. A provincial team, he insisted, is vital to the preservation of a "distinct local identity," to a local "imagined community."[3] In Kirov's case, a city and region in economic decline and subsequent loss of national prestige, a vibrant Dinamo would have been all the more important for the sustenance of civic pride.

In today's Russian Federation, a largely untrammeled free market in players makes football, even at its lower ranks, more than ever an expensive proposition. For a team to participate, however poorly, in the second division, it needs 30–40 million rubles ($500,000–$667,000 at the current exchange rate).[4] A national Dinamo organization can no longer support teams in the provinces. In a relatively poor region such as Kirov, one without oil, neither government nor private business possesses the resources to fund professional sports. The region's minor-league hockey team in Kirovo-Chepetsk folded in 2016. Several years later, it reemerged as an entrant in the National Junior Hockey League, professional hockey at its lowest rung. Kirov's bandy club, Rodina, continues to experience never-ending financial crises and a position year in and year out at or near the bottom of its league.

In early December 2017, President Vladimir Putin's plenipotentiary for the Volga superregion, Mikhail Viktorovich Babich, commented on the state of Kirov's Dinamo and Rodina at a meeting with journalists. As reported by Radio Echo Moscow, Babich chose to return to a position somewhat reminiscent of that of the Soviet state in the 1920s. He insisted that the national budget support efforts to promote the nation's physical fitness and amateur sports. Professional teams, he added, must be privately owned and financed.[5] He was at his disingenuous best. He was fully aware of the central government's lavish support of the nation's most prominent professional hockey and football teams.

Kirov's regional government increased its support of Rodina for the 2019–2020 season to help it recruit better athletes. It was not enough. The team finished the season in thirteenth place among fourteen teams (with four wins, three ties, and nineteen losses). In the 2020–2021 season, it finished in twelfth place in a league of fourteen teams. And yet despite the poor showing by Rodina and the need for even greater financial support of it, in early 2022, Kirov's municipal and regional governments decided to resurrect Dinamo. The team will be a faint reminder of its former self, even in its worst years. The new Dinamo played in Russia's third division, the lowest rung in Russian professional football, with over one hundred teams arranged in ten zones (among 112 additional teams in three other domestic leagues). Teams in this zone and the division at large might best be characterized as semiprofessional. Dinamo did manage to complete the season atop its zone of ten clubs. It is doubtful, however, that it will advance in 2023 to the modestly reputable third division.

Dinamo, the team of the past, remains alive in documents, memoirs, and books such as this one. But in so many other ways, Kirov's Dinamo has perished regardless of the name emblazoned on the jerseys of the "new" team. Losing can have consequences beyond the scoreboard. In Dinamo's case, the "else" in "win or else" has proven fatal.

NOTES

1. Minor league teams have been devastated by underfunding, dilapidated stadiums, plummeting attendance, match fixing, fans' obsessive allegiance to faraway squads in England's Premier League, and incompetent as well as corrupt administrators of leagues and teams. See David Goldblatt, *The Age of Football: Soccer and the 21st Century* (New York: W. W. Norton, 2020).

2. Artur Masal'tsev, "Otmaialis'!," *Viatskii krai*, no. 29, July 21, 2017, 15. The recent book *Soccernomics* emphasizes that almost all football clubs have been and continue to be notoriously unprofitable. The successful ones depend on "sugar daddies." The authors also point out that in Europe since the early 1980s, most clubs in midsize cities lack the funds to successfully compete. See Simon Kuper and Stefan Szymanski, *Soccernomics: Why England Loses, Why Spain, Germany and Brazil Win, and Why the US, Japan, Australia—and even Iraq—Are Destined to Become the Kings of the World's Most Popular Sport* (New York: Nation Books, 2014). See especially chap. 3, "The Worst Business in the World: Why Soccer Clubs Don't (and Shouldn't) Make Money," 49–71. Most teams in England's Premier League, however, now turn a profit: Daniel Geey, *Done Deal: An Insider's Guide to Football Contracts, Multi-Million Pound Transfers and Premier League Big Business* (London: Bloomsbury, 2019), 72.

3. David Goldblatt, *The Game of Our Lives: The Meaning and Making of English Football* (New York: Penguin, 2015), 133.

4. This information is in Kirov's newspaper, *Kirovskii nabliudatel'*, July 21, 2017, 21.

5. Radio Ekho Moskvy, December 4, 2017: http://echokirova.ru/news/44322.

SELECT BIBLIOGRAPHY

Archives

Russian State Archive of Contemporary History (RGANI, Rossiiskii gosudarstvennyi arkhiv noveishei istorii)
f. 5. Administrative Organs of the Central Committee of the Communist Party (Apparat TsK KPSS)
State Archive of the Kirov Region (GAKO, Gosudarstvennyi arkhiv Kirovskoi oblasti)
f. R-1363. The Regional Soviet of the Union of Sports Societies and Organizations
f. R-2169. Executive Committee of the Kirov Regional Soviet
State Archive of the Russian Federation (GARF, Gosudarstvennyi arkhiv Rossiiskoi Federatsii)
f. R-7576. USSR's Sports Committee
State Archive for the Social and Political History of the Kirov Region (GASPI KO, Gosudarstvennyi arkhiv sotsial'no-politicheskoi istorii Kirovskoi oblasti)
f. P-1656. Kirov Municipal Committee of the Young Communist League
f. P-3141. Primary Party Organization of the Kirov Regional Committee of Physical Culture, October District, Kirov
f. P-6766. Kirov Regional Soviet of the Dinamo Society
f. P-6818. Kirov Regional Committee for Television and Radio

Journals and Newspapers

Fizkul'tura i sport
Futbol (*Futbol-Khokkei* after 1964)
Izvestiia
Journal of Sports History

Kirovskaia pravda
Komsomol'skoe plemia
Krasnyi sport
Leningradskaia pravda
Ogonek
Pravda
Soccer & Society
Sovetskii sport
Trud

Collections of Documents

Chudinov, I. D., ed. *Osnovnye postanovleniia, prikazy i instruktsii po voprosam fizicheskoi kul'tury i sporta, 1917–1957*. Moscow: Fizkul'tura i sport, 1959.
Dmitrii Shostakovich v pis'makh i dokumentakh, edited by I. A. Bobykina. Moscow: RIF "Antikva," 2000.
Tomilina, N. G., and M. Iu. Prozumenshchikov. *Igra millionov pod partiinym kontrolem: Sovetskii futbol po dokumentam TsK KPSS*. Moscow: Mezhdunarodnyi fond "Demokratiia," 2017.

Reminiscences

Bubnov Aleksandr. *Spartak: 7 let strogogo rezhima*. Moscow: Eksmo, 2015.
Buford, Bill. *Among the Thugs*. New York: Norton, 1992.
Chudinovskikh V. A. *Ispoved' "perevertysha": Iz zhizni reportera*. Kirov: Avtor, 2008.
Dement'ev, Petr. *Peka o sebe, ili Futbol nachinaetsia v detstve*. Moscow: Izvestiia, 1995. See the downloaded copy in Word format at https://royallib.com/book/dementev_petr/peka_o_sebe_ili_futbol_nachinaetsya_v_detstve.html.
Hornby, Nick. *Fever Pitch*. New York: Riverhead Books, 1992.
Merzhanov, Martyn. *Igraet "Spartak."* Moscow: Fizkul'tura i sport, 1963.
Romanov, N. N. *Trudnye dorogi k Olimpu*. Moscow: Fizkul'tura i sport, 1987.
Simonian, Nikitia. *Futbol—tol'ko lli igra?* Moscow: Agenstvo "FAIR," 1998.
Starostin, Nikolai Petrovich. *Futbol skvoz' gody*. Moscow: Molodaia gvardiia, 1989.
Toussaint, Jean-Philippe. *Soccer*. Translated by Shaun Whiteside. New Brunswick, NJ: Rutgers University Press, 2019.

Secondary Literature

Armstrong, Gary. *Football Hooligans: Knowing the Score*. New York: Berg, 1998.
Butov, Sergei Valer'evich. "Razvitie sovetskogo futbola v 1921–1941 gg." PhD diss., Sibirskii gosudarstvennyi tekhnologicheskii universitet, Krasnoiarsk, 2007.

Critchley, Simon. *What We Think about When We Think about Soccer.* New York: Penguin Books, 2017.

Demeter, G. S. *Ocherki po istorii otechestvennoi fizicheskoi kultur'y i olimpiiskogo dvizheniia.* Moscow: Sovetskii sport, 2005.

Downing, David. *Passovotchka: Moscow Dynamo in Britain 1945.* London: Bloomsbury, 1999.

Dunning, Eric. *Sport Matters: Sociological Studies of Sport, Violence and Civilization.* New York: Routledge, 1999.

Dushkin, E. *Oni igrali za "Dinamo": Fotoal'bom: Istoriia komandy, predstavliaavshei v pervenstvakh RSFSR i SSSR po futbolu Kirov. obl. sovet Vsesoiuz. fizkul'turno-sportivnogo obshchestva "Dinamo."* Kirov: Kirovskaia oblastnaia tipografiia, 2013.

Edelman, Robert. "Romantic Underdogs: *Spartak* in the Golden Age of Soviet Soccer, 1945–1952." In *Euphoria and Exhaustion: Modern Sport in Soviet Culture and Society,* edited by Nikolaus Katzer, Sandra Budy, Alexandra Köhring, and Manfred Zeller, 225–244. New York: Campus, 2010.

———. *Serious Fun: A History of Spectator Sports in the USSR.* New York: Oxford University Press, 1993.

———. "A Small Way of Saying 'No': Moscow Working Men, Spartak Soccer, and the Communist Party, 1900–1945." *American Historical Review* 107, no. 5 (December 2002): 1441–1474.

———. *Spartak Moscow: A History of the People's Team in the Workers' State.* Ithaca, NY: Cornell University Press, 2009.

———. "Sport on Soviet Television." In *Sport and the Transformation of Modern Europe: States, Media and Markets, 1950–2010,* edited by Alan Tomlinson, Christopher Young, and Richard Holt, 100–112. New York: Routledge, 2011.

———. "Stalin and His Soccer Soldiers." *History Today* 43, no. 2 (February 1993): 46–51.

Edelman, Robert, and Christopher Young, eds. *The Whole World Was Watching: Sport in the Cold War.* Stanford, CA: Stanford University Press, 2020.

50 let "Dinamo." Moscow: Fizkul'tura i sport, 1973.

Football Facts. https://footballfacts.ru (an encyclopedic source of information on professional football teams in the USSR).

Galeano, Eduardo. *Soccer in Sun and Shadow.* Translated by Mark Fried. New York: Nation Books, 2013.

Goldblatt, David. *The Ball Is Round: A Global History of Soccer.* New York: Riverhead Books, 2008.

Grant, Susan. *Physical Culture and Sport in Soviet Society: Propaganda, Acculturation, and Transformation in the 1920s and 1930s.* New York: Routledge, 2012.

Harte, Tim. *Faster, Higher, Stronger, Comrades! Sports, Art, and Ideology in Late Russian and Early Soviet Culture.* Madison: University of Wisconsin Press, 2020.

Haynes, John. "Film as Political Football: The Goalkeeper (1936)." *Studies in Russian and Soviet Cinema* 1, no. 3 (2007): 283–297.

"Interv'iu s M. Iu. Prozumenshchikovym." *Sotsiologicheskoe obozrenie* 17, no. 2 (2018): 173–194.

Katzer, Nikolaus, Sandra Budy, Alexandra Köhring, and Manfred Zeller, eds. *Euphoria and Exhaustion: Modern Sport in Soviet Culture and Society* (New York: Campus, 2010).

Keys, Barbara J. *Globalizing Sport: National Rivalry and International Community in the 1930s.* Cambridge, MA: Harvard University Press, 2006.

———. "Soviet Sport and Transnational Mass Culture in the 1930s." *Journal of Contemporary History* 38, no. 3 (July 2003): 413–434.

Kuper, Simon. *Soccer against the Enemy.* 2nd ed. New York: Nation Books, 2006.

Levent, Nina Sobol. *Healthy Spirit in a Healthy Body: Representations of the Sports Body in Soviet Art of the 1920s and 1930s.* New York: Peter Lang, 2004.

Luzianin, Vladimir. *Futbol na vsiu zhizn'.* Kirov: Al'fa-Kom, 2009.

———. *Futbol'nyi snaiper.* Kirov: Al'fa-Kom, 2010.

Maguire, Kieran. *The Price of Football: Understanding Football Club Finance.* Newcastle: Agenda, 2020.

Matveev, Aleksei. *Dogovorniak-2: Kak pokupaiut i prodaiut matchi v rossiiskom futbole.* Moscow: Eksmo, 2011.

Merzhanov, Martyn. *Eshche raz pro futbol.* Moscow: Fizkul'tura i sport, 1972.

Murray, Bill. *The World's Game: A History of Soccer.* Urbana: University of Illinois Press, 1996.

O'Mahony, Mike. *Sport in the USSR: Physical Culture-Visual Culture.* London: Reaktion Books, 2006.

Pribylovsky, Leonid Pavlovich. *Trenery bol'shogo futbola.* Moscow: Fizkul'tura i sport, 1980.

Prozumenshchikov, Mikhail. "Action in the Era of Stagnation: Leonid Brezhnev and the Soviet Olympic Dream." In *The Whole World Was Watching: Sport in the Cold War,* edited by Robert Edelman and Christopher Young, 73–84. Stanford, CA: Stanford University Press, 2020.

Prozumenshchikov, M. Iu. *Bol'shoi sport i bol'shaia politika.* Moscow: ROSSPEN, 2004.

———. "Obratnaia storona sovetskogo futbola." In *Igra millionov pod partiinym kontrolev: Soivetskii futbol po dokumentam TsK KPSS,* edited by N. G. Tomilina and M. Iu. Prozumenshchikov, 5–37. Moscow: Mezhdunarodnyi fond "Demokratiia," 2017.

———. "Za partiinymi kulasami velikoi sportivnoi derzhavy." *Neprikosnovennyi zapas,* no. 3 (2004). https://magazines.gorky.media/nz/2004/3/za-partijnymi-kulisami-velikoj-sportivnoj-derzhavy.html.

Rabiner, Igor'. *Spartakovskie ispovedi.* Moscow: Olma, 2011.

Riordan, James. *Sport in Soviet Society: Development of Sport and Physical Education in Russia and the USSR.* New York: Cambridge University Press, 1977.

———. "Sport in Soviet Society: Fetish or Fair Play?" In *Home, School, and Leisure in the Soviet Union*, edited by Jenny Brine, Maureen Perrie, and Andrew Sutton, 215–238. Boston: Allen & Unwin, 1980.

———. "The Sports Policy of the Soviet Union, 1917–1941." In *Sport and International Politics: Impact of Fascism and Communism on Sport*, edited by Pierre Arnaud and James Riordan, 67–78. New York: Routledge, 1998.

———. "Worker Sport within a Worker State: The Soviet Union." In *The Story of Worker Sport*, edited by Arnd Krüger and James Riordan, 43–65. Champaign, IL: Human Kinetics, 1996.

Riordan, Jim. "Football: Nation, City and the Dream. Playing the Game for Russia, Money and Power." *Soccer & Society* 8, no. 4 (2007): 545–560.

———. "Playing to New Rules: Soviet Sport and Perestroika." *Soviet Studies* 42, no. 1 (January 1990): 133–145.

———. "The Strange Story of Nikolai Starostin: Football and Lavrentii Beria." *Europe-Asia Studies* 46, no. 4 (1994): 681–690.

Starks, Tricia. *The Body Soviet: Propaganda, Hygiene, and the Revolutionary State.* Madison: University of Wisconsin Press, 2008.

Veth, K. Manuel. "The Berlusconization of Post-Soviet Football in Russia and the Ukraine: Money Scores Goals, Goals Win Titles, and Titles Win Popularity." *Journal of Sports History* 41, no. 1 (Spring 2004): 55–72.

———. "Selling the People's Game: Football's Transition from Communism to Capitalism in the Soviet Union and Its Successor State." PhD diss., King's College, London, 2016.

Zeller, Manfred. "'Our Own Internationale,' 1966: Dynamo Kiev Fans between Local Identity and Transnational Imagination." *Kritika* 12, no. 1 (Winter 2011): 53–82.

Zharavin, V. "Iz istorii stadiona 'Dinamo' v gorode Kirove." In *Pamiatnaia knizhki i kalendar' na 2017 god*, 294–303. Kirov: Federal'naia sluzhba gosudarstvennoi statistiki po Kirovovskoi oblasti, 2016.

INDEX

All-Union Council of Physical Culture, 26, 27, 72
All-Union Council of Physical Culture and Sport (the Sports Committee), 27, 72
Aktiubinets, a team from Aktiubinsk (now Aktobe), 119-120
amateur players, 48, 77; squads/clubs/teams, 7, 30-31, 44, 48, 59, 62, 80, 103, 107, 115, 165, 175, 181; sport/athletics, 10, 13, 35, 58, 79, 97, 102, 130, 133, 149, 165, 194
Arsenal (football club), 2, 44, 46

ban (on football), 36; on departures, 138; games, 149; of player(s), 84, 131-133, 140, 150; of teams, 187
Basques, 31, 39-43, 44, 60-62, 73, 181, 183, 190
benefits (for players), 7, 10, 13, 30, 31, 38, 57, 74, 76, 77, 82, 89, 103, 114, 129, 130, 163, 180, 182, 185; illegal, 13, 75, 76, 78,-79, 83-84, 90, 130, 131, 136, 170; inappropriate /excessive 84, 116, 129, 131, 138, 139
Beria, Lavrentii, 81

bonus (for players), 7, 30, 57, 74, 76, 78, 98, 108, 112, 114, 145, 170; illegal/excessive/inappropriate, 78, 80, 131, 134, 135-36, 182
Brezhnev, Leonid, 9, 82
bribe, 83-85, 92n63, 92n67, 130, 131, 186
British teams, matches with, 32, 44-47
Bubnov, Aleksandr, 82, 84
Bubnov, Sergei Arkad'evich, 100, 101, 113, 114, 116, 123, 129, 147, 167, 175
buyers (sports agents), 74, 100, 129

Cardiff City football club, 44-45.
Central Committee, 9, 11, 25-26, 32, 48, 57, 58, 72, 78-83, 84-85, 131,135, 180, 184; letters to, 75-76, 80
Chelsea football club, 32, 44, 45, 46, 47
Chernozubov, Viacheslav Alekseevich, 105-107, 113, 114, 116, 123, 134, 137, 145, 150, 151, 161
Chudinovskikh, Viktor Andreevich (sports correspondent), xiii, 9, 100, 102, 112, 115, 117, 119-120, 123, 145, 148, 149, 150, 151, 153, 154, 162, 164-166, 167, 168, 170, 176, 177, 181
Czechoslovakia, play against, 48, 50

Dinamo Kiev, 43, 69n122, 75, 92n61, 184
Dinamo Kirov, 7-8, 11, 12, 73-74, 99-100, 103, 107, 123-124, 130, 146, 161, 164; fall from grace, 175- 179; financing, 97-98, 114, 119, 122, 169; illegal activities, 78, 83, 133-135, 136, 139, 148, 163; travel, 121, 144-145, 152
Dinamo Moscow, 40, 42, 43, 44, 46, 48, 59, 81, 82, 116, 161, 163, 184, 187
Dinamo society, 12-13, 27, 73, 89n32; for the Kirov Region, 9, 10, 13, 73, 97, 108n10, 114, 133, 134, 154; for the Russian Republic, 11, 73; Proletarian Sports Society 'Dinamo' (holdings), 98
Dinamo soviet, 73; for the Kirov region, 87, 97, 100, 102, 103, 114, 122, 133, 134, 163, 165, 167, 168, 182, 185; for the Russian Republic, 98, 102, 107, 114, 119, 122, 134, 144, 153, 169, 182
Dinamo Sports Factory, Kirov, 98
Dinamo Stadium (Moscow), 40, *41*, 42; for Kirov's Dinamo Stadium *see* facilities
Dinamo Tbilisi, 43, 82
disbandment (of teams), 49, 181-182, 193
draft (drafting players), 75-76, 84, 184
Dziuba, Anatolii (chair of Kirov's municipal soviet), 119, 123, 134

Edelman, Robert, 1, 8, 39, 47, 76, 82, 184
European Football Championship, 50, 59, 181

Facilities (for Dinamo Kirov). Dinamo Stadium (Kirov), 97, 99, *100*, 101, 102, 112, 118, 120, 121, 132, 146, 149, *178*, 185; repairs, 103, 115, 119, 122, 145, 149, 154, 166, 170, 193; Manpower Reserves (Trudovye reservy) stadium, 103; Poroshino (training base), 115, 148, 153, 176; Rodina (stadium and sports club, Kirov), 148, 176; Shinnik, the tire factory's stadium, 145-146, 148, 163-164
fans, 13, 45-46, 50, 51, 52, 53, 58, 77, 122-123, 188; relationship with the game, 1-3, 184-185; relationship to Dinamo Kirov, 7-8, 9,10, 100-101, 113, 116, 117, 121, 124, 145, 147, 148, 155, 163, 165, 177, 181, 183; attendance, 32,53, 98, 99, 112, 118, 120, 123, 139, 146, 149, 152, 163, 164, 169, 170; complaints from, 11, 75, 119, 149, 166
Fediakov, Gennadii (sports correspondent), 112, 113, 118, 123, 149, 152
fictional jobs (ghost jobs), 7, 30, 57, 78, 80, 89n32, 130, 131, 132, 134, 136
financing, 8, 97, 122, 135, 183; financial backing, 8, 177; financial support, 31, 124, 154, 170, 186, 194; funding, 7, 10, 97, 103, 104, 107, 114, 139, 178
First League, 5, 8, 12, 74, 76, 80, 116, 118, 121- 124, 130, 136, 138, 144-149, 150, 151-155, 161, 162-163, 166, 170, 175-177; promotion to, 7, 115, 124, 134, 144, 155, 182
Fizkul'tura i sport, 30, *41*, 43, 46, 49, 52, 55, 61
Franco, Fransico, 51, 52, 73
Futbol /Futbol-Khokkei, 9, 50, 53, 54, 56, 124, 146, 147, 149, 151, 152, 166, 176, 180

INDEX

Galeano, Eduardo, 3, 181, 186, 187
Glasgow's Rangers football club, 32, 44, 47
Goalkeeper, The (Vratar'), 32, 42

Higher League, 12, 74, 76, 78, 80, 84, 114, 116, 136-137, 145, 161, 170; for hocky and bandy, 138-139
housing, 79, 115; apartment, 38n39, 74, 75, 76, 98, 101, 142n41, 184; dacha, 74

Iakovlev, Aleksandr Nikolaevich, 78, 80
Iakovlev, Boris Evgen'evich (coach), 161-163, 165-166, 167-169
Iakushin, Mikhail Iosifovich (coach), 46
illegal (activities), 8, 134, 135, 139, 182, 185; off the books, 7, 79, 98, 108n6, 124, 134, 136, 181; for a discussion of illegal benefits, *see* benefits, for a discussion of illegal bonuses *see* bonus, for Dinamo Kirov's illegal actions *see* Dinamo Kirov
Izvestiia, 42, 43, 49, 52, 53, 183

Kachalin, Gavriil Dmitrievich (coach), 50, 150
Kampuchea (Cambodia), 152
Kassil', Lev Abramovich, 42-43, 61n14
Kavazashvili, Anzor Amberkovich, 78, 91n58, 122
Keller, Aleksandr Andreevich (coach), 78, 99-100, *101*, 105, 107, 109n14, 180
Kharchenko, Ivan Ivanovich, 43
Kiev's Army Sports Club team, 146, 152
Kirovskaia pravda, 9-10, 100, 101, 116, 117, 121, 123, 146, 147, 151, 167, 168
Kirov's regional soviet, 10, 72, 97, 105, 114-115, 119, 123, 138, 170, 181

Kirov's television station, 6, 9, 101, 112, 117, 142n41, 146
Kolchanov, Evgenii Petrovich, 97, 98, 102, 116, 119, 123, 134, 142n41, 145, 148, 157n30, 158n49, 165-166, 167, 178n5
Kolomensky, Boris Aronovich (reporter), xiii, 9, 101, 102, 103, 112, 113, 115, 118, 121-122, 123, 145, 146, 148-149, 151, 152, 153, 162, 164, 165, 168, 181, 185
Koloskov, Viacheslav Ivanovich, 83, 90n51, 131, 136
Komsomol, 23, 27, 40, 122, 145, 170, *see also* Young Communist League
Komsomol'skoe plemia, 9-10, 101, 103, 112, 118, 121, 148, 149, 164, 166, 168, 176
Kozlovskikh, Aleksandr Georgievich, 116-117, 119, 121, 123, 129, 147, 149, 156n22, 162-163, 164, 175, *178*, 185
Krasnyi sport, 31, 42, 46, 49, 180
Krivbass, a team from the city of Krivoi Rog, UkSSR, 79, 119, 120
Kryl'ia Sovetov football team, Moscow, 82
Kryl'ia Sovetov football team, Kuibyshev/ Samara, 116; scandal, 129, 130-134, 136-137, 139, 140n14, 142n37, 177, 181
Kucherenko, Oleg (sports correspondent), 53-54, 56

Laos, 152
Lenin, Vladimir, 24, 33, *100*
Lokomotiv football club, Moscow, 40, 41, 43, 74, 79, 149

Malenkov, Grigorii Maksimilionovich, 49, 73, 78, 82

major league, 32, 40, 43, 51, 57, 73, 78, 99, 100
Master of Sport, 27, 47, 84, 89n30, 132, 138, 166
Mazurenko, Aleksandr Iakovlevich, 104-105, 107, 111n 36, 111n42, 113, 114-115, 116, 119, 120, 123, 134, 137, 142n41, 151, 153, 154, 158n49, 167, 170, 175, 185, 186
Merzhanov, Martyn Ivanovich (sports correspondent), 43, 44, 49, 54, 56
Ministry of Internal Affairs, 10, 12, 73, 75, 82, 85, 89, 99, 102, 104, 105, 107, 113, 134, 175, 185; People's Commisariat for Internal Affairs, 12, 81, 82, 85
minor league, 5, 7, 31, 57, 99, 107, 193, 194
Molotov, Viacheslav Mikhailovich, 81
Moscow's Universal Military Training Administration (Vsevobuch), 23

Ochnev, Vasilii Egorovich (chair of the regional sports committee), 114, 115, 133, 137-138, 155, 168
Ogonek, 45, 46, 47, 49, 53, 54, 56
Olimpiia, Kirovo-Chepetsk's hockey team, 138, 174n60
Olympics, 44, 48, 49, 52, 53-54, 55, 56, 59, 76, 103, 181, 186; refusal to compete in, 25, 58
Orwell, George, 45
Ovchinnikov, Valerii (coach), 105-107, 112-113, 114, 116, 119, 121, 123, 124, 134, 144, 146, 147, 149, 153; bribes/match fixing, 83, 84; rebuke, 145, 150; fired, 151-152, 158n49, 161

Pavlov, Sergei Pavlovich (chair of USSR's sports committee), 57, 58, 76, 80

payment, for utilites, 104, 114; of players *see* salary
physical culture, 23-26, 27, 33, 57- 59, 138, 153
Pravda, 39, 42, 43, 45, 50, 52-53, 180
Proletarian Culture and Educational Organizations (Proletkul't), 24, 32
Prozumenshchikov, Mikhail Iur'evich, 8, 52, 72, 80, 103

Racing (French football club), 31, 39
Red Army football club, Moscow, 48-49, 75, 83, 84, 181
Red Army football club, Rostov-on-Don, 75
Red Army football organization, 184
Red Sports International (Sportintern), 25, 30, 39
regional soviet's committee for physical culture and sport (the sports committee), 10 ; Kirov's regional sports committee, 114, 133, 152, 155, 168, 185 Kuibyshev's regional sports committee, 131
relegation, 6, 8, 12, 84, 85n3, 136, 146, 151-153, 155, 161, 166, 168, 170, 175, 182 ; of Rodina the bandy team, 138, 139
remuneration, *see* salaries and benefits
Rodina, Kirov's Bandy team, 138-139, 194
Romanov, Nikolai Nikolaevich (head of the USSR's Sport Committee), 46, 48-49, 73, 78, 79, 89n32
Rostsel'mash football club, Rostov-on-Don, 129-130, 136
Russian Republic's Sports Committee, 11, 123, 132-134, 135, 137, 138, 182

salary (salaries), 3, 10, 31, 38n39, 47, 74, 76, 77-78, 80, 97, 98, 103, 107, 114, 134, 135; payment of players, 32, 47,57, 74 -78, 79, 131-132, 134, 135, 139, 181-182, 187
Sal'nikov, Sergei, 82, 184
second league, 5, 8, 12, 74, 80-81, 105, 106, 118, 121, 129, 130, 135, 136-137, 138, 147, 152, 161, 163, 164, 175-177; relegation to, *see* relegation
Sergeev, Mikhail Nikolaevich, 97, 133-134, 137, 153
Simonian, Nikita, 50, 82
Sovetskii sport, 9, 49-50, 51, 53-54, 56, 75, 78, 81, 123, 180, 183;
Spartak football club, Moscow, 6, 13, 32, 42-44, 48, 56, 75, 81-82, 83, 86n3, 146, 150, 161, 183, 184; sports club, 27, 61n14
Starostin, Andrei, 50-51, 55, 56, 81, 130
Starostin, Nikolai Petrovich, 13, 55, 81-82,105, 183
Strel'tsov, Eduard Anatol'evich, 82-83
subsidies, 80, 130
Supreme Council of Physical Culture, 24, 26, 72

training camp, 74, 103, 116, 119, 144, 155, 160n69, 180, 183
Traktor, Stalingrad, 99
transfer (of players), 30-31, 38n39, 75, 77, 82, 92n61, 129, 131, 163, 184, 186; of hockey players 174n60; of funds, 79, 98, 107; of Dinamo holdings, 99
Torpedo football team, Gor'ky, 99
Torpedo football team, Moscow, 78, 82-83, 114
Torpedo football team, Vladimir (scandal), 135, 137, 139, 117, 182

tournament, 50, 52-53, 118, 121-122, 127n55, 144-145, 151, 163, 165, 170, 176, 187
Trud, 39, 55, 183

Usatov, Anatolii Pavlovich, 101, 114
USSR's Committee for Physical Culture, 31
USSR's Football Federation, 50, 55, 72, 104, 132, 133, 163; presidium of, 11, 50, 122, 130, 150
USSR's Sports Committee, 11, 31, 39, 40, 42-43, 44, 46, 48, 51, 55, 57, 72-74, 76, 79, 80, 81, 84, 123, 149; appeals to, 114,138, 152; chastisement of teams, 122, 129- 139

Van'iat, Iurii Il'ich (sports correspondent), 55, 183
Viatlag, 83, 99, 107
Vietnam, 152, 153
Vostrikov, Andrei Andreevich, 116, 129

West Germany, played against, 51-53, 54, 56
World Cup, 3, 44, 49, 51-57, 183, 187

Young Communist League, 9, 23, 48, 116, 122-123, 155; *see also* Komsomol
Yugoslavia, play against, 48-50, 64n48, 65n60

Zalialiev, Ravil (assistant coach/coach), 113, 134, 152, 153, 161,163, 168-169; rebuked, 165, 167
Zaria football club, Voroshilovgrad, 75-6, 88n21
Zhidenitse football club, Czechoslovakia, 31

Larry E. Holmes was Professor Emeritus of History at the University of South Alabama. He passed away on November 30, 2022, in Kirov, Russia. He is author of several books on Soviet Russia, including *The Kremlin and the Schoolhouse: Reforming Education in Soviet Russia, 1917–1931* (IUP, 1991) and *Revising the Revolution: The Unmaking of Russia's Official History of 1917* (IUP, 2021).

Samantha Lomb is Assistant Professor in the Department of Foreign Languages at Vyatka State University in Kirov, Russia. She is author of *Stalin's Constitution: Soviet Participatory Politics and the Discussion of the 1936 Draft Constitution*.

For Indiana University Press

Brian Carroll, Rights Manager
Anna Garnai, Indiana University Press
Sophia Hebert, Assistant Acquisitions Editor
Samantha Heffner, Marketing and Publicity Manager
Brenna Hosman, Production Coordinator
Katie Huggins, Production Manager
David Miller, Lead Project Manager/Editor
Bethany Mowry, Acquisitions Editor
Dan Pyle, Online Publishing Manager
Pamela Rude, Senior Artist and Book Designer

www.ingramcontent.com/pod-product-compliance
Lightning Source LLC
Chambersburg PA
CBHW030650230426
43665CB00011B/1030